More & More
about
Less & Less

Suresh Subrahmanyan

INDIA • SINGAPORE • MALAYSIA

ISBN 979-8-89322-856-4

This is not an easy time for humourists because the government is far funnier than we are.

– Art Buchwald

Knowledge is knowing a tomato is a fruit; wisdom is not putting it in a fruit salad.

– Miles Kington

One morning I shot an elephant in my pyjamas. How he got in my pyjamas I'll never know.

– Groucho Marx

CONTENTS

CONTENTS

FOREWORD

Our homegrown Wodehouse

Mani Shankar Aiyar

In Suresh Subrahmanyan, India has its own Wodehouse. Like several of his own and my generation, it was more from P.G. Wodehouse than from William Shakespeare that we learned the nuances of the English language and the uses to which turns of phrase, often drawing on high literature, could be put to the service of satire, characterization, and sustained displays of wit and humour.

Of course, the Master cannot be bettered. He can only inspire. So, whatever lesser mortals write is but a pale imitation of Jeeves and Marcus Aurelius, Bertie and his gang of engaging dimwits, Gussie Fink-Nottle and others of his brainless but well-padded ilk, Madeleine Basset and other dreamy, besotted young women who, all unasked, throw themselves, however unsuitable, at Bertie Wooster till Jeeves arrives to the rescue.

In peopling his books with the jaded aristocracy, which by his time was in steep decline, Wodehouse's delightfully amusing novels constitute a running commentary on the social and political transition of an Imperial Britain from a society dominated by the landed gentry to one where the middle class and professionals – 'the Commoner' – had emerged as the ruling elite. When one considers the lunatic Duke of Dunstable and the potty Lord Emsworth, the godawful women like Hermione and the other Blandings sisters, and the desire of all the young upper class to marry unsuitable young men from the lower orders, egged on by the likes of Uncle Fred (in the Springtime) and the ever-resourceful Galahad Threepwood, one sees the genius of the upper classes confined to hilarious adventures involving young love but hardly suited to ruling Britannia. In his own way, Wodehouse succeeded better than Karl Marx in teaching us to laugh our way to a profound understanding of the passing of an era in the early years of the 20th century and the emergence of another world by the end of the Second World War – the transition, if you like, from the world of Palmerston and Roseberry to Clement Atlee and Harold Wilson.

In significant measure, Subrahmanyan uses the twists and nuances of the English language to comment on social and political transition in today's India even while regaling us with stories like those that Wodehouse attributes to Ukridge and Mr. Mulliner. As well as a host of other stand-alone characters, like Senator Opal and the Vicomte de Blissac, who have left on our minds the impress of hours of giggling and falling over ourselves at the uses to which the intricacies of the language can be put to current use to subtly reveal a serious story of a world and India in transformation, even transmogrification. Truly revolutionary.

Among the many who have attempted to convert Wodehouse language into an exercise in drawing attention to contemporary events in contemporary India, Suresh Subrahmanyan most merits the prize coconut. Thus, he deftly wields his command of the English language into hilariously portraying two senior citizens in a park on their morning walk recounting to each other with mock horror the implications of the Supreme Court's ruling on consenting adults. It is a gem of a column – certainly my favourite.

However, Subrahmanyan has a more serious vein too. Dropping from his usual Wodehousian take, he comments quite seriously on issues that trouble his conscience. All of a sudden, we see beyond the raconteur and the satirist into a serious side of his writing, reflective of a mind anchored in the core civilizational values of our ancient composite heritage. This is when one realizes that his irony and wit are often a mask for telling sociological commentary and penetrating political insights.

I am delighted to commend to the reader this collection of his writings, which follows several other such volumes. Subrahmanyan has vacated David Davidar's magisterial judgement that 'books of columns do not work.' This one does.

(Mani Shankar Aiyar is a former Union Minister and Social Commentator)

PREFACE

'From my earliest years I had always wanted to be a writer. It was not that I had any particular message for humanity. I am still plugging away and not the ghost of one so far, so it begins to look as though, unless I suddenly hit mid-season form in my eighties, humanity will remain a message short.'

Let me say, straight off the bat, that I did not write the above purple passage, which is why I have put it in single quotes. I do not much care for double quotes unless it happens to messily insinuate itself within a single quote sentence, if you are still with me. I could have written that gem, about humanity remaining a message short. I should have written it but Sir Pelham Grenville Wodehouse was much quicker off the blocks. About a hundred years quicker, give or take, if you must know. This is the existential problem we hack writers of the present age must face.

Every time I think of something snappy to tap on my keyboard, it will be painfully brought to my attention that Shakespeare has already said that. If not Shakespeare, then Shaw, or Wilde. Or, as in this case, Wodehouse. But we bash on regardless. Hence quotes, single or double, play such a seminal part in our lives. Originality is strictly for the birds. With any luck, most readers will scarcely remember who said what eons ago, but fair's fair. If you are quoting, and *know* you are quoting, be man enough to acknowledge it. Those who pass off other people's quotes as their own are part of the dregs of our society. Incidentally, the title of this book is an inversion of a Wodehouse gag (a ruse the Master frequently indulged in), rendering the employment of quotes superficial.

The point I am striving to drive home, if you are still holding this volume of my ramblings in your hands, is that I do not have anything of importance to say to anyone. If you are looking for a message, you will not find it here. I am a bit like the late, lamented Beatle John Lennon's *Nowhere Man*, 'sitting in his nowhere land, making all his nowhere plans for nobody.' However, I do work hard to entertain my flock of faithful readers (around eleven of them when I last checked), who are being fed daily on a diet of earth-shatteringly weighty missives by all and sundry about all the nasty issues that bedevil our little lives these days. Of course, at times, if the mood takes me, I do touch upon some of these aspects but only if I can unearth something risible out of them. Times without number, well-meaning friends goad me to write something serious. I respectfully decline. I do not have a serious bone in my body, though there is something unpleasant going on in my spinal cord between the second and third vertebrae that threatens to be quite serious. I shall let sleeping vertebrae lie lest I should find myself lying prone on an orthopaedist's table.

A quick caveat. The pieces in this volume have been collated over a three-year period. Some references, therefore, will necessarily be dated. I only ask that you read them for their own sakes.

In that carefree, devil-may-care spirit of live and let live, I present to you my fourth volume of stray thoughts and reflections on whatever came into my head every week, on the spur of the moment. Stream of consciousness? Perhaps. If only I knew what it really meant. Perhaps I should try and re-read James Joyce's *Ulysses,* which I last visited twenty years ago, with my bookmark (an airline boarding stub) still securely lodged between pages 16 and 17. It will take an iron will but I shall grit my teeth and give it another shot. As the poet Longfellow had it, *Life is real! Life is earnest! / And the grave is not its goal.* You nailed it, Mr. Longfellow, I think.

A special word of thanks to veteran politician, perennial gadfly and coruscating commentator Mani Shankar Aiyar, for readily agreeing to write the Foreword to this volume.

And now, I really must be off and get those vertebrae checked out.

Read on Macduff!

Suresh Subrahmanyan
Bangalore, April 2024

A PARROT IS GRILLED

And when I awoke, I was alone, this bird had flown.
– The Beatles

Once every so often, we come across some weirdly amusing nuggets of information from our daily newspapers. Not all of them do I find arresting enough to expound upon, but here's one that aroused my interest. Even if I wasn't actually rolling in the aisles with helpless mirth, it had my dormant creative juices flowing. A few days ago, I came across a headline in my daily, tucked away in one of the inside pages, which went something like, *Police interrogate parrot at crime scene.* Swear to God and hope to die. That may not have been the exact wording of the headline, but it comes within a toucher of being accurate. The nub of this apparently true event is that, somewhere in the vast hinterlands or boondocks of our country, a bunch of well-heeled thugs were enjoying a rambunctious, Rabelaisian party with plenty of booze, illicit drugs along with a bit of illicit sex thrown in on the side. As I am unable to find the said issue of the newspaper, the exact location and date of this wild revelry remains a closed book. You will simply have to take my word for it, though much of what follows is admittedly a product of my imagination.

Getting back to the scene of action, clearly plenty of unwanted ruckus into the small hours was generated causing much disturbance to the neighbours, who decided to invite the long arm of the law to put a stop to the unseemly and, in their eyes, immoral shindig. Somehow, word got round to the party revelers that the cops were on the way to play the role of party poopers, and they had better hightail it to somewhere safe. When the police duly arrived at the shady (as in illegal or immoral) villa or bungalow, there was not a soul to be seen. Plenty of empty liquor bottles and glasses but no sign of human habitation. One of the cops even lamented that the goons could have at least left a few bottles of beer for them. It's thirsty work, the job of a policeman and one entirely sees his point of view. It was as they were about to dejectedly leave the premises, empty handed, that one of the policemen caught sight of the caged parrot. He was a sharp one, this young cop. 'Parrots are supposed to be smart aren't they,' he told himself. 'They observe and they can talk, nineteen to the dozen. My smart phone is full of snippets of talking and warbling parrots posted on social media. With a bit of encouragement, they can even sing the national anthem. A bit off key, but still. Well then.'

The earnest, young policeman motioned to his boss to join him in front of the parrot's cage. The inspector, one suspects that was the boss' designation, walked across to his junior and looked somewhat bewildered. The young man was staring at the parrot, and the parrot was doing exactly the same at the cop, with a fixed glaze. Unseeing eyes, if you get my meaning. At this point, the inspector gave tongue.

'What exactly are you trying to do, constable? And why have you called me to stand in front of this bird.'

'It's not just any bird, Sir. It is a green parrot.'

'I can see that. I am not colour blind. So, it is a parrot, green in colour, all present and correct. Well done. What of it?'

'Parrots talk, Sir. It might have seen something. We can try and engage it in a bit of a chat. No harm in trying. We have nothing to lose.'

The inspector was cynical. In his long career with the police, he had never been called upon to interrogate a parrot as a material witness. In fact, barring humans, he had never spoken to anyone from the animal, vegetable or mineral kingdom. He turned to his young charge.

'Next you will ask me to hug a cow. Well go on, then. You seem to know all about parrots. Say something and see if it responds. This ought to be fun, should brighten up our evening.'

'Right ho, Sir. Hullo there, Polly. Can you talk to us?'

There was no answer from the winged one. The boss butted in.

'Look, the parrot's eyes are open, which means it is awake. Do you think the bird is deaf?'

'Sir, there are many birds that sleep with their eyes open. Could be playing possum. Let me try again.'

'Gosh, we have an avian expert in our midst Who would have guessed! Go ahead and have the time of your life.'

Ignoring his boss' sarcasm, the young constable raised his voice. 'Polly, POLLY! How are you?'

The startled bird finally cocked its head up and spoke. 'I am not Polly. Why does everyone think my name is Polly? If all the parrots in the world were called Polly, imagine the confusion that would create. Next thing you'll be asking me to put the kettle on. Call me Solly.'

The two cops, after their initial surprise and delight at this sparkling piece of dialogue from Solly, whispered among themselves. The boss spoke. 'I say, is Solly male or female? Can you check it out? I don't want to offend our fine, feathered friend in any way. As you said, he or she could be a vital witness.'

'Sir, how can I check it out? The gender, I mean. They are not like dogs. Things are not immediately apparent with birds. It will be rude to ask. And how does it matter, anyway? Let me continue.'

The inspector resignedly agreed. 'Make notes.'

'All right, Solly. So glad to have made your acquaintance. We have some questions for you. Do you mind sparing the time?'

'Not at all, but no recording. I am just sitting in this cage. It is not even gilded. I have all the time in the world. Do you have a nut?'

'Pardon?'

'Nut, you nut. Almond, cashew, walnut, even your common or garden groundnut will do nicely. I am starved. And while you are about it, pour some drinking water into that little bowl, there's a good chap. Nuts first, then we talk.'

'Sir, where do I go for nuts at this time of night?'

'Don't worry son. You keep talking to Solly. I am sure there's some nuts in the house. They always keep nuts and small eats when they drink.'

'Fine, Solly. Nuts and some drinking water coming up. Tell me, why is there no one inside the house. The neighbours were complaining about some awful noise and plenty of boozing and other funny business going on. Frankly, I am not worried about alcohol and the proverbial roll-in-the-hay with the girls, but do you think drugs were involved? You know, snorting and shooting up, that kind of stuff?'

'Listen brother, some of those who scooted when they got wind of you lot approaching, happen to be my masters. I have been with them for nearly four years. I owe them big time. I am afraid my beaks are sealed.'

'Look here Solly, my master has gone hunting for nuts and things. Just for you. I expect something in return. Otherwise, your masters will find you lying on your back, legs pointing upwards, stiff as a board. Now what is it going to be? Starvation or cooperation.'

'Boy, you cops drive a hard bargain, but be warned. You can ruffle my feathers only up to a point. As I am hungry and could, speaking metaphorically, eat a horse, I am willing to part with some information. First let me see the colour of those nuts. Then we will talk turkey. Till then, you can clip my claws.'

'Sorry Solly, I am not a vet and I do not have a nail-clipper handy. Ah, here comes my boss. Found some nuts, Chief? Solly is really being difficult.'

The inspector whispers to his constable. 'Look, I just found some dried peas in the freezer. Everything else has been cleaned out. Solly will just have to make do. Who the hell does he think he is, anyway? Walnuts and almonds indeed. Even I don't get that at home.'

Solly squawks angrily. 'Who told you I was a he, inspector?'

Caught off-guard, the inspector sputters, 'Well I mean, I have no way of confirming, what with all the feathers covering everything. Lovely feathers, by the way.'

'Relax inspector, I *am* a "he." Just pulling your leg, else you should have been calling me Sally. Ha, ha.' A parrot with a sense of humour, though laughing at his own jokes.

The inspector, red-faced, turned to his deputy, who was desperately attempting to hide his broad smile. 'Listen you, I don't think I can take any more of this parrot. It's a pity it's an endangered species and I can't harm it. For the last time, try and get something out of this blasted Solly.'

In a conciliatory tone, the junior cop turned to Solly, 'Look, for your own sake, give us something to take back to the station, else our jobs are at stake. I know these frozen peas are not quite up to your exacting standards. Promise I will bring back something really yummy if you can tell me something, anything. Just throw me a crumb.'

Solly seemed somewhat mollified. 'Look fella, I do feel for you. Your boss is a louse, but I will whisper into your shell-like ear, as you have a nice face. Ask that idiot, your boss, to take a hike. First, push those peas in and pour the drinking water into the bowl. You will need to take the bowl out first. At which point the cop opened the cage door, and 'whoosh,' Solly flew clean out of the cage to freedom. The two policemen distinctly heard a squawky version of Frank Sinatra's *Fly Me to the Moon,* as the bird flew higher and higher, up, up and away into the late night meeting the first light of dawn.

Crestfallen, but recovering fast, the young cop told his senior, 'Obviously, the renegade gang had a nice collection of CDs, Sir. I mean, Sinatra and everything.' Before his bilious boss could explode, the young man added helpfully, 'Not to worry, Sir. I have made copious notes as instructed.'

The two guardians of the law drove wearily off into the bleary sunrise.

MY RIGHT FOOT

The much-acclaimed movie, *My Left Foot (1989),* is based on the true story of Christy Brown as revealed in his autobiography and brilliantly portrayed by Daniel Day Lewis in his Oscar-winning role of the handicapped protagonist. Afflicted with cerebral palsy, the only functional part of his body was his left foot. He could paint, write, and do extraordinary things with it. I was reflecting on this heart-rending, wonderful film after many years for a reason. A week or so ago, I discovered that my nails needed clipping, and the nails on my big toes had grown conspicuously. So much so that people had begun to take notice; not in a nice way. *Would you look at those toes. Ugh!* Until that fateful moment, it never occurred to me that people looked at other people's toes. It was the work of a moment for me to fish out my nail-clippers and get to work on the big toes.

Now here's what impelled me to start writing about my right foot, and let me state right away, the concerned trotter is not really deserving of being billed in capitals as My Right Foot. Just a normal foot that happens to be at the end of my right leg. As I got to work in right earnest with the clipper, I had to struggle a fair bit with the nails of my big toes, particularly the one attached to my right foot. Those of you who visit fancy salons for an outrageously expensive pedicure may not realise it, but cutting the nail of one's big toe, left or right, is no mean task. For unfathomable reasons, these nails are much harder and more inflexible than the nails on the smaller toes or your finger nails.

Finger nails, on the other hand, can be easily bitten off without any mechanical aid. Just observe some youngsters watching the end of a tense cricket match and you will know what I mean. Bite it and spit it out. Nails scattered all over the floor. Why only youngsters, just watch former Australian cricket captain and coach Ricky Ponting, a notorious nail biter, sitting in the dugout. He could be playing a mouth organ the way his fingers are clamped to his mouth. It's a wonder he has any finger left to chew. A nervous habit, and a filthy one, if the frequent admonition of our elders is anything to go by. Incidentally, did you know that nails and hair keep growing even after you are gathered up and buried. In the poet John Donne's words, *A bracelet of bright hair about the bone.* Just as well much of the world cremates its dead.

Let me get back to my right big toe. There I was straining my back muscles to reach my big toe with the clipper. As you enter your 70s, or even 60s for that matter, these apparently routine tasks take on a different degree of difficulty. Once you have finished managing to clumsily cut your toe nails, a visit to your physiotherapist is in order to take care of your knotted back muscles. Perhaps those who deem it worthwhile to spend a small fortune at the tender mercies of their fashionable pedicurist, have a point after all. However, in my case a visit to a footsie (my *nom de guerre* for a pedicurist) would have been infinitely preferable to what, in fact, happened to me.

My inexpert handling of my right big toe led to some serious medical issues. As explained, because of the toughness of the nails, I literally cut off more than I could chew. Is that how the expression 'tough as nails' came about? Or does that aphorism refer to the other 'nails' that you hammer into wooden planks and joints? I wonder. Be that as it may, to my shock and horror, I discovered that I had been ignoring my toe nails, at least the one on the right foot, to a point where it had started growing inwards; an ingrowing toe nail. While I sat staring at the royal mess I had created for myself, a trickle of blood started oozing. Without wishing to alert and alarm my better half, I locked myself up in the bathroom, and did whatever I could with wads of cotton wool, Dettol, and some clean strips of cloth. A stop-gap measure. While the bleeding was momentarily staunched, the pain got worse and the best way I can describe what was achingly happening to my right big toe, onomatopoeically, is 'boing, boing' indicating a repeated throbbing sensation.

At this point, my wife had to come into the picture and I made a clean breast of it. She would have found out anyway. You can never keep a messed-up, painful toe under wraps for long. 'My foot got caught in the door jamb' would come across as a limp lie, to tie in with my limp gait. Next thing I knew, I was being driven off to our nearby friendly GP. By now, the fleshy part of the toe had developed a conspicuous, white tinge, possibly an incipient sign of pus formation. I feared I might be going under the knife, but made no mention of it to the better half. Little did I know that she was thinking on similar lines. Septicemia briefly flashed across my fevered brain. Anyway, off we went to the man who had taken the Hippocratic oath. He took one, disgusted look at the toe, let out a volley of oaths and pointed firmly to the surgical room, called his nurse to prep me for surgery, pronto. I wanted to tell him that the pain was subsiding in the hope that some medication might be prescribed instead of the 'chop chop' option.

'But Doc...' he did not let me finish.

'No buts, no ifs, I have seen it and that's that. Off you go to the surgery.' Evidently, the errant nail had macheted its way through the nerves and any further burrowing would have led to serious consequences. He might have been condemning me to the gallows. (If you want a good laugh over this, watch the Fawlty Towers episode on YouTube featuring Sybil Fawlty's in-growing toenail.) I swallowed and slunk off to the surgery and waited with trepidation, the good, old ticker pounding away like nobody's business. Sting's timely song, *Be Still my Beating Heart* played around in my head, but provided little comfort. After an uneasy half hour or so, the doctor breezed in, and announced that he will be injecting my toe with an anaesthetic ('this won't hurt') to numb the digit while he waded into my toe with surgical knives and other implements of torture. The local anaesthetic was a blessing, as I felt nothing during this minor surgery but as my hearing was not impaired, I could take in all manner of sounds aided by a few 'oohs,' 'aahs' and 'ayyos' from the nurse. Clear as a bell. Which did nothing to help restore my equanimity. It was all over in about 5 minutes at the end of which, the doctor's parting words to the nurse, 'clean and dress it up,' came like a soothing balm. End of ordeal.

I still felt absolutely nothing and had no idea what had transpired. In a quaking voice, I mock-ironically asked the doctor, 'have you lopped off my entire toe Doc, or is it still there?' He just gave me an enigmatic smile and whooshed off the room, leaving me still uneasy. The nurse, who appeared to possess a macabre sense of humour, comforted me by saying, 'you will be able to walk after a few days, even without the toe, Sir.' I craned my neck and nervously peered at my right leg, and was greatly relieved to see a clean, white bandage round my right toe, while the nurse giggled, enigmatically. After the mandatory rest and recovery for about ten minutes I walked out, rather, limped out, my toe intact and the operation successful. The nurse asked me if I would like to take the severed toenail with me. I did not detect any irony in her voice, so I guess she meant it. I fleetingly considered having it mounted and displayed as a trophy, but wiser counsel prevailed.

So, there you have it. The story of My Right Foot, the capitals now fully earned. My point, quite simply, is this. If Daniel Day Lewis can be awarded an Oscar for going on and on about his character's left foot, or rather His Left Foot, I don't see why I should not go to town somewhat on the travails of My Right Foot. Granted My Right Foot is incapable of writing or painting, or doing anything at all other than mindlessly (in)growing itself a useless nail that is impossible to cut at home. A total nuisance in fact, but one can draw some salutary lessons from my trivial episode. The gentler sex, at least many of them, love to grow their nails and daub all manner of paints and polishes on them. We males are not called upon to similarly indulge ourselves, unless we are real odd balls. So, if you spot a nail growing more than it should, particularly on your toes, get thee to a pedicurist or chiropodist, as fast as your feet can take you. Take care of your toes because your toes will not take care of themselves.

Leonardo da Vinci once said, 'the human foot is a masterpiece of engineering and a work of art.' That's all very well for Leonardo. He was fully limbed from hand to foot enabling him to paint that famously enigmatic smile of you-know-who. Spare a thought for the palsied Christy Browns of the world, not to speak of amateur toenail cutters.

It was a big day for enigmatic smiles. And giggles.

DROWN A RAT, GO TO JAIL

'You dirty, yellow-bellied rat…' James Cagney in *Taxi*

Let me state, straight out of the box, that I am not terribly fond of rats. That goes for mice, bandicoots, hamsters and other representatives of the rodent species. I could add lizards to this list but they are not rodents. It is rats that I am focussed on for now. It is a prejudice I share with millions of people all over the world. Never mind if these critters are black, brown or white, rats are rats, even if cuddly, and I do not fancy spending a relaxed evening with one of their number. The comic book cliché of a woman screaming, 'Eeks, a rat,' is well documented. This is no reflection on the female of the species. I don't mind admitting that I will do the same on sighting a dormouse, except that my expletive, as opposed to 'Eeks,' might not be printable. One appreciates, somewhat reluctantly, that scientists and medical researchers, in the line of duty, are compelled to spend most of their waking hours communing with members of the rodent family. Lab rats, they are called (not the scientists, the rats) and usually they are white in colour (the rats that is, not the scientists), if Hollywood is anything to go by. I have not analysed this leaning in favour of white mice against black or brown, but I am satisfied that there is no racial bias involved. Injecting these furry creatures with all manner of germs and viruses is part of the research ritual, and good luck to them. They seem quite happy doing it and observing the results, even if the rodents are not. Mark Twain once said, 'Nothing is made in vain, but the fly came near it.' He could have added the rat to his quote.

Now let me come to the nub of my piece and the provocation behind this rather unsavoury obsession with rodents. Earlier this week my daily brought the cheerful news that a gentleman, if one can so describe him, from the state of Uttar Pradesh, where bandits and bandicoots abound in profusion, was arrested, address unknown but residing somewhere in that vast state, on the charge of killing a rat. To protect his identity let us just call him Ratso. Those of you who are going, 'What a horribly contrived pun of a name,' I would urge you to hold your horses. Remember Dustin Hoffman in that classic film noir, *Midnight Cowboy* all those years ago? His name was 'Ratso' Rizzo. If it was good enough for Dustin Hoffman, it should be good enough for our anonymous rat killer.

I can detect many of you reading this piece clicking your tongues restlessly (if tongues can be clicked restlessly) and exclaiming, 'Why don't you come to the point and what is the big deal about some guy snuffing out a rat? We are doing it all the time. Government agencies are employed to put to death rats on an industrial scale. Why the fuss?' Good point, and your irritation is understandable. You see, this Ratso was no ordinary rat killer. Not for him the spraying of an insecticide or leaving a bit of chemically treated poisoned cheese in a caged rat trap. Even employing the services of a predatory cat was not in his complex scheme of things. To cut to the chase, here is how our Ratso went about killing his rodent victim.

Apparently, the Indian version of Ratso the rat killer's *modus operandi* was simple in the extreme. Or was it? We dig deeper into the criminal's method. Curiously, Ratso's weapons of choice were a brick and a piece of string. Once thus armed, he apparently goes about looking for a stray rat. Now here's the damndest thing. When rats are the last things you have on your mind and all you are seeking is a bit of mindless television, watching some pervert being arrested on charges of vivisecting and refrigerating some poor, innocent teenager, rats will appear out of nowhere, completely destroying your sleep-inducing, idiot box goggling. You get up with a start, look for broomsticks or other lethal domestic implements and by the time you wrap your hands round the rusty can of Flit, the gas having evaporated eons ago, your agile Stuart Little has scurried away. Yet, when an avowed rat-seeker like Ratso is searching high and low for a rat, never mind black, brown or white, he draws a blank. Where is the local Pied Piper of Hamelin when you desperately need him? It's a cruel world. However, Ratso is a determined, young man. He will have his rat.

Clearly this obsession with wanting to bring a rat to book is some sort of mental disorder. And since rats were brought to this earth only to be killed in their millions, no one took a blind bit of notice of Ratso's strange way of spending his nocturnal hours. Nocturnal, because that is when the rats come out to play. And since cats do the same to catch the rats, the problem for Ratso increases manifold. No sooner does he tell himself, 'I smell a rat,' Grumpy Cat gets ahead of the game and the chase is on. Now my interest in Ratso's rat-hunt expedition is not so much to do with why he does it as how he does it. As stated earlier and duly recorded by the police, a brick and a piece of string play a vital role in the plot. As to being interrogated with the philosophical question, 'How long is a piece of string?' Ratso was equivocal.

'It does not matter, one way or the other,' he replied, 'so long as the rat cannot slip out of the loop and make good its escape.'

'And what part does the brick play in your murderous scheme of things?' continued the insistent police officer, trying to make sense of this complexity.

'It provides the weight to take the rat down to the bottom of a well, pond or drain. If there is no brick, the rat can swim back up to safety. Simple physics.' Ratso was a failed science graduate, which is a contradiction in terms, but let us not nit-pick. Suffice it to say that he knew a thing or two about Archimedes' displacement of water principle and that sort of stuff.

The local cop had barely scraped through high school, so he was a bit fogged. 'Why could you not just bonk it on the head with a hockey stick or something?'

'Good question, officer. Firstly, I am not in possession of a hockey stick and before you ask, no cricket bat either. And even if I had either of those, the rats run very fast and hide. Impossible to bonk them on the head and run the risk of waking up the household at one in the morning. It would have been simpler to bonk Grumpy the Cat.' Ratso was persuasive, but the cop was not convinced.

'In that case, how did you catch this rat alive and tie it with a string to a solid brick? Surely, the creature would have struggled and even attempted to bite you. You might even have contracted rabies.'

'Another good question. You are in fine nick, officer. I do not want to reveal trade secrets. I do this for other households in the neighbourhood for a fee and I have no wish to have some copycat rat killer imitating my methods. Competition can kill my business. Incidentally, rats do not carry rabies. I have checked it out.'

By now, the cop was getting exasperated. 'Look, you are aware that there is a government rule prohibiting the killing of rats with bricks and strings and so on. It constitutes cruelty to animals. Rats can only be exterminated by authorised government agencies, if the problem is brought to their notice.'

Ratso was also beginning to get peeved. Refraining from inquiring about cruelty to humans, he protested, 'Look officer, in the middle of the night, if I am bothered by rats, I can't be calling the government rat catchers. They will all be asleep. Are you not worried about the plague?'

'*The plague?* The plague was gone hundreds of years ago. History. I have read Camus' *The Plague*, the local translation, naturally. So please, don't get too cute with me. Now look, you will be in the lock-up for a day or two till the local magistrate arrives and decides on the final punishment. For the last time, just to satisfy my curiosity, how exactly did you secure a live rat with a brick and a length of string?'

'Right, ask me nicely and I will tell you, provided you put in a good word for me with the magistrate and help me get off lightly. Deal? Good. Now here is what you do. Get hold of a strong piece of string, preferably a twine and tie it tightly to a brick, which must be lying around somewhere in your shack. Having done that, you now sit with your kerosene lamp and wait for the rat to appear.'

The policeman was not impressed. 'Suppose the rat does not oblige and sees through your ruse. What then?'

'You just go back to sleep and try again the following night. It is a chance you take - a game of patience.'

'All right, into the lock-up you go. And here is a piece of string and a brick. Also, a large bucket of water for the drowning act. There is a huge bandicoot resident here and we can't seem to get rid of it. I will leave it in your capable hands. It's against the law, but I'll look the other way. Good night.'

'Pssst,' Ratso was not done. 'I'll let you into a little secret. I actually kill the rat with the brick, tie it with the string and chuck it down a well, but don't tell a soul. Bad for my image.'

The cop was aghast. 'Then what is the point of it all? Why confess to cruelty when you are not guilty? Bashing a rat to death is not a crime. Drowning it alive is.'

Ratso's lips were sealed. He just smiled enigmatically. He was released immediately.

Postscript: Well, what do you know? As I am putting this reflection on rats to bed, news comes through that the Mayor of New York City has appointed one Kathleen Corradi as the city's first director of rodent mitigation. In plain speak, rat catcher, or as Mayor Eric Adams grandiloquently put it, NYC's first ever 'Rat Czar.' Her task? To send the rats packing and create a cleaner New York. In the Mayor's compelling words, 'The rats are going to hate Kathy, but we're excited to have her leading this important effort.' All together now, three 'eeks' for Kathy! Rats will no longer be nibbling at the Big Apple.

Oh, and one other thing. If I am invited out for dinner and find *ratatouille* on the menu, I shall give it a wide berth.

OPEN FLIES IN OPEN SKIES

At the very outset, let me make it plain as a pikestaff that being urinated upon by an inebriated idiot is no laughing matter, even at a light-headed 40,000 feet up in the air, on Air India's business class service. The 71-year-old lady who was thus obscenely assailed was certainly not amused. Neither is being snuffed out prematurely and chopped into little pieces, a pastime many of our insane murderers seem to be overly partial to. Add to this list of macabre horrors, being trapped under a car full of drunken louts and dragged for miles after which it is only a matter of picking up the pieces. We are left dumbfounded and speechless. Which, of course, is an affliction that garrulous talking heads on our television news channels do not in any way, shape or form suffer from.

Let us examine the Air India incident first. Celebrity anchor, shouter and fist-waver Arnab Goswami on Republic TV went berserk and ballistic (this time with some justification), throwing hashtags around like confetti and repeatedly referring to the 'drunken creep' who 'exposed his private parts' in order to do his number one business on business class on an elderly lady. Not that the dastardly deed would have carried even an iota of merit had it been perpetrated on a younger person. Without getting too technical about it, I suppose the drunken slob's pathetically weak defence would have been that exposing one's private parts inevitably goes hand in hand, as it were, with having to relieve oneself, and that he was not quite himself after several large single malts. Had he been well-read, he might well have paraphrased King Lear and protested his innocence by claiming he was more pissed against than pissing.

Where this misguided poop went horribly wrong was in supposing that the reclining seat, where the unfortunate victim was enjoying her forty winks, dreaming of home and hearth, was a convenient toilet receptacle for him to unzip his fly and blissfully disgorge the liquid contents of his bloated bladder. Imagine the lady's shock and horror. She could not have had a ruder awakening than the poor girl who found herself trapped under a swiftly moving car in Delhi.

As if all this was not ridiculous enough, news reports tell us that another similar incident occurred on an Air India international flight of a man mistaking a passenger seat for his private bathroom to aim (not very well), shoot and flush. Is this a nasty habit that one catches, like the flu? This time, mercifully, the passenger was not physically present in the plush, seat urinal. Actually, you can forget about the flushing bit. These sloshed sons of Belial were only interested in drawing and shooting, wherever and whenever it took their urges and fancy. A modern-day Quick Draw McGraw of yesteryear cartoon fame! One of the perpetrators now has a name, but I shan't demean my column by giving him publicity, even if it is of the extremely cheap variety Our television, print and social media are doing the honours, with knobs on.

Inevitably, the endless, tasteless jokes must follow on social media. Toilet humour has been with us for centuries and when provided with an opportunity on a plate, such as in the present instance, Facebook and Twitter go to town with puns, cartoons and wisecracks to keep them all rolling in the aisles with helpless mirth. The Air India fracas is presently enjoying top billing in the media and is, by some distance, the lead story. Keeping close company is the pathetic tale of the girl who was fatally trapped under a car. The girls who were killed and vivisected have, for the nonce, faded into the background, if not complete oblivion. My preoccupation is not with the criminality or otherwise of all these grim tales. The law, if there is one operating in our country, can take care of such matters, even if our dilatory justice system often moves at a snail's pace to pass sentence and mete out justice. They are far too tied up jousting with the government over appointment of judges and other such weighty matters. I can see where the Supreme Court is coming from. If you don't have the requisite number of judges, who will do the judging?

My primary focus of attention is on our television media channels. There can be no arguing on the fact that heinous crimes like grisly murders are grist to our channels' voracious mills. What I am not able to come to grips with is why, for a certain length of time, say a week to ten days, they behave as if nothing else is happening anywhere in the country, or indeed, in the universe that is worthy of even a passing mention. If a lady has been defiled by a drunken passenger on an international flight, by all means report it, give it the due coverage it deserves. Then, for crying out loud, move on to other things. Make Air India, deservedly, the whipping boy. Come back later to the urinary track if things move and you have some important development to convey. Perhaps Arnab's 'creep' had a prostate issue and couldn't keep it in. Who knows? Who gives a toss?

However, if every channel has nothing better than to, day after dreary day, hour after lurid hour, repeat the same story, raising an almighty stink to high heaven, you have irretrievably lost the plot and the viewer's interest. As we used to say as school kids, 'stale news stinks, and so do you.' And guess what, after a week or so, the story dies a natural death and all the channels grow tired of it and we hear no more on the subject. It is as if nothing ever happened. Once the goons are apprehended, it is pretty much curtains as far as that story is concerned. The viewers have switched off and so have the television channels. Perhaps the Tatas are counting on this familiar pattern. We can now revert to Rahul Gandhi's Bharat Jodo Yatra, scuffles in parliament, analyses on forthcoming state elections, the Nifty's erratic behaviour, the never-ending Russia-Ukraine war, India's decline in world cricket, and so on and so forth.

Let's face it. There must be innumerable other horrendous happenings taking place all over India and elsewhere in the world that we may not even be aware of. So let us display a sense of proportion in how much coverage we allot to these stories, and not inundate the public with minutiae of these incidents that have no bearing on the overall development of the newsbreak. In assessing the seriousness of a crime, a man urinating on a lady, in-flight, disgusting as it is, cannot compare with the severity of a girl being put to death under the wheels of a car. However, you could be forgiven for feeling otherwise, judging by the way the respective news items are covered. My own sense is that our channels love a high-profile target to lash out at. And who could be more high-profile in India's corporate ether than the venerated Tatas and their pride and joy, India's very own flagship airline which they once owned, lost and regained recently. It was too good an opportunity for the media to miss and they are going about it with a vengeance. This will be a supreme test of the Tatas' resilience and PR skills to see how this highly admired institution will deal with the situation. Thus far, they have maintained a stoic silence, doubtless burning the midnight oil with their PR and advertising agencies to chalk out a suitable response. I am not sure about what the nation wants to know and how our TV channels are responding to this insatiable thirst for knowledge. Speaking for myself, I shan't be holding my breath.

Finally, as a note of abundant caution, all passengers, if they are finicky about being pissed upon, should make a special request to the airline to provide a seat next to an abstemious teetotaler. An extra charge may apply, but look on the bright side. You will save big on laundry and dry-cleaning charges. On a less flippant note, it is high time airlines placed a cap on how much alcohol a passenger should be allowed to consume during the journey. There ought to be a cap, after which a red sign should flash, *'THE BAR IS CLOSED.'* This may tempt some hopeless, gone-case lush to tank up before boarding, but that is a chance we are going to have to take. And it lets the airline off the hook.

Postscript: As I put this blog to bed, news is filtering in that the CEO of Air India has expressed regret at the unsavoury incident. This has set the cat among the pigeons, again, as the hyperventilating news channels go yakety-yak over whether an expression of regret constitutes an apology. Or not. I cannot even say 'watch this space,' because I have no intention of revisiting this subject again.

WANTED: JEEVES AND WOOSTER IN JAIL

Stone walls do not a prison make, / Nor iron bars a cage / Minds innocent and quiet take / That for an hermitage.

17th-century English poet Richard Lovelace from his poem *To Althea, from Prison.*

My heart goes out to the well-known human rights activist, Gautam Navlakha. I shan't go into the whys and wherefores or the rights and wrongs pertaining to the justification or otherwise of his confinement in a prison in Mumbai, where he is holed up in a high security cell. Let the lawyers and the judges break their heads over matters that go over my head. That is not part of the mandate I have set for myself in setting out to pen this piece. Reports tell us that he is allowed a 30-minute constitutional 'in the open space' and must clean his own cell. So far so bad, but it gets worse and this is where my heart does its bleeding act. Mr. Navlakha has been denied, on the face of it a most reasonable request, for a copy to savour of one of master humourist P.G. Wodehouse's books, evidently from the Jeeves-Wooster canon. That went through my heart like a flaming arrow.

Now anyone who knows me even remotely or have read some of my weekly outpourings, will surely be aware that I am more than an avid Wodehouse fan. During my callow, wet-behind-the-ears phase of writing, I would unabashedly imitate the great man. Like any avowed fan, I would read many of his books over and over again (and still do), sitting quietly somewhere and chortling uncontrollably to myself while the rest of the household or fellow passengers on a train or flight, would conclude that I have become discombobulated, disoriented or even slightly demented. The more perceptive, bless them, will turn to me and say, 'Another Wodehouse fan, I see. Which one is it?' There's a man after my own heart. Any Wodehouse devotee will relate, word for word, to what I have just said.

Under the circumstance, it should come as no surprise that I was shocked to the core on learning of this insane refusal, on the part of the jail authorities, to allow this incarcerated activist his daily fix of Bertie Wooster's imbroglios while his personal gentleman's gentleman, Jeeves, pours oil over troubled waters. All Mr. Navlakha wanted was some respite from the gloom of his darkened cell, and who better to provide that relief than Wodehouse? To add to the ridiculousness of the prison authorities' position, we learn that the Maharashtra government argued that this request by Mr. Navlakha for a Wodehouse novel happened during the Covid-19 pandemic, and that it was the postal department that viewed this request as a 'security risk.' Thus, a case was made out that it was not the jailers who had anything against Wodehouse, but the postal department. A wag noted that neither our jail wardens nor the boffins at the post office would be able to tell a Wodehouse tome from a hole in the ground. The matter was laughable, only no one was laughing. Certainly not Gautam Navlakha. As the court asked the prison administration tersely, 'Why was he not given the book? Is humour banished from jail?' That's telling them. On being told that there are only 2800 books in the jail library, the court observed pithily if ungrammatically, 'That is very less.' However, they went on to add that something should be done, and right speedily, to obtain more books of greater variety to keep the feast of reason and flow of soul in good order. Those are not their exact words of course, but you get the idea. They did conclude, in that admonishing tone which judges tend to adopt, that access to books is an important step towards the reformation of cell inmates. Well said, Your Honours. Bravo!

This strange plight of Mr. Navlakha's set me thinking. What if I decided, one fine day, to stick a knife into someone I could not stand the sight of? Then, like Dostoevsky's anti-hero in *Crime and Punishment*, Rodion Romanovich Raskolnikov, who takes an axe to a corrupt, elderly lady pawnbroker's head, resulting in a messy, gory murder. Having done his dread deed, consumed with guilt and remorse, he walks into the nearest police station and confesses. It takes all sorts. The punishment? Nothing short of a lifer. There is much stuff about subsequent redemption in an existential kind of way, and you can expect Russian authors to go on forever wallowing in that vein. Dostoevsky was no exception. Putting myself in Raskolnikov's position, I visualised sitting in a cell and wondering, between the daily plate of cold gruel, liberally sprinkled with crawling insects, with some friendly bandicoots scurrying around for company, and only a mugful of turbid water to slake my thirst. Not a very pleasant situation, I grant you, but surely nothing a good, cheerful book can't set right. So, at the appointed hour, one of the reprieved prisoners (for good behaviour) who has been given library duty, wheels into the cell corridors with his trolley full of books. He is whistling a happy tune from some obscure Hindi film I am unable to recognise.

'Good morning,' this cheerful dispenser of books greets me. 'Any particular book you fancy reading over the next few days? Has to be returned inside a week mind you, otherwise your sentence will be increased proportionately by a week.'

'Ha, ha. Very funny. You mean they will keep my body in the cell for another week after I die? I am here for life, you know.'

'Just kidding. Where's your sense of humour? Speaking of humour, any funny books you want to borrow? I can give you Truman Capote's *In Cold Blood,* if you wish.' He was beside himself, laughing.

'You are in fine form this morning, aren't you? Look, my convict librarian friend, I am in no frame of mind for black humour. *In Cold Blood* indeed! How about good old P.G. Wodehouse? Have you any of his books in that miserable trolley of yours?'

'Sorry mate, Wodehouse is banned in this prison. No can do.'

I was flabbergasted. 'Why, for heaven's sake? Because the authorities are worried that I might laugh myself to death? I see you have Enid Blyton's *Noddy in Toyland,* A.A. Milne's *The House at Pooh Corner* and an illustrated comic book of *Snow White and the Seven Dwarfs.* I didn't know we have convicts under the age of ten serving extended sentences here. Come on, fish out *Jeeves and the Feudal Spirit.* I have read it only twenty-five times. Dying for another go at it.'

'You are a glutton for punishment. I am sorry mate, but the big nobs at the office think Wodehouse is a pernicious influence,' he said rather pompously.

'Where did you learn words like that? Pernicious? I can see you've been reading too many Noddy books.' I was feeling quite sardonic. Prison can do that to one.

My mobile librarian found his voice again. 'Look, I do not know or understand the details. Come to that, I do not even know why people think this author is funny. Can't understand a word he writes, but each to his own. However, I did read somewhere that Wodehouse once made some controversial broadcasts on behalf of the Nazis when he was under house arrest somewhere in France during the Second World War. That led to him being virtually blackballed in his home country, England, and he went and settled down in America. That is the story they tell about this funny man.'

I was beginning to get exasperated. 'I am very impressed by your knowledge, but my good man, what has all that got to do with my wanting to read his book in prison. His works are not banned in India. In fact, my information is that there are more Wodehouse readers in India than anywhere else in the world, including the United Kingdom. Can you pass that on to your bosses?'

He rubbed his chin thoughtfully for a while and said, 'Tell you what, I'll slip through the bars a copy of R.K. Laxman's cartoons. They are pretty funny. Even if the courts decide to hear your appeal, the prison management will have to get a budget approval for buying some new Wodehouse books through Amazon, Flipkart or whoever. That is going to take time. Plenty of papers to be signed in triplicate and all that bureaucracy stuff. For the moment have some fun with R.K Laxman, and I'll see what I can do next week about Wodehouse.'

I sighed resignedly and said, 'OK, I'll take the Laxman, and while you're about it, give me that Charlie Brown and Peanuts hardbound volume, plus two of those Amar Chitra Katha comics on the Ramayana and Mahabharat.'

'Coming up right away Sir, and you can keep them all for an extra week on the one ticket. Only don't tell anyone.' And off he went, humming a tune I recognised from that old Raj Kapoor blockbuster, *Sangam.* Jolly jailer.

BOOKED FOR LIFE!

I have found the most valuable thing in my wallet is my library card.
– Laura Bush

The library card: Laura Bush, former first lady of the United States of America hit the nail on the head in assigning to this precious ticket such a generous accolade. Madam Bush's claim to fame was not merely as the better half of George W. Bush (few would argue with that), but in her own right, she was widely regarded as an author, librarian and memoirist. Enough to be getting along with, I should think. When I came across this quote, quite by chance, it set me thinking about my college years in Calcutta. My wallet, if I did possess one, contained pocket money of around Rs.20/- in notes and coins, my college identity card and, you guessed it, my British Council and U.S.I.S. (United States Information Service) library membership cards. I had not the faintest what a credit or debit card even looked like, if at all they existed in the early 70s. I did have a driving licence, a bulky, little red booklet which permanently nestled in my dad's car glove compartment. Having crossed 18, I got to zip around in the legendary Ambassador about twice a month, not without the family driver usually in tow. Failing which, transport meant Calcutta's smoke-belching buses, its sedentary trams and brisk perambulation, if the distances were not forbidding. In sum, the two library cards, liberally date-stamped, were my sole prized possessions (if two cards can be characterised as 'sole').

In hot and steamy Calcutta, during the late 60s and 70s, with power cuts all day long being the norm, the library was a cool and cloistered haven to spend pleasurable hours in. For one thing, the air-conditioning ran even during what was laughably referred to as 'load shedding,' thanks to these foreign-funded establishments being able to afford back-up generators. That alone was worth the price of the membership card. Our college too had a well-stocked library on the premises, but to move to the library in the same building complex where you had just spent five stultifying hours was not a pleasing prospect. You wanted to get the academic fug out of your system once the closing bell rang.

The British Council, being located in tony Theatre Road, later renamed quite appropriately to Shakespeare Sarani, was a mere ten minutes stroll from my college in nearby, swinging Park Street. The Council may not have been quite The Bodleian Library of legend, but good enough for us students. Wasting no time, off I would trudge to BC, as we fondly nicknamed the best library in town. Walking into the precincts of the library with the 'whoosh' of the air-conditioning washing all over you, was nothing short of ecstasy. Once inside, you took things as they came. No unseemly rush. Studious looking bookworms were bent over their tomes, some making feverish notes. Others would be strolling along the book racks, randomly picking up a book, putting it back and walking on to the next corridor of shelves. There were usually two or three librarians on duty, located in the well of the library, busily date stamping books being borrowed or being returned. If you were late in returning a book, even after the grant of an extra week's extension, a small fine had to be paid, which the librarian accepted somewhat apologetically, as if to say, 'Sorry, I understand you were down with chicken pox, but those are the rules. The due date is sacrosanct.'

Speaking of the librarians on duty, invariably there would be an attractive lady doing the honours along with a couple of earnest looking gentlemen. The younger male visitors to the library would invariably try and make a beeline for the fetching lady librarian, often repeatedly going back to her to ask silly questions.

'Excuse me Madam, but where would I find Kingsley Amis?' That's about as silly as it gets in a library.

'Did you try the A to D Section?'

'Ah thanks, I was looking at the K section. You know, Kingsley.'

'Books are stacked as per the author's surname and not first name,' she replies tartly. 'You've been a member long enough.'

The poor sap is not sure if he should be blushing at the unmistakable ticking off or be happy that she remembers him to be a long-time member. He is not finished, however. Glutton for punishment.

'And what if I am looking for a book title, and not sure of the author's name? Say, *The Code of the Woosters.* Do I go to C and hunt for *Code of the Woosters, The* or should I go to T looking for *The Code of the W?* Sorry to bother with you all these silly, but necessary questions.'

'Not at all. I have all day and nothing better to do than to answer all your silly questions. You said that. There's only another twenty people standing patiently behind you in the queue. Tell you what, go to the W section and look for Wodehouse P.G. You'll find it there, unless it's out. I take it you have heard of that author, since you seem to know the book title. And further, I could also recommend, if you visit the C section, *The Body in the Library* by Christie, Agatha.'

The young visitor couldn't put a finger on it, but felt she sounded quite threatening. There was an edge to her voice and she spoke through clenched teeth. He took the hint seeing as she was getting quite shirty, and responded calmly.

'Thanks a lot. I shall visit the W section and look for Wodehouse and not Wooster. I shall give *The Body in the Library* a wide berth. Be ready with your date stamping machine, miss. And if you are not a miss, do forgive me.' He was now blabbering. He could have added, *a la* Tony Hancock, 'I suppose *Lolita* is still out,' but thought better of it.

I guess the point I am attempting to make is that the library was not just a quiet, comfortable place to browse, borrow and return books but was also an excellent forum for enlightening exchanges like the one I just narrated. The Council recruited librarians who were more than just mechanical dispensers of books. They were lively personalities who had something about them. Lest we forget, young boys and girls often met surreptitiously in the library, pretentiously pretending to be reading *The Catcher in the Rye* or *The Lord of the Flies,* books that were not only in vogue, but calculated to impress the hell out of your girl or boy friend, as the case may be. From there to popping round the corner for a cup of cheap tea and a puff of Charms was but a simple step.

Another section in the library that many of us made a beeline for was the newspaper section. All the main English newspapers from London were filed in long, wooden slats for us to be able to read in comfort. They were back issues, of course, but it was always a pleasure to read The Guardian or The Times, particularly the Sports pages and some Opinion columns. The Sunday editions were so thick you had to lift them carefully if you suffered from a bad back. Excellent reportage and incisive insights. Mind you, what Margaret Thatcher thought of the Labour Party was of scant concern to me, but it was great fun reading her quotes. 'The lady's not for turning,' being one of her memorable one-liners.

Later on, BC added a selection of long-playing records at a nominal additional charge. Not The Beatles or The Rolling Stones, not on your nelly! However, audio recordings of plays by G.B. Shaw, Oscar Wilde and their ilk were made available. I do fondly recall borrowing *Pygmalion* and *The Importance of Being Earnest* with a superb cast headed by the likes of Sir John Gielgud and Sir Ralph Richardson, playing it at home on our Grundig radiogram till the grooves almost ran out. Nowadays all this and much more are freely available at the tap of a key on YouTube. The pleasure of obtaining something rare one experienced in the days when YouTube was not even remotely visualised, can only be experienced wearing the proverbial rose-tinted glasses of nostalgia.

I mentioned the U.S.I.S earlier in this piece. The American library was not my favourite destination of choice. Unlike the British Council, it was located in a very busy and crowded area of Calcutta. Every area in Calcutta was crowded and this one even more so. Nevertheless, they had an outstanding collection of records of American jazz and popular musicals. So once a month or so, I would set out to the U.S.I.S and go home with an armful of Broadway musicals like *West Side Story* or *Camelot* and some rare vinyl records of Louis Armstrong, Duke Ellington and Miles Davis. Once in a way, the U.S.I.S also organised film shows of rare classics featuring the likes of Orson Welles' *Citizen Kane* and Humphrey Bogart's *Casablanca*. The small auditorium was invariably packed to the rafters.

I do not know when I last visited a library. Do today's young generation even know what the inside of a library looks like? I have wondered about that. As one wise man recently said, 'Many authors are selling books by the truckloads, but most well-furnished households have books on their shelves which have not even been opened, leave alone read. The expression 'well-thumbed' book has ceased to hold any meaning. I mentioned Tony Hancock a little earlier in this column. To those who are unaware, go to YouTube and punch in 'Tony Hancock – The Missing Page.' If you do not laugh your guts out, you are not a better man than I am, Gunga Din.

THE SECRET INGREDIENT

One of the earliest advertisements I can recall, and this was much before I took up advertising as a profession, was for Signal toothpaste. The tag line for the brand was, *'the red stripes contain hexachlorophene,'* which promised to take care of bad breath. Many of us rushed to the nearest provision store (Amazon was not even a twinkle in Jeff Bezos' eyes) to get hold of a family-size tube of Signal. This was not because we were taken in by the unique chemical properties supposedly contained in those snazzy red stripes, but mainly because we thought those snazzy red stripes were, well um, snazzy. Truth to tell, we had not the foggiest what hexachlorophene was, but it sounded mighty impressive. Chances are all brands of toothpaste contained this chemical, but when one brand makes the claim clamorously and adds some red stripes to it, we will follow that brand to the ends of the earth, like so many mindless and gullible sheep. Are sheep gullible? You can think on that when next you are tucking into your mutton *rogan josh.*

During my working days at the ad agency, they used to call this the Unique Selling Proposition (USP), a concept that has been consigned to the rubbish bin in subsequent years, I know not why. On reflection, I think I know why. Rosser Reeves, the American ad guru credited with discovering USP, could be turning in his grave. On reflection, I think I know why other ad gurus gave USP the short shrift. There's not much percentage in claiming bragging rights simply because you were the first to make the USP claim with no genuine exclusivity to back it up. Others will follow, splurge more money and shout even louder, completely drowning out the first mover. It's not quite the same thing as

Edmund Hillary being immortalized as the first *Homo sapiens* to set foot on Mount Everest with his faithful Tenzing (Sherpa) Norgay hot on his heels. Brands, however, must needs shout from the rooftops, if not from the mountain tops.

To get back to Signal, at the time most toothpaste brands extruded plain white paste from the tubes, and when some new kid on the block startled us with blood red stripes, we were sold. Speaking of which, if our gums were prone to bleeding due to caries or gingivitis or whatever tooth or gum-disorder we teenagers were prone to, thanks to not brushing our teeth after dinner and not saying our prayers before going to bed, the red mush in the paste camouflaged the actual, bloody discharge – an added advantage the advertising campaign failed to latch on to. Other brands promised whiter teeth, stronger gums and killing bad breath (...*But no one kisses Katie*). Colgate (or was it Forhans?) may have been created by a dentist and we would have died wondering where the yellow went when we brushed our teeth with Pepsodent, but in the end, the red stripes and Signal won the day. Here's the irony. I once visited a dentist in Calcutta who suffered from an awful case of halitosis and like the advert says, *even his best friends wouldn't tell him.* I was tempted to blurt out, 'Dentist heal thyself,' but thought better of it as he was holding the pliers. What is more, this Dr. Ghosh (or it could have been Dr. Bose) had this disconcerting habit of tapping the affected tooth and solicitously inquiring, *'Do you fill pen?'* It took me awhile to figure out he wasn't asking me about my fountain pen's ink-filled status, but if I felt any pain! An endearing aspect of Bengali English. Sadly, for the dentist that is, I had to switch my custom to another molar-mangler, after taking the initial precaution of chatting with him at close quarters!

On a quick aside, as we are on toothpastes, another brand came up with a very novel idea. Or so they thought. They advertised heavily exhorting their clientele to spread the paste only up to half the toothbrush, claiming it will more than do the job of brushing, cleaning, removing bacteria, reaching every crevice, and all this with plenty of foam. This way the tube will last twice as long as any other brand. It was a clever ploy but as it happened, too clever by half; and it backfired. The advert worked only too well for its own good. Sales of this brand plummeted owing to the reduced usage. In short, the brand managers and their agency were hoist with their own petard and had to abruptly call off the campaign. Whether the agency was shown the door or not, I am in no position to say. For the record, I can assure you, from personal experience, that any brand of toothpaste will pretty much give you satisfactory results with just half the brush 'pasted.'

In case you were wondering, this piece is not so much about the power of advertising *(It pays to advertise)*, as it is about how gullible we consumers can be (like those sheep) when cunningly fed with a good deal of pseudo-scientific gobbledygook on products we use daily. It's a strange phenomenon that marketers and their advertising agencies have cottoned on to. Sometimes it is not the advertising, but what is on the bottle label or packaging that brings home the bacon. Which is where we enter the brave, new world of medicine, or more properly, medicines. There are those amongst us who know precious little about how our body works and at the slightest feeling of discomfort rush off to our family doctor, if such a one still exists, feeling much better when we come away clutching a prescription. I am a life-member of that club. Not a full-blown hypochondriac but apt to keep taking my temperature six times daily if I am feeling even a wee bit out of sorts. In recent years, I came to learn, after a routine blood test, that my thyroid functions were not quite within the normal range.

This is as good a time as any to confide in your shell-like ear that I had not the foggiest idea what the thyroid gland was supposed to do. (I refused to consult Google as that would have been the death of me). Until my doctor looked gravely at my test results, tapped his nose contemplatively with his pencil, removed his reading glasses (always a bad sign) and declared that my thyroid numbers were not all that it should be. It is one thing if my doctor had said my blood-pressure was high (or low). I could grasp that as a broad concept – 120/80 excellent, 140/90 fidgeting time, 150/100 call the ambulance. However, I was swimming in uncharted waters when it came to thyroid. 'Should I worry about it, Doc? You can tell me.' The man with the stethoscope replied that I *should* worry about it, but all is not lost, and a proper course of medication should set it right, whatever *it* was.

He then proceeded to gently massage my throat, just under the chin, grunted vaguely to himself and wrote out a prescription for a bottle of Thyronorm 25 mcg, two tabs a day for three months and return for a review. He said nothing more and I decided not to probe further. Best to leave well enough alone. Ignorance is bliss. I just kept popping the pills till my next test. Let me just cut to the chase. These tablets, amongst other things, contain something called thyroxine sodium and evidently my body needs them. Which is all I needed to know, rather like Signal's hexachlorophene-filled red stripes. When I called my doctor and asked him what this thyroxine sodium was, he told me curtly not to pry into matters I knew nothing about. Some sort of secret ingredient, I surmised. 'Just take the pills and stop reading the label on the bottle,' harrumphed as the line went dead.

So much for the healing touch. The point I am trying to make, in my somewhat orotund way is that, were it not for my GP mentioning those magic words, thyroxine sodium, I might have gone home without feeling any sense of reassurance. The moment I became aware that my thyroid medicine was armed with the equivalent of Signal's hexachlorophene, my mood lifted distinctly. If I had been appearing for an ad commercial for Thyronorm 25, you would have seen me, bright-eyed and bushy-tailed, looking smilingly straight into the camera, my teeth sparkling thanks to Signal's hexachlorophene and mouthing the words, *I have no worries about my thyroid because I take Thyronorm 25 every morning. If you are concerned about your thyroid, ask your doctor to prescribe the same. Thyronorm – with thyroxine sodium.'* Ting-tong! Only I cannot do all that because medicine brands are not allowed to advertise, but you get the picture. Bottom line, I am still no wiser about the functions of the thyroid gland, any more than I am about strontium 90, but at least I am able to sleep better, secure in the knowledge that I have the gland under control, thanks to thyroxine sodium. Mind over matter. As that celebrated wag Mark Twain put it in another context, *'If you don't mind, it doesn't matter.'*

WITH GOD ON OUR SIDE

The words fill my head / And fall to the floor / That if God's on our side /
He'll stop the next war.
– Bob Dylan

This past week or so has witnessed members of leading political parties, not just leaning towards one political ideology or the other, as in left or right of centre (that's old hat), but also implicitly or explicitly promoting one religious cause over another and going hammer and tongs at each other. So what else is new? In so doing, words have been exchanged which, at best, can be described as incendiary. In India politics and religion are inextricably joined at the hip. Usually, such differences of opinion are expressed on our so-called television debates. These cacophonous exchanges can get incoherent, raucous and unpleasant, with the programme anchor making futile attempts to keep a lid on things and on an even keel; futile being the operative word. Oftentimes, the anchor himself or herself is the cause of the unseemly flare up.

However, things have never gotten completely out of hand, necessitating the party bosses to step in and take action against the errant loose cannons, namely, some of their garrulous spokespersons. That part of the script has now undergone a sea change as India's ruling party has suspended two of its members for making utterances they would have been well-advised not to, over the airwaves. Or anywhere, for that matter. A couple of members from rival, opposition factions are also in the dock, presumably for retaliating in kind. Predictably, supporters of the ruling party claim that they were the ones retaliating under extreme provocation. Ultimately it all boils down to 'your word against mine,' or in the current Indian parlance, *'tu tu mein mein.'* Whataboutery rules the day. Notwithstanding, we are probably in for a long battle in the courts, and violent threats to life and limb, even beheading, being a constant refrain on the streets. In India, we regularly face such powder keg situations given how our politicians and populace react to religious tensions, each vying to take advantage of the fraught situation, and the latest cause of trouble has seen the ruling party take the extreme step of suspension. And not a moment too soon, many would aver.

A troubling sidebar. As if not to be left out of the action, a DMK politician in Tamil Nadu has decided to add fuel to the fire by calling his brethren to eliminate the already dwindling and, by and large, peaceable Brahmin community wherever they may be found. Apparently, he is seeking revenge for all the suffering the non-Brahmin lot allegedly endured historically under the 'superior' caste members. This fire-breathing activist goes by the improbable name of Rajiv Gandhi! When it comes to wreaking vengeance or inciting violence, it looks as if there are no half-measures to be entertained. The thirst for blood is insatiable. Not surprisingly, BJP firebrand lawyer and politician, Subramaniam Swamy, himself a member of the Brahmin denomination, has moved the Election Commission to take the strongest possible action against this misguided individual and his party, which has thus far maintained a stoic silence on the matter. Mr. Swamy, a feisty lawyer who will not hesitate to take any issue to court at the drop of a *veshti,* has threatened judicial action if he does not get satisfaction from the Election Commission. To be fair to Mr. Swamy, he is not playing the Brahmin victim card to gain sympathy. His position is simple. You cannot go around threatening mass extinction of communities in a civilized society and he now seeks that the political party that supports such statements themselves ought to be in the dock. The days of pogroms are a thing of the past. Or so we hope. We shall eagerly await further developments.

To revert to our original subject, the BJP's action of suspending two of its spokespersons has been characterized cynically by the opposition parties as pandering to international criticism, particularly from the oil-rich Islamic nations in the middle-east. They have reasoned, with some logic, that when similar critical noises have been confined within the borders of India, the ruling dispensation has tended to look the other way. The Government, in turn, could riposte by saying 'you are damned if you do and damned if you don't.' As objective outsiders looking in, most of us are left in the dark because we have not been clearly told precisely what the two spokespersons said that has so incensed the opposition and the minority community. And in what context? Suffice it to say that serious offence has been caused, taken and suitable punishment meted out. Apparently, Nupur Sharma of the BJP allegedly said some unsavory things about the Prophet, though what the provocation was is not entirely clear. That was enough for those who felt grossly insulted, to bay for her head. Quite literally. The television and print media have been scrupulously silent on the specifics of the issue, though the argument rages across all media channels. This means those who actually heard the remarks have spread the message about, with suitable ornamentation and the rest have been left to speculate on what might have been. In such an event, social media that thrives on canards, comes into its own and all hell breaks loose. Samuel Johnson once described patriotism as the last refuge of the scoundrel. He could so easily have been talking about today's insufferably self-righteous social media.

At the end of the day, I am left scratching my head wondering why human beings find it impossible to live with each other without polarizing themselves into all kinds of binaries – race and religion, to name just two. This is by no means a new phenomenon unique to India. The problem goes back several hundred years and never looks like coming to any kind of sensible and amicable end. Whether it is the Bible, the Koran or the Ramayana and Mahabharata, battles have been fought and blood spilt in an infructuous effort to arrive at any solution, leave alone the Final Solution. This continues even as I write this piece, and one must wonder how something sacred like religion, which is meant to guide humans towards leading a decent existence and point them in the right direction, should in fact be the cause of so much strife. I am reminded of King Henry II scolding one of the senior bishops from the clergy in Jean Anouilh's play *Becket* – 'All wars are holy wars, Bishop.' Staying with historical literature, Queen Margaret's 'off with his head' command in Shakespeare's Henry VI can hardly find resonance in the 21st century. And so say all of us, but medievalism exists in the hearts and minds of so many constituents around the world and they wouldn't bat an eyelid carrying out such barbarous deeds under any pretext they deem offensive to their tenets. Never mind the laws of the land and civil codes. It is an appalling situation because so many people are not really appalled by it.

Whether it was Salman Rushdie's *Satanic Verses,* French satirical magazine Charlie Hebdo's and Denmark's Jyllands-Posten cartoons on the Prophet, the simmering anger of Islamic fundamentalists has frequently taken a violent turn. The question of tilting at windmills, against the inalienable right of freedom of expression, struggles to meet at the crossroads. Perhaps the twain shall never meet.

I return to the here and now, when religious and political differences have become so toxic that even family members have to mind their Ps and Qs at social gatherings lest they commit an unpardonable solecism, without intending to do so. Bones of contention are crumbling through an irreversible case of osteoporosis. We keep treading on hyper-sensitive toes and are unable to put forth arguments without offence, intended or otherwise, being taken. In a recent television debate (a misnomer if I ever heard one), while the participants appeared to lose their cool and their heads, my old friend, the multi-faceted speaker and brand-builder Suhel Seth, who is never short of a word, appeared to be the lone, sane voice. As he tellingly and gently chided, and I am paraphrasing from memory, 'let us agree to disagree, but let us not become disagreeable.' Seth might well have been echoing Paul McCartney's famous lyrics, 'speaking words of wisdom, let it be.'

Karl Marx's memorable quote, 'religion is the opium of the masses' rings true today in ways he may or may not have envisioned.

VENOMOUS SIDESWIPES WITH SIDEWINDERS

I have written at length in the past on the vexed subject of having to deal with the well-known affliction bloggers like me periodically confront, viz., Writer's Block. I marvel at many professional columnists who, at the drop of a Homberg, can reel off three 2000-word columns a week without batting an eyelid. The operative word here is 'professional.' If some publication is paying you good money to churn out a certain number of columns a week, and you are paid by the word, then you jolly well hitch up your trousers and get down to it. I am, happily, under no such compulsion. Au contraire, I pay this blogsite a pretty penny every year to allow me to use their space in order to spread the good word to my faithful, if limited, reading public. The commitment to write one blog a week is entirely of my own making. For the most part, I keep reading my own blogs times without number (having already proof-read them several times) and marvel at my own brilliance, saying to myself in the manner popularised by Little Jack Horner, 'What a good boy am I.' I have been advised to get urgent psychiatric help.

Once in a rare while, I do dash off a piece or two to some friendly newspaper which will carry the piece, if the editor is in a good mood. In the fullness of time, they may (or may not) pay me. A pittance, I'll trouble you. I suppose the honour of being published ought to be payment enough. I take the moral high ground and exclaim, 'I do it for the sheer pleasure of it, and not for cheap dross.' However, I do not cavil, even if some junior sub mangles my prose beyond recognition.

'The apostrophe was meant to be after the *s* and not before, you cretin.' And that is the least of it.

Just when all seems lost, someone of substance somewhere, says something stupid and the creative juice, for what it is worth, starts flowing. A couple of days ago, the President of the redoubtable Congress Party of India, Mr. Mallikarjun Kharge, likened the Prime Minister of India to a poisonous snake. I wish to make no comment on the appropriateness or otherwise of this hare-brained remark. To quote the Congress President, if the English translation from Kannada in leading newspapers is accurate, he said, 'Modi is like a poisonous snake. Don't try to lick this snake to check whether it is venomous or not. If you taste it, you are dead.' I am not sure of Kharge's familiarity with the works of Shakespeare. Had his school syllabus contained the play Julius Caesar, he would have quoted Brutus word for word, 'It is the bright day that brings forth the adder and that craves wary walking.' In Kharge speak, that translates roughly into, 'tread warily before you get within licking distance of the Prime Minister.' Not much chance of that Sir, what with all the hawk-eyed security detail in place.

There is no lyrical beauty here, and I refer to Kharge's quote, not the Bard's. That could be just the translator's fault. Perhaps in Kannada, the dormant poet in Kharge came to the fore. We can but surmise. Nevertheless, the good Mr. Kharge evidently had a rethink on his unthinking faux pas, issued a hurried apology and 'clarified' that it was not a personal remark targeting the Prime Minister but at his party and their ideology. Nice try, Sir. Had Mr. Modi been aware of the phrase, he might have riposted with a 'you can tell that to the marines, Kharge Saheb.' Or in schoolboy banter, 'put it in the Ripley's Believe It or Not!' This will be scrumptious cannon fodder for all our television channels for a few days, before someone from the ruling party returns the compliment in kind, and we will be off again.

Almost on cue, as I keyed in those words. an over-zealous BJP MLA in Karnataka unwisely decided to get his own back, presumably on behalf of his party, by reportedly calling former Congress President and MP, Sonia Gandhi a vishakanya, meaning a venomous woman. The snake poison motif has clearly caught the imagination of some of our politicians. With the number of loose cannons that abound in our political circles, there is never a dull moment. Battle is now truly joined. Seconds out of the ring, first round, fight. I could have added, and no hitting below the belt, but I would have been laughed out of court.

One can only hope someone does not go to the courts with a defamation suit against Kharge, whereby the latter finds himself holding hands with his young leader, Rahul Gandhi who is already facing the prospect of a sentence for defamation against the Modi collective, both wondering what the harvest will be. With elections looming, the last thing anyone would want is for these two worthies playing patience on the wrong side of the iron bars. And who knows, they may even have for dubious company, the errant BJP MLA who shot his mouth off indiscreetly against Madam Sonia Gandhi.

Vile invective being hurled at political leaders, particularly at hustings during the elections, is not a new phenomenon. Not in India, not anywhere in the world. In fact, if history teaches us anything, it is that political leaders from time immemorial have never been short of an abusive word when it comes to describing their political opponents. For the most part these politicians give as good as they get. Prime Minister Modi has himself brushed off these diatribes against him by quipping that he has digested several kilos of gaali (insults) and is none the worse for it. While that may be so, his party apparatchiks as well as those of other parties, are so thin-skinned that they are quick to take offence at any comment made against them and as we are witnessing, ready to run to the judiciary and the media and make maximum capital out of it. It is in this regard that one can take a few salutary lessons from those leaders from other nations who abuse and have been similarly abused in much viler, if wittier, fashion.

At the dawn of the 19th century, former U.S. President John Quincy Adams described his predecessor Thomas Jefferson as 'a slur upon the moral government of the world.' This may be regarded as high obloquy given the less vituperative times in which these two worthies operated on the political landscape. Contrast that with this salvo from erstwhile British PM Boris Johnson who greeted Labour leader Jeremy Corbyn as 'a mutton-headed old mugwump.' Never one to hold back, the garrulous Boris did not hesitate to take a sideswipe at former U.S. President George W. Bush characterising him as 'a cross-eyed Texan warmonger.' Speaking of British PMs, even the iron lady, Margaret Thatcher was not spared. Parliamentarian Jonathan Aitken opined that Mrs. Thatcher 'probably thinks Sinai is the plural of sinus.' Arguably one of Britain's most fearless and dynamic political figures, Thatcher's authoritarian ways tended to rub a lot of people the wrong way. Politician Tony Banks was at his acerbic best, 'she behaves with all the sensitivity of a sex-starved boa constrictor.' Again, with the snakes! As I have not had the privilege of observing a boa constrictor on heat, I am unable to visualise the level of sensitivity they exhibit at such charged moments.

In Syria, where they go straight for the jugular, their defence minister General Mustafa Tlass said of PLO Chief, Yasser Arafat, 'He is the son of 60,000 whores.' Religious heads were not spared, as Zimbabwean President Robert Mugabe had no hesitation in calling the much respected and admired Archbishop of South Africa, Desmond Tutu 'an angry, evil and embittered little bishop.' We will let the feisty Boris Johnson have the last word as he describes former US Secretary of State, Hilary Clinton thus, 'she's got dyed blonde hair and pouty lips, and a steely blue stare, like a sadistic nurse in a mental hospital.' Boris probably had Nurse Ratched, the main antagonist from Ken Kesey's One Flew Over the Cuckoo's Nest in mind.

I guess what I am driving at is that we in India should try and not get too hot under the collar if our leaders are called names, even vile ones, during the frenetic cut and thrust, rough and tumble of elections. It does not make for very civilised discourse, but then, with rare exceptions, who ever expects politicians to be civil to one another? Certainly not at the hustings. Our judiciary is already creaking under the intolerable strain of too many cases and too few judges. Give them a break and stop running to court, wailing, 'Mamma, he is calling me bad names.'

I would like to end with a quote from a contemporary writer, the brilliant satirist Marina Hyde, who had this to say on former British PM Theresa May's final days in office. 'May loses her majority and is effectively left on life support for the rest of her premiership. (Boris Johnson spends a lot of time hanging around the plug socket looking shifty.)' At the end of the day, even the most reviled politicians are not known for their Dickensian Uriah Heep's 'umble, 'umble persona. When asked how he would rate his performance as President, Donald Trump said, 'I would give myself an A+.' Not for him all that false modesty, school exam report stuff like 'could do better,' 'room for improvement,' and all that guff. Only a straight A+. What a man!

So, I say to our politicians in India. Develop a thick skin. You can shed it later, as the snakes do. On the other hand, like Cleopatra, if you have 'immortal longings,' slide your hand into a little basket of figs containing a venomous asp, and let the slithery reptile do its deadly stuff.

IDIOMS FOR IDIOTS

I do not believe in pure idioms. I think there is naturally a desire, for whoever speaks or writes, to sign in an idiomatic, irreplaceable manner.
– Jacques Derrida

The word idiom, if one were to be pedantic, means 'an expression whose meaning is different from the meanings of the individual words in it.' I picked that up from one of the many dictionaries that are readily available to us if one made a reference to any of the established search engines on the internet. I would not set too much store on their spellings as most of them are locked into the American school of English, about which the less said, the better. Anyhow, getting back to idioms, we are also provided with a helpful example. The idiom 'bring something home to somebody' means 'to make somebody understand something.' As a quick aside, if anyone knows how to switch to English (UK) on my Word document from the dreaded English (US), please let me know pronto. The option is available but never works. If I take my eyes off my keypad for a second, 'honour' quickly becomes 'honor.' And to rub it in, 'honour' sports a red underline as if to say, 'watch it buddy, we don't hold with that needless "u". Get rid of it. Then again, don't bother, we will do the needful.' Don't miss the sneer. You see what we have to put up with? My response is clear. 'Up with it, I will not put. My honour is at stake.' I shove the "u" back where it belongs. Sorry, I digress, I ramble, but all in a good cause.

Let me get back to idioms. From a writer's point of view, idioms are an excellent tool to drive home a point. In fact, to bring home something to somebody, as my digital dictionary so artlessly and inelegantly puts it. We employ idiomatic expressions all the time, often without even being conscious of it. They are so ingrained in our psyche. One assumes that many of these expressions have been with us for hundreds of years. The greatest writers of the English language have honed their writing skills by introducing homespun idioms which, over time, have become part and parcel of the way we speak and write. All fine and dandy, which ought to mean, everything is hunky-dory, but evidently it is now said in a patronising, sarcastic tone, meaning just the opposite of what it was originally meant to convey. Excuse me while I bang my head against the wall.

That said, I do have a gripe against quite a few of these idioms that have gained currency over the centuries. If you examine them closely, as I am about to, you will find that quite a few of them do not make much sense. I could be inviting vitriol and the wrath of God to rain down on me. And the devil take the hindmost, to employ another idiom. Which is as good a place to start as any. I am reliably informed that the origins of the expression 'and the devil take the hindmost' date back to the 1500s. Apparently, the idea is that if everyone is running away, the devil will get its nasty hooks on those who are farthest away from the front. So much for nice guys finishing last! Implying, presumably, that those who get left behind from the group, are at great risk. From what? That is the question. The devil? Give me a break. For some obscure reason, from the 16th century onwards, the meaning of the expression was simplified to mean selfishness. Confusing? Of course. Which is why, at times, it may be better to employ some of these idioms without being overly conscious of its meaning. Let it just flow naturally, like James Joyce's stream of consciousness passages. If you followed with clarity some of JJ's outpourings from *Ulysses,* you are a better man than I am, Gunga Din. If people don't quite get it, hard cheese. And the devil take the hindmost!

Did you notice what I just did, without even thinking about it? Hard cheese. An idiom, to understand which I have never sought any learned soul out to ascertain what it actually meant. By itself, hard cheese sounds nonsensical, but in the context of the flow of a running dialogue, you get the gist of it. I must have come across it in a book or a play or something. What it means, and I need hardly spell it out, is 'tough luck, old chap,' said sympathetically. It can also be used with a dose of irony, 'you spurned my offer, hard cheese, go and cry on someone else's shoulder.' Just two words, and so much to explain.

How often have we come across someone who is described as being so gentle and soft that 'he wouldn't hurt a fly.' This one really beats the bejeezus out of me. Let us assume, for one insane moment, that I actually wish to hurt a fly. Let's face it, they are annoying things, flies, and we keep trying to swat the damn things with a folded newspaper, more in hope than with any real intent. But how does one go about hurting it? I suppose if you are one of those sadistic boys in William Golding's *Lord of the Flies,* you might be inclined to inflict harm to a fly, as they do to a pig, but that is fiction. If I did catch a fly, even by a huge stroke of luck, I will just let it out of the window, dead or alive. I make no such promises about cockroaches or lizards, but flies? I can take them or leave them. And the devil take the hindmost!

How about 'burning the candle at both ends?' A well-known, if idiosyncratic, idiom that means a person working his socks off, round the clock, virtually working himself to a standstill until he is drained of all energy. My question to the nutcase who thought up this phrase is this. Is it possible to burn a candle at both ends? And to what end? By definition, a candle has a wick at one end, and is flat at the other, such that you can make the candle stand on any smooth surface after a drop of wax from the wick end (if you are still with me). If you light the wick and show a flame to the flat end, surely the wax would melt, rendering your ability to make the candle stand upright, a non-starter. You are now free to call me a literal-minded idiot, as we are discussing idioms and idiots. I shall, however, firmly stand my ground. The person who burned the midnight oil (there's another one) to come with this candle classic clearly did not think it through. He would have been better off lighting one candle at one end than to risk waxing lyrical by daftly burning it at both ends. As a complete *non sequitur,* I am reminded of a line one of my teachers wrote in my autograph book, 'better to light one candle than to curse darkness.' Make of that what you will.

When I first heard the expression 'never give a sucker an even break,' I could not make head nor tail of it. After much asking around and researching, I arrived at the conclusion that the idiom was just another way of saying 'one should not suffer fools gladly.' However, the 'sucker' idiom gained a great deal of currency after a 1941 Hollywood film starring the incomparable W.C. Fields, with the same title. The expression started appearing frequently in American novels, pop song lyrics and of course, movie scripts. To say nothing of P.T. Barnum's immortal contribution to our idiomatic lexicon, 'there's a sucker born every minute.' Now here's the thing. Every time I have attempted to use this idiom (I refer to the W.C. Fields version) in casual conversation, people tend to look at me strangely. Whether this is because they did not understand it, or thought I was being pretentious, I cannot say, but I am a bit chary of using it these days to avoid being branded as a bumptious idiot.

I can go on in this vein till the cows come home, but then, all those carpers who are already fed to the back teeth with these tired, old aphorisms, will come crawling out of the woodwork, and I might end up laughing out of the other side of my mouth. Why in heaven's name would you ask someone to break a leg, when you intend to wish him good luck? And why is something you are deeply impressed by, the best thing since sliced bread? The problem is that when it comes to scattering idioms about, everyone wants to jump on the bandwagon and grab a piece of the action. I bash on regardless, in for a penny, in for a pound. Tell you what, I shan't beat around the bush anymore. I have bitten off more than I can chew and between you, me and the gatepost, I am ready to hit the sack. I am calling it quits.

Good night.

LARRY, KING AT NO. 10

By now, the whole world knows that Rishi Sunak, at the ripe young age of 42, is the youngest Prime Minister that the United Kingdom has had over the past 216 years. If you are not aware of this earth-shattering, historic statistic, you must be in deep meditation in the dark, damp caves of the Himalayas, your blissfully ignorant body encrusted with anthills. These political milestones are invariably expressed within the limits of certain time frames. Reason being, prior to a couple of hundred years and a bit, there was one William Pitt the Younger, who took the oath of office as PM when he was barely 24 years old, just a few years after he passed his driving test, always assuming one drove cars during the Younger Pitt's reign. Wet behind the ears? Tell me about it. If William Pitt the Younger made his precocious mark in British politics, could William Pitt the Elder have been far behind? Not on your nelly. The father of the son was also the Prime Minister several years before the chit of a scion walked into No.10, always assuming there was a No.10 during that time. Not that it matters really, as one is merely employing the expression No.10 as an imperishable symbol of Britain's highest executive official residence. Anyhow, as we in India know only too well, these things run in families – fathers, daughters, sons, grandsons and granddaughters – they all tilt ever so frequently at our own political windmills.

As for Rishi Sunak, since we set much store by numerology, there is a statistical, serendipitous symmetry at play, if you'll excuse the serendipitous alliteration, between him and the Younger Pitt. Sunak is 42 as he takes over as PM. Flip that number round and what do you get? 24 of course, which was Pitt's age when he took over the reins to reign.

This must be a good omen for Rishi. Why that must be so, I haven't the foggiest, but then, the logic of numbers brooks no argument. Rishi, his wife Akshata, their two daughters, pet dog Nova and the Downing Street cat Larry, are by now, well ensconced at No.10, toasting their feet with the logs crackling merrily at the fireplace, what with winter almost at their doorstep and energy costs soaring through the chimneys.

When I say, 'the Downing Street cat' in that off-hand way, I am doing a great disservice to this brown and white tabby, Larry. This is no ordinary cat mate, this is the officially designated 'Chief Mouser to the Cabinet Office' who has served for 11 years in that distinguished capacity, seeing off four Prime Ministers, namely, David Cameron, Theresa May, Boris Johnson and Liz Truss. And now the fifth, Rishi Sunak to contend with. Most people would view Larry as just a regular house cat but in political circles, his status is akin to the magical Jellicle cats of T.S. Eliot's *Old Possum's Book of Practical Cats,* later set memorably to music by Andrew Lloyd Webber for the musical, *Cats.* In her immensely readable, best-selling book of satirical columns, the incandescent Marina Hyde posits thus on PM David Cameron's priorities, 'The Prime Minister was at pains to address one of the dominant news preoccupations over the past 48 hours. To wit: the future of Larry, the Downing Street cat.' Furthermore, Downing Street's tryst with cats goes all the way back to 1929. Among the many cats that have served at No.10, two of them in more recent times were christened Humphrey and Sybil, named after two unforgettable characters from British sitcoms, Sir Humphrey Appleby from the *Yes, Minister / Yes, Prime Minister* series and Sybil Fawlty from the hilarious *Fawlty Towers.*

When I started writing this column, it had entirely skipped my mind that only a few weeks ago, when Boris Johnson was eased out of office, while Liz Truss and Rishi Sunak went hammer and tongs at each other, attempting to cajole the British public to make the right choice for PM, I had written an extensive piece on Rishi's chances, how such a result might resonate in India blah, blah, blah, the relevance or otherwise of his

Hindu Indian origins, his billionaire Indian in-laws – in fact everything that everyone is now talking about after Liz Truss' brief and disastrous stay at No.10, and Rishi's dramatic entry into that storied residence. Meanwhile, we will have to live with American Presidents murdering the new incumbent's name. Biden called him Rashid Sunook, for crying out loud. No better than Trump's Swami Vivekamundan!

Point being that rather than going over all that guff again, I thought it would be better from the point of view of public interest, to speak with Larry the tabby cat and get a unique perspective on these amazing goings-on at one of the most famous addresses in the world. After all, no one has had a closer view of the frenetic comings and goings in and out of No.10 than Larry, the residence's celebrated feline mascot. Accordingly, I approached Larry cautiously. You never know with cats. They can be temperamental.

'Good morning, Larry. I trust you are well. Can you spare a few minutes and take some questions?'

Larry looked at me with suspicion, his hackles rising ever so slightly. 'Have you been cleared by Security? I cannot speak to any old hobbledehoy without the PMO's clearance. No offence.'

I quickly scribbled "hobbledehoy" in my note pad. Some vocabulary! For a cat, I mean. 'None taken Larry, I have obtained permission from the authorities. Here's my card issued by the PMO. Can we start? I hope you don't mind the cameras. This will be a great photo-op for you.'

'Look I will give you 10 minutes, not a second more. And what do you mean, great photo-op for me? More like, for you. I am the most photographed cat in the world, and you should be grateful I am giving you the time of day. Better get a move on, because waiting in line are the New York Times and Washington Post, those rags The Sun and Daily Mirror from my neck of the woods, and nearly a dozen newspapers and television channels from India. Pravda and Izvestia from Russia are also trying to muscle in, but I have refused on account of the Ukraine - Russia war. I am a very busy and principled cat.'

'Right, Larry. Noted and understood. Why don't you give me a quick, snappy sketch of the four PM's you have served so far?'

'I am prevented by the Official Secrets Act from saying too much about them but just for you, here goes. Cameron was fairly pleasant, a hail-fellow-well-met kind of guy, May was up a gum tree, tying herself up in knots over Brexit, Bo Jo was a one-off, gave the impression of being mad as a March hare but he was sharp as a tack. And great fun when in the mood. He scratched my belly every time he stepped out. And that hair! As for Truss, she was hopping around like a cat on a hot, tin roof. She was not here long enough for me to judge her properly, but she blinked a lot.'

'Blinked a lot? Meaning?'

'Meaning, blinked a lot. Are you dumb? It must have been the tension. Makes people do strange things.'

'And now you have Rishi. What do you make of him?'

Larry took a long stretch and yawned before answering, 'Yes, now as you so shrewdly point out, I have Rishi Sunak. Early days yet, but he was occupying No.11 when he was Chancellor under Boris, and he used to keep popping into No.10 frequently. However, I am the Chief Mouser at No.10, and don't fraternize much with the lower orders at No.11.'

'What, by the way is a mouser?'

'That's Mouser to you, with a capital M. Show some respect.' Larry was pretty haughty at this unintended solecism of mine. 'Mouser, because I make short work of the rats and mice that keep scurrying around these parts. Ever since The Plague.'

'The Plague? Spotted those capitals this time. But that was way, way back in…..never mind. Getting back to Sunak and family, are they looking after you well, Larry?'

'I have to wait and watch. For a start, he is a teetotaler, which is fine with me as I am abstemious myself. Three saucersful of milk is my limit. But I am dead in the water if he is a vegetarian, as some rumours seem to suggest. Where will I get my daily supply of fish from? I'll have to swallow my pride and sidle through Chancellor Jeremy Hunt's cat flap at No.11. He is bound to have a portion of salmon or tuna, or even a tin of sardines in the fridge.'

'Good thinking, Larry. And how are you on the subject of Rishi being the first brown Briton from an Asian background becoming the PM of what has thus far been a Caucasian preserve?' I thought that would fox Larry, but I was wrong.

'Aren't we getting a bit racist here, Mr. Whatever-your-name-is? We did have Gordon Brown, but that doesn't count. Ha, ha that was just me being witty. Look, I am more or less colour blind, so it does not make a blind bit of difference to me what colour Rishi is. I am only worried about the food. I'll go batty if they keep dishing out rice and dal, morning, noon and night. Can't eat rats all day long, either. My digestion will go for a six.'

'One last question, Larry, after that I am out of here. I hear Rishi has brought a dog, Nova, along with him. Where does that leave you in the pecking order?'

'A brown Labrador, yes. Had to be brown! Look, as long as the canine keeps to herself, I have no issues. I'll stay aloof, but if she pulls any tricks and tries to be super Nova, she will feel the benefit of my sharp, manicured claws. Previous PMs have also brought in dogs to No.10, but the dumb chums knew their place. One good thing, though. I can't see the pooch surviving on rice and dal. So, I am looking forward to some left-over mince or steak or something I can get my teeth into.'

'Brilliant, Larry. *Bon appétit.* Unlike your PMs, you have nine lives. Make the most of it. Thank you for your time. Much appreciated.'

Before I knew what was happening, the security detail had thrown a ring of guards round Larry. It was time for his afternoon siesta. As I walked away, I could hear a gentle, musical purr, which, to my fevered brain, sounded like *Memory* from *Cats.* Larry was in dreamland, tucking into a juicy halibut. The Chief Mouser may or may not have been awake, but he showed himself to be very woke.

MIND THOSE MEDICAL CHECK-UP OFFERS!

I don't know about you, but for some time now, my mail inbox has been inundated with all manner of freebie messages. Notoriously regular among them are offers of 'full body medical check-ups at unbelievable prices.' There are others such as servicing of my car (including free washing and special chemical cleaning), free inspection of my apartment for delousing and routine electrical line checks, and not to forget, combo cleaning offer of all our carpets and curtains by specially imported machines, all done *in situ*. However, it is the medical check-up wallahs, pounding my inbox daily like there's no tomorrow, who hold my particular attention. A word of caution. Do not get taken in by the seductive 'free.' There is nothing free in any of this. What they mean, in their own elliptical way, is that they will not charge you for coming over and taking a close look at your carpets. Once they unleash their sales spiel, they have you by the short and curly. When they start the actual work, the meter starts ticking. *Caveat emptor* applies. Get a close look at the estimate first, sign on the dotted line and the devil take the hindmost.

That said, let me get back to the subject that interests me most. Every day, without fail, I will receive a mail from some pseudo-medico organization (their provenance a big question mark) stating dramatically that 'YOUR APPOINTMENT FOR A FREE MEDICAL CHECK-UP IS CONFIRMED FOR 11AM ON SEPTEMBER 1.' When I first came across a message of this nature, I naturally thought I had fixed an appointment and that it had slipped my mind. I had no idea all this was being offered gratis. Perhaps I should check out one of those ayurvedic concoctions to aid memory power. Closer inspection revealed the truth, that this was just a crude, sales hoax. One has to read the small print carefully with a magnifying glass to figure out there's nothing free here. The following day I would receive an almost identical message from some other lab testing company. It did not take me long to realise that these messages should be ignored and deleted straight away. I even tried to block these evangelical messengers so concerned about my health. No way, they just kept coming back like a reverberating echo. Skins as thick as buffalo hides.

Gone are the days when you just trotted round the corner to a pharmacy, behind which in a small, dank room sat a sad-looking general practitioner reading the daily newspaper. When you told him you had a slight tummy upset or thought you were running a temperature (actually it did not matter what you were ailing from), his course of action was unfailingly the same. 'Stick your tongue out, say aaahh,' then out comes the stethoscope which will be pressed at different points on your chest and back during which you had to essay a cough or two, just to ensure your lungs are clear. When all that was done, he will write out a prescription for some awful-tasting patent mixture to be taken for three days. The 'compounder' at the pharmacy actually put together the liquid concoction. No second visit to the doctor was required. Life was simple.

Truth to tell, I was a bit of a sickly child. Every couple of months or so, I would invariably come down with some form of streptococcal infection (sore throat), graduating to high fever and if the mood took me, my stomach would start playing up and all in all, I was a miserable wreck for about a week to ten days. I was once told I had para typhoid, which sounded very impressive to relate to your friends who hadn't had it, like some dubious badge of honour! At heart, we are all hypochondriacs. The funny thing though, not that anyone was laughing, was that I do not recall blood being drawn and ten pages of platelet count, red blood cells, white blood cells, hemoglobin, clotting factor and all manner of other nauseating details of my A+ blood group being revealed. Maybe I was too down in the dumps to have noticed all these sly tests taking place behind my back. I think the general theory those days was that you just lay around feeling like death warmed up, drank plenty of fluids (provided you didn't bring it up) and your natural immunity system would kick in and fight off those awful germs attacking your frail body. However, if the doctor came round to administer an injection, you feared the worst, the jab being worse than the disease.

Let me stress that such treatment as one received in the days gone by happened only when you actually fell ill. Things are different today. You could be in perfectly robust health, but you are encouraged to take an annual medical check-up. *Just in case.* Any number of hospitals and private clinics offer this service, and it is an excellent revenue stream for these institutions. Now, I do not wish to sound too cynical about all this, but the fact is most of us have fallen prey to these medical blandishments, and we dive headlong into the waiting arms of their seductive offers. Next thing you know, after another ten months or so, you get a call saying your next check-up is due in a fortnight's time and can we confirm your appointment. Rather like the reminders you receive nowadays from your car service company.

It helps that if you are over the age of 60, you are entitled to special discounts on the tests. Medical insurance does not provide coverage for diagnostic tests, but you had better take one out on the off-chance that you might get knocked over by a bus and be wheeled in for emergency surgery. Or worse. It is a carefully calibrated world, this whole medical check-up lark, but you have been sucked into it, so you had better lie back and enjoy it. A brief word on medical insurance. When you actually need it, you have to work doubly hard to get the compensation you deserve and have paid for, year on year. Extracting blood out of a lump of rock could be easier, such is the runaround you are given by the companies. That said, I must confess that if you have the ability and the patience to fill up hundreds of forms and answer all their questions to their satisfaction, they usually cough up. My own advice is to take out a policy by all means, but try not get into a situation where you must make a claim. Better you take advantage of the 'no claim bonus.'

I come back to these regular advertising mails one receives on one's mobile phones luring me to come and take a medical check-up on the never-never, because they have apparently actually 'fixed an appointment' for me. Do not touch these invitations with the proverbial bargepole. If, out of curiosity, you respond in any shape or form, you are done for, my friend. You will get calls, day and night, at the end of which you may need to actually go and get yourself tested for high blood pressure. Leave well enough alone, is my sage advice. Stay with your trusted family doctor, if such a tribe still exists, or visit a reputed hospital and consult the same doctor every time, as he or she will get to know you, your family history and will ensure that you do not need to go haring off to get tested for all manner of ailments, real or imagined. I do realise that I reckon without those who simply love visiting doctors, and spend a pleasant morning or evening chatting about their innards and perhaps politics and the cricket scores. To them I say, you are beyond hope and you may as well have the time of your lives discussing your gout, lumbago or sciatica in excruciating detail with your doctor. If that is what gives you your jollies. Speaking for myself, if I do not have to visit a doctor or wait to take a blood test for the next five years, it will be too soon.

MORE THAN THE SUM OF HIS PARTS

My morning newspaper brings me glad tidings. The MCC or Marylebone Cricket Club to give it its full nomenclature, has just announced that its next President will be none other than the celebrated English actor, screenwriter, author, playwright, polemicist, television presenter and film director, 64-year-old Stephen Fry. Not to mention that he is a gripping and side-splittingly witty public speaker. My research on the man also reveals that Fry has been a long-time advocate for mental health and has been President of Mind, the mental health charity, for well over a decade. The more astute and observant among you are probably reading this and going, 'All that is very well but we do not detect the word cricket anywhere in that brief, though awesome, resume of MCC's somewhat unusual choice for such an exalted position.' On the face of it, dear reader, you would have made a telling point, but you would have been guilty of missing the wood for the trees. The MCC is not a body that takes decisions on a whim, even if this particular choice bears close scrutiny.

Around 20 years ago, on BBC Radio's much-loved *Test Match Special* broadcast at the Oval, Stephen Fry was invited to the commentary box to have a chat with Jonathan 'Aggers' Agnew at The Oval, a day on which Sachin Tendulkar made 54 on his 100th Test appearance. Amongst other things, including high praise for India's little master, Fry shared his world view on the game. 'It's a whole cultural world and the marvellous thing is it's not just a British one. I can't bear the snobbery that says real cricket is cricket played within sight of a spire and an English field. It's wonderful, village cricket, but cricket on a coir mat or on a beach or in an alleyway in Calcutta – that's cricket as well. It's a game that's much bigger than its roots. That's what's so wonderful. Rather like the English language.'

That pretty much sums up Stephen Fry. A lifelong cricket lover, supporter and a patron of the MCC Foundation, the multi-faceted Fry was invited last year by the MCC to deliver its prestigious annual MCC Cowdrey Lecture, a sure sign that the once undisputed headquarters of world cricket had Stephen Fry in its sights for bigger things. Expressing his overwhelming emotions at the invitation to speak, Fry pointed out that he was only the second non-cricketer to be so invited after the Reverend Bishop Desmond Tutu of South Africa - 'big shoes to fill.' Fry will take over as President of the MCC from former England women's captain, Clare Connor in October this year. Connor had notched up a unique distinction when she became the first woman president of the MCC in 2021.

While Fry's love for the game of cricket needs no elaboration, his appointment to this august position underscores his deep concern and anguish at some of the darker aspects that have bedevilled the game in recent years. Yorkshire cricket's infamous racism row last year, when Pakistan-born cricketer Azeem Rafiq had to face racial abuse in the dressing room, had the British thespian feelingly expressing his solidarity with the victim. 'When he (Rafiq) said today that he didn't want his son to go anywhere near cricket my heart fell to my boots. But actually, that simple statement crystallises everything, it gives us a clear human image that says it all. It is a rallying cry.' In a typical example of Fry flamboyance, he described the handling of that abhorrent incident in Yorkshire as having exuded a 'mephitic stink.' He rounded off his observations on this unsavoury incident thus, 'Unless all our nation's sons and daughters with the talent and desire to have a life in cricket are confident that cricket will want to have a life with them, the spirit of cricket, its very flame, will flicker and go out. Let's dedicate ourselves to ensuring that that will never happen.' That is the kind of language one would like to hear from a president-elect.

While I was driven to hastily pen this appreciation of Stephen Fry's rise to cricketing stardom, in a manner of speaking, I cannot but take this opportunity to recall some of his brilliant moments on print and television. His comic double act with fellow British actor Hugh Laurie in *A Bit of Fry & Laurie* and the same partnership delighting fans the world over in their televised interpretation of P.G. Wodehouse's immortal creations, *Jeeves and Wooster,* his hilarious partnership with Rowan 'Mr. Bean' Atkinson in the memorable *Blackadder* series – we can watch these again and again and never tire of them.

Fry's atheistic views on religion saw him take on the high and mighty of theology without taking a backward step. He often stood solidly side-by-side with friend and fellow non-believer, the brilliantly coruscating late Christopher Hitchens. You, dear reader, could do a lot worse than spend a relaxed evening watching these titans at their eloquent best on YouTube. Lest I forget, Stephen Fry's role in the film *Wilde,* in which he portrays the protagonist, author and playwright Oscar Wilde, is so eerily uncanny. That Fry is a dead ringer for the controversial Wilde and given Fry's own unabashed sexual orientation which meshes with Wilde's, one could be forgiven for mistaking the one for the other. Fry is happily married to British comedian, Elliot Spencer, who is 30 years his junior. Stephen Fry even gained a brief period of notoriety when he was sent to prison for three months for a credit card fraud at the age of 17. Never a dull moment.

As a writer, Stephen Fry is an unmitigated delight. From his hilarious columns which are available in book form *(Paperweight, The Stars' Tennis Balls),* his autobiographical works *(The Fry Chronicles, More Fool Me),* his magnificent retelling of Greek myths *(Mythos, Troy* and *Heroes)* – just a few dishy morsels from a wide and impressive body of work.

There you have it. Stephen Fry, a man of many parts and I may even be guilty of merely scratching the surface in describing his astonishing variety of achievements. In inviting such an extraordinary personality to helm the affairs of the MCC for the period 2022-23, the cricketing mavens at Lord's should be warmly congratulated for their choice. One is confident Stephen Fry will carry out his responsibilities as MCC's President with erudition, compassion, skill and above all with his renowned wit and humour – qualities the game and the world need more than ever, right now. The silver-tongued orator and soon-to-be cricket boss once famously said, *'Better sexy and racy, than sexist and racist.'*

May the force be with you, Stephen.

CASHLESS IN LA-LA LAND

'He lends out money gratis and brings down the rate of usance here with us in Venice.' Shylock, *Merchant of Venice.*

Most of us have credit and debit cards these days, tucked away in slits in our bulging wallets and squeezed into our back pockets. Not to mention driving license, Aadhaar card, medical insurance card and all things plastic, contributing to the battle of the bulge. Hard cash plays a minor walk-on part, if that. Credit and debit cards are essentially the same things, only the credit cards take a while longer to inflict the pain on your bank balance, but that is compensated by their charging a punitive interest rate. You know what they say. There is no such thing as a free lunch. Debit cards, however, are more direct. Swipe one of those and it is bye-bye moolah. Hasta la vista. These cards are linked to our bank accounts and one's credit card brand could be any one of the well-known names like Mastercard, Visa, American Express and a host of others. In addition to these cards, various online vendors like Amazon, Flipkart, Big Basket et al, from whom we place orders on a regular basis, entice and exhort us to deposit varying sums of money in their 'wallets,' the easier to place orders online without having to go to the trouble of credit / debit card rigmaroles like keeping an eye on the expiry dates, the monthly limits, mad rush to key in the OTP and so on. Forgive me, dear reader, if I am preaching to the converted. Are these the 'plastic revolutionaries' that poets and songwriters of yesteryear wrote so presciently about?

Lest we forget, there are also various UPI digital payment options like BHIM, Google Pay, Phone Pe, Pay Pal and Paytm amongst others. The embattled Paytm is currently in strife and under the scanner while we poor sods are still trying to figure out the implications. Meanwhile their chief executive has been shown the door and those of us who have placed our trust and money in Paytm are left wondering if we have not been taken for a right royal ride. Welcome to the rarefied world of cashless transactions. It is by now a well-worn cliché that our next-door dhobi or vegetable vendor transacts business digitally. Dystopian fancy conjures up images of women giving birth to babies, the mobile phone firmly in the clutches of the baby's hand showing up first out of the womb followed by the parent body. 'It's an iPhone 15 Pro Max 256 GB,' cries the proud father, as he hands out the customary celebratory cigars to his friends. Make that *laddoos*, if you are a non-smoker.

A brief aside. In the world of trading and commerce, the word cashback is intriguing. I am struck by the word cashback that has now become an integral part of our commercial lexicon. For reasons I have not been entirely able to fathom, the word discount has been cast into outer darkness. Totally discounted. The nobs tell us there is a subtle difference between the two terms, but I am still trying to get my head around it. The only plausible reason I can come up with for this change of terminology is that the word cashback sounds so much more alluring. It is only a mirage of course, but one gets the idea that the company is doling back cash to us every time we buy something. In a sense they do, but only after hiking up their recommended list price. And when we are not actually forking out hard currency from our wallets to pay but swiping plastic cards, or placing our mobiles in front of obliging QR codes, life seems to be a breeze. What you don't know does not hurt you. Until you check your bank balance at the end of the month. Many people do not even do that. If they do, they flinch and quickly avert their eyes. *'I couldn't possibly have spent that much.'* Tell that to the Marines.

There is a deeper question to be addressed. Is the ease of transacting business through credit or debit cards, digital wallets, QR codes and in the case of larger amounts, NEFT / RTGS and so on goading us to spend more than we might normally have done? In other words, are we often buying things we do not really need? There's a silly question for you during this silly season. Purely rhetorical, don't bother answering. I know for a fact that every time I visit Amazon with something particular in mind to buy, other products slyly insinuate themselves and proffer attractive offers and you are that sucker that is born every minute, in the immortal words of P.T. Barnum. Rather like Eve in the Garden of Eden seductively reeling Adam in to bite into the apple, giving birth to the original sin.

'Based on your recent buying patterns, we think you might be interested in these products.' That is a dead giveaway. If you pay heed, on your head (or bank account) be it. A slew of items will stream in front of your eyes and before you can say 'two for the price of one,' you have just tapped a few keys on your mobile phone and bought four printing ink cartridges which you may not use for the next four months, by which time they would not be fit for purpose. Same day delivery of course, which is unfailingly the clincher. They call it bundling. I recently bought the redoubtable and feisty Congressman Mani Shankar Aiyar's autobiographical peregrinations (the first of a trilogy, not clear if the other two are in the market or on the anvil), *Memoirs of a Maverick,* online from Amazon. Just to avoid confusion, my searches revealed there are half a dozen other published books titled, 'Memoirs of a Maverick,' with slight variations. That said, they are all foreign mavericks, as opposed to our very own desi variant. For reasons best known to themselves, Aiyar's book had been bundled with another title, *Dethroned,* by one John Zubrzycki. If I had not been sharp about it, I would have had two books for the price of two! What is more, I never buy books written by authors whose names I cannot pronounce, which rules out most Polish writers. However, each to his or her own. If you wish to try out Nobel Prize awardee Wislawa Szymborska, Henryk Sienkiewicz or Olga Tokarczuk for size, be my guest and have the time of your life. And mind you don't get your tongue in a twist.

There you are. The wonders of free-form writing. Stream of consciousness, some may call it. Psychologist William James called it exactly that in 1893 and it stuck. For myself, I just meander, as the mood takes me. I started off talking about cashbacks and discounts and ended up quoting obscure psychologists. Obscure for me, that is. I am sure William James was the toast of his intellectual circle and a household name way back when. Particularly around the pubs in Warsaw. Had I run into the great man, which I could not have on account of my having been born 100 years (give or take) later, I would have doffed my hat to him. Had I been wearing a hat that is, which I never have. Then again, should I have met him in some third dimension, having cast off my mortal coil, I would have probed him closely about cashbacks and discounts, to say nothing of UPIs, thereby hoping to stymie him. Chances are, the celebrated psychologist would have responded with some such nugget as, 'A difference which makes no difference is no difference at all.' Pithily put. In fact, that priceless gem has been attributed to William James, Esq. Somebody once said, 'Procrastination is like a credit card: it's a lot of fun until you get the bill.' That pretty much sums up my thoughts on cashbacks and discounts.

ONCE IS NOT ENOUGH

How well he's read, to reason against reading!
– William Shakespeare, *Love's Labour's Lost*

I have long since come to the profound conclusion that really good books ought to be read more than once if one is to derive full value from all the riches of the language that the author has sought to so joyously share with his or her readers. Not unlike listening to your favourite piece of music, repeatedly. It is entirely possible that a whodunnit could have been written extremely deftly, but once you know who it was who put the strychnine in the soup, there is little point in revisiting the narrative. The suspense has been laid to rest. You will always know that it was the butler who did it. As a category, by definition, murder mysteries do not generally merit a second reading, however well written. With due apologies to Agatha Christie, Raymond Chandler, Ruth Rendell and their ilk. The other issue I have with best-selling crime novels, even those written by *éminence grises* of the supreme quality of Arthur Conan Doyle, Dorothy Sayers or P.D. James is that most of their works have also been adapted to film and television serials, and very well produced too. In fact, in the case of the Sherlock Holmes *oeuvre,* over the decades many of his famous stories have been filmed in a variety of adaptations such that we have a surfeit of *The Hound of the Baskervilles, A Study in Scarlet, The Sign of Four,* et al. There is such a thing as having too much of a good thing. Let me reiterate, lest you get the wrong impression, that I yield to no one in my admiration for these great authors and their works. I am merely emphasizing that the genre tends to preclude a second reading for its own sake. I am open to a divergence of opinion.

Speaking of building suspense and climaxing with the final denouement, I would urge readers of this blog to key in on YouTube, *The Missing Page*, featuring that lugubrious British comedian of the 60s, Tony Hancock. The episode hilariously demonstrates what happens when our protagonist, Hancock, borrows a murder mystery novel, *Lady Don't Fall Backwards,* from his local library, only to mortifyingly find the revelatory last page missing, presumably torn out by the previous sadistic reader. He spends sleepless nights trying to outguess the author and takes the librarian to task for his lack of diligence in keeping books with pages missing. He even attempts to locate the author to uncover the mystery only to learn that he has died, and the book is out of print. It's a laugh-a-minute episode, not slapstick, brilliantly scripted and wonderfully acted. A single viewing will not suffice.

Let us now take P.G. Wodehouse. Between you, me and the gatepost, I can take Wodehouse all the year round. Weaned on the master of farce, as he has often been described, from an early age, I have read most of his famous novels at least twice, if not more. You may well ask why. As I write this column, I am well into chapter five of *The Code of the Woosters,* a Jeeves / Wooster classic. This could quite possibly be my 10th reading of this ageless wonder involving Bertie Wooster's escapades in an old English country pile, with his gentleman's personal gentleman, Jeeves, on hand to rescue his master at every turn from a fate worse than death. A silver 18th century cow creamer plays a sterling part! There are, of course, several other novels by Sir Pelham featuring the likes of Lord Emsworth and his frightful sisters, not forgetting his magnificent sow, the Empress of Blandings, Galahad and Freddie Threepwood, Uncle Fred, aka Lord Ickenham and his greatly put-upon nephew, Pongo Twistleton, the Mulliner tales, the Golfing stories, Ukridge, Psmith (the P is silent), Gussie Fink-Nottle and so many more. On reflection, why do I waste words when I can quote one of our contemporary comic geniuses, Stephen Fry (who essayed Jeeves on television) on Wodehouse.

'Had his only contribution to literature been Lord Emsworth and Blandings Castle, his place in history would have been assured. Had he written of none but Mike and Psmith, he would be cherished today as the best and brightest of our comic authors. If Jeeves and Wooster had been his solitary theme, still he would be hailed as the Master. If he had given us only Ukridge, or nothing but recollections of the Mulliner family, or a pure diet of golfing stories, Doctor Sir Pelham Grenville Wodehouse would nonetheless be considered immortal. That he gave us all those – and more – is our good fortune and a testament to the most industrious, prolific and beneficent author ever to have sat down, scratched his head and banged out a sentence.'

I will move on from Wodehouse, but not before leaving you with a couple of gems, among hundreds, that demonstrate why we read the man over and over again. 'The fascination of shooting as a sport depends almost wholly on whether you are at the right or wrong end of the gun.' *The Adventures of Sally*. 'The great thing in life, Jeeves, if we wish to be happy and prosperous, is to miss as many political debates as possible.' *Much Obliged, Jeeves*. The last quote resonates like a ton of bricks with me every evening when I tune in to the chaos that is our so-called television debates here in India. As to those unfortunates who have never laid their eyes on a Wodehouse tome, they are more to be pitied than censured.

Evelyn Waugh, a contemporary of P.G. Wodehouse's, had this to say of the great humourist, 'Mr. Wodehouse's idyllic world can never stale. He will continue to release future generations from captivity that may be more irksome than our own. He has made a world for us to live in and delight in.' It is a quote that adorns many of Wodehouse's book jacket covers. Waugh himself was no slouch when it came to the telling phrase that rousingly celebrates the English language. Author of some of the finest novels you could hope to get your hands on, special mention must be made of *Brideshead Revisited, Put Out More Flags* and *The Decline and Fall*. Mr. Waugh clearly did not care much for newspapers, about which he said, 'News is what a chap who doesn't care much about anything wants to read. And it's only news until he's read it. After that it's dead.' As with any great writer, words are Waugh's stock-in-trade. As he memorably puts it, 'One forgets words as one forgets names. One's vocabulary needs constant fertilizing or it will die.' That's one in the eye for the lay person who keeps carping about writers 'who use big words.' Evelyn's son Auberon, himself a journalist and satirist of note during the 80s, didn't quite achieve his father's everlasting fame.

It is rare, in the world of English Literature to witness a father and his son achieve stardom almost contemporaneously. The exception to the rule, Sir Kingsley Amis and his son Martin Amis, managed to do just that. Overly fond of his daily libation than was good for him, Kingsley Amis nevertheless wrote a clutch of highly acclaimed novels, most notably his 1954 debut *Lucky Jim,* a trenchant, rollicking send-up of the literary world, academia and those who peopled it. Here is the highly articulate atheist commentator, gadfly and essayist, the late Christopher Hitchens on Amis' novel. 'If you can picture Bertie or Jeeves being capable of actual malice, and simultaneously imagine Evelyn Waugh forgetting about original sin, you have the combination of innocence and experience that makes this short romp so imperishable.' *Lucky Jim* requires to be read twice, at least, to savour its subtle and heady flavours. Again, not to miss the reverberating Wodehouse reference. Two great quotes from *Lucky Jim* - 'If you can't annoy somebody, there is little point in writing.' And this classic, 'His mouth had been used as a latrine by some small creature of the night, and then as its mausoleum.'

The Amis scion, Martin, a close friend of Christopher Hitchens' has earned the sobriquet of being the *enfant terrible* of contemporary English Literature. A prolific novelist, essayist and memoirist, Martin Amis is a modern-day literary celebrity on a par with the likes of Salman Rushdie, Ian McEwan, Julian Barnes and of course, Hitchens himself. Among his many books, he may be best remembered for three novels, collectively referred to as the London Trilogy – *Money*, *London Fields* and *The Information*. Martin Amis' stories and essays are often dark, dense, thickly portentous and his descriptions and dialogues can take you into uncharted territory. Hence the need to re-read and get a grip on his amazing felicity and razor-sharp observations. His elegant prose can traverse comfortably from high-minded sublime to absolute down and dirty, but the Force is always with him. 'Someone watches over us when we write,' he says disarmingly. 'Mother. Teacher. Shakespeare. God.' How true, even if we are not aware of it and even if we are non-believers. And my personal favourite – 'What we eventually run up against are the forces of humourlessness, and let me assure you that the humourless as a bunch don't just not know what's funny, they don't know what's serious. They have no common sense, either, and shouldn't be trusted with anything.' Strong stuff, but as a lifelong follower of humour as a genre, I concur unreservedly.

What I have shared with you, dear reader, is only a smidgen of a sample which does not even scratch the surface of the riches that are available in terms of reading material. Before you hastily order your next best-seller from Amazon, take a quick look at the stack of books in your home library and ask yourself this question, 'Should I be re-reading some of these great novels and discovering hidden literary treasures that might have escaped me at the first reading, 'born to blush unseen and waste its sweetness in the desert air,' before splurging on new books with no space to keep them?' You might duck that issue by turning to the digital Kindle, which obviates the space problem but that, in my humble opinion, would be indulging in prevarication.

As Oscar Wilde, who can never be kept out of any literary discussion, said, 'If one cannot enjoy reading a book over and over again, there is no use in reading it at all.'

PS: In case you're wondering, I have excluded Shakespeare from the ambit of this discussion for obvious reasons. We quote extensively from the

Bard's complete works, as I have at the top of this piece. but we do not pass an idle hour reading his plays from cover to cover, inviting cervical cricks. Unless, of course, it was part of our school or university syllabus, or if we were treading the boards in fancy dress, playing Richard III or Hamlet.

TAKING SMOKERS DOWN A PEG

Giving up smoking is the easiest thing in the world. I know because I've done it thousands of times.
– Mark Twain

How times have changed. Not all that long ago, actually it *was* a long time ago in the 70s, when I first started working in an advertising agency in Calcutta, smoking was all the rage. I'll come to drinking in a while. At the ad agency, pretty much everybody, men and women, lit up a Wills Filter or a Charminar or, if you belonged to the higher echelons of the corporate ladder, India Kings would be the order of the day. Those privileged few who returned after a trip to the United States, United Kingdom or any other part of the world, flashed a duty-free carton each of Dunhill, Marlboro or Benson & Hedges, courtesy Indian Customs' munificence. A pack or two was all it took to grease the palms of some of the customs officials to chalk a tick mark on your bulging suitcase, enabling it to pass unhindered through the green channel. If you were an inverted snob, as some of our creative writers and designers at the agency were, even the humble rolled up *beedi* was in the mix. For the more discerning, a pouch of Prince Henry scented tobacco (peeping out of a shirt pocket) was also part of the smoker's paraphernalia. Pipe or cigar smokers were sighted, though rarely, but there were the odd big shots who sported them with much ostentation.

I am not certain if the poet and novelist Rudyard Kipling was a male chauvinist of the porcine persuasion, but he is 'credited' with the quote, *'A woman is only a woman, but a good cigar is a smoke,'* whatever that was supposed to mean. Speaking of women, in the late 60s in America, Virginia Slims launched an eponymous brand of elegantly slim cigarettes, with the women's lib inspired catchphrase, *'You've come a long way, baby.'* All in all, there was so much smoke swirling around the office you would have been hard pressed to see the person standing in front of you. All right, so I am exaggerating a trifle here, but put it down to literary hyperbole to drive home a point.

This was a phenomenon that was not unique to our organization. The whole of corporate Calcutta, or for that matter corporate India and possibly the world, was lighting up like there was no tomorrow. To employ celebrated British author Nancy Mitford's coinage, very *au courant* during the 60s and 70s, smoking was U and an abstaining non-smoker was, well, non-U. In other words, if you smoked you were 'with it' while the non-smokers were out of the charmed inner circle. *'You're never alone with a Strand,'* was a famous cigarette ad slogan in the UK. Here in India Wills' *'Made for Each Other'* swept the honours boards in the popularity charts. When you consider the fact that one of India's largest advertisers of the day, ITC Ltd., market leaders in branded cigarettes was headquartered in Calcutta, the biggest client for some of the leading ad agencies at the time, one smoked the company's brands almost out of a sense of bounden duty. If ITC told you to jump you asked, 'how high?'

In sharp contrast, in my own family circle, smoking was considered not just an abhorrent habit, but calculated to shorten your life by at least a third. Medical science strongly supported that view. More to the point, the filthy habit was seen as the worst kind of moral turpitude. Smoking was placed on par with immorality of the highest, or do I mean lowest, order. Debauchery might have just about pipped smoking to the post, as far as scraping the bottom of the morality barrel was concerned, but not by much. My father would view anyone seen with a cigarette dangling from his lips like something the cat had brought in. If it happened to be a woman puffing away, she was a gone case, banished to everlasting perdition. Even if he had to reluctantly tolerate a smoker in his midst, say at an official party, if the showoff smoker had the temerity to blow smoke rings in the air, that spelt the end of their relationship. Since my pater was still in service when I started my career in advertising, I would dread the day he would decide to casually walk into the agency to see 'how his son was faring.' That is, of course, if he could have floundered through all the smoke and found my cubicle in our 'den of vice.' Fortunately, that day never arrived and he retired soon after and settled down in pious Madras.

Speaking for myself, I was not a great fan of the habit. However, on the specious reasoning that one had to keep up with the Joneses, one would puff the odd fag now and then in a spirit of camaraderie, just to show there was no ill feeling. As I was a bachelor at the time and living with my parents, a couple of strong mint chewing gums on returning home provided rigorous exercise to my dentures, in the hope that any residual evidence of tobacco odour would have been obliterated. I think it worked, else my mother would have thrown an apoplectic fit and my father would have had to manage anger and depression (my mother's) at the same time.

A quick word about drinking. Alcohol, I mean. Much as my folks would not have been patting me approvingly on the back for downing a couple of beers or something even stronger, the lack of overt visual unsightliness while drinking, unlike smoking, did not seem to greatly bother them. Gin and water would look just like a plain, odourless glass of water. An uncle of mine was overly partial to this innocuous looking, but lethal, potion. Kindly bear in mind that we are talking about someone, that's me, who had just broken out of his teens, in his early twenties, stepping out into the big, bad world where vice and sin stalked the innocent lamb at every corner. Or so it was perceived. Another uncle of mine, who did not wish to utter the word beer within his wife's earshot, would invite me to go out with him for a spot of 'malt and yeast.' By the same logic, chewing paan with treated tobacco and shaved betel nuts, was considered kosher. Subterfuge was the order of the day. My father was an occasional, social imbiber. He sedulously stored a bottle of Chivas Regal in his cupboard for what I believe was at least twenty-five years! Whether that gave it an extra vintage halo or not, I could not say. What little was consumed of it was usually by our next-door neighbour, who would pop round once in a while to down a convivial peg or two, much to my mother's chagrin.

At some stage, I found even casual smoking provided little joy and much discomfort, and the world had started talking aggressively about the ills of the habit. Advertisements of tobacco and related products were banned and even cigarette packs carried ghastly visuals of skeletal bodies at terminal stages of cancer or lung disease. Ad agencies were going bankrupt. International airports were fitted out with special booths for smokers to congregate, shoulder-to-shoulder and smoke their hearts, or lungs, out to kingdom come. In fact, it's been a complete turnaround. Mitford's U and non-U appellation has been totally reversed. Smokers are now almost treated like *pariahs* (outcasts). In offices, they need to step out of the premises if they desperately need a drag. Thankfully, the little I myself indulged in the habit, after a fashion in the 70s, I gave up soon thereafter. You wouldn't catch me touching a fag with the proverbial bargepole. Hardly anyone I know smokes nowadays, barring an occasional gasper or two at a party where alcohol is flowing freely. Somehow, even those who puff on a ciggy infrequently are tempted to light up when they are involved in some serious elbow-bending with a glass of single malt or Bloody Mary.

As for drinking, as I had suggested earlier, if you are an alcoholic beyond repair you don't belong to the land of the living. Abandon hope. However, a glass of beer, a goblet of wine (red or white), or even something stronger in strict moderation, comes under the definition of social drinking, and not too many eyebrows will be raised. Assuming, of course, that you are an adult and know how to hold a drink. This hocus-pocus of 'my doctor told me two large pegs a day does wonders for my heart,' is just that, absolute balderdash. The problem is that most doctors lead tension-filled, hectic professional lives, and feel the need to let their hair down once in a while, and who can blame them? Have a civilized drink or two by all means, but don't justify it by pretending it's great for health. Only a loony doctor will ever actually say that. Let's face it. At the end of the day, there will always be smokers in our midst, but at least they cannot say they were not warned of the consequences.

I'll raise a small peg to that!

CELEBRATING WORLD BEE DAY

*If the bee disappeared off the surface of the globe, then man would only
have four years of life left. No more bees, no more pollination, no more
plants, no more animals, no more man.*
– Albert Einstein

Let us raise a toast to the humble bee. Or if you prefer, the bumble
bee. I cannot assert with any degree of authority if the bee, be it
ne'er so humble or bumble, can lay any genuine claim to humility as
an inborn trait. I just put that in because the two words, humble and
bumble, rhymed. Which is usually a good enough reason for any hack
writer to get started on an article. Naturally, that raises the valid question
as to why I woke up yesterday morning and decided to write a paean
on the bee or, to give it its biologically generic name, *Anthophila*. My
research on the subject further reveals that there are more than 20,000
known species of the bee and possibly, several hundred more variants.
That's a lot of bees to be getting along with, and the one thing you want
to avoid are these flying insects buzzing around your head at any time.
Get your head caught in one of these angry swarms, and your face could
be rearranged forever - with the help of plastic surgery. If you spot a
beehive anywhere in your line of vision, pause and admire a stunning
marvel of nature, but on no account touch it.

On World Bee Day, however, I have no wish to dwell on the more
unpleasant aspects of the bee's behavioural characteristics. There are
plenty of perfectly good things to say about the bee (honey for starters),
and I shall manfully strive to focus on these. Particularly because we

have been celebrating World Bee Day on May 20th, to mark the birth anniversary of Slovenian beekeeper Anton Janša, widely regarded as the pioneer of modern beekeeping. Seeing as he was born in 1734, it is clear that beekeeping as a hobby and profession has a hoary old tradition. I am somewhat handicapped by the fact that there exists no further useful information on Mr. Janša barring his strange obsession with these busy, winged creatures. This bee lover was of Austrian descent which explains his appointment as the first beekeeping teacher at the Viennese imperial court. From early childhood, he was as dedicated in his quest to suss out information about the bees as the latter themselves were in single-mindedly focusing on hive building and honey producing.

We can set the domestic scene. I imagine the young Anton coming home every evening, joyously showing off to his parents the many stings he has had to endure from his favourite insects. 'Look mummy, I got seventeen red stings on my arms and cheeks today. Aren't they lovely?' Mummy freaks out and heads towards the kitchen looking for some ancient herbal ointment to ease the pain and lessen the swelling while muttering under her breath, 'he *will* not listen, he *will* play with those bees.' But the boy will have none of it. Anton had firmly made up his mind to keep bees – a few stings here and there were little more than a flea-bite, a necessary collateral damage. Beekeeping was thus born not just as an interesting if dangerous hobby, but one that was to become a cottage industry of considerable financial significance in the years to come. The stings and arrows of outrageous fortune, to paraphrase Shakespeare and begging his pardon. Yes, we will come to the honey part of it presently.

On this very significant day, when we are doffing our hats to bees of every genus and recognising their immensely industrious nature, their innate architectural genius in building those picture-perfect beehives and honeycombs, it is not my intention to take you on a National Geographic type excursion into the habits and everyday chores of the bee species. If they reproduce like rabbits, I shan't go into the hows and whys. Some of their habits are pretty weird, mind you, like the queen bee literally making a meal of her king bee, assuming there is one, if he fails to obey her slightest command. Not unlike her other distinguished colleague from the insect kingdom, the highly poisonous 'black widow' spider which wouldn't think twice about gobbling up its kith and kin at the drop of a hat, having invited them to her parlour. At the human level, there have been dark suggestions that in 1567 Mary Queen of Scots did her husband Lord Darnley in, but it remained in the realm of rumour and saucy palace gossip. Unlike the Scottish queen, the queen bee from the Queendom of Anthophila does not leave anything to idle speculation. It goes about its murderous business with cannibalistic efficiency.

Moving away from the darker side of bee life, as we are celebrating World Bee Day and singing hosannas to Anton Janša and his pioneering efforts in the arcane hobby of beekeeping, my thoughts turned to music. So many songs have been written and sung, leaving the hit parades buzzing the world over. (This is where I introduce the honey motif.) I felt this is a good time to look at some of these memorable numbers by famous artists that celebrate the sweetness of honey and the bee that is responsible for bringing the sticky sweet syrup into our homes and our breakfast tables. We are, thanks to Hollywood, familiar with the many terms of endearment this sticky, gooey substance has inspired in men – honey / hon / honey-bunch / honey-kins and so on. From there to bursting into song is but a lilting step.

This is a purely personal and subjective selection and could be conspicuous by the songs that went missing from your list. So here is a list of my personal song favourites on the subject of bees and honey. In so doing, I once again bow to this singular, largely unsung individual, Anton Janša, who gave us something sweet to cheer and sing about even if, in the process, he was stung pleasurably.

A Taste of Honey. I first heard this beautiful song performed by The Beatles though the original composition is credited to Scott / Marlow. The song featured in their debut album, *Please Please Me* in 1962. While there have been many other cover versions of this song, for me the young Paul McCartney sets the benchmark and shows early signs of his melodic crooning talent as he takes the lead - A taste of honey / Tasting much sweeter than wine. It was one of those rare Beatles albums where they covered other composers' songs, till they became the most prolific singer-songwriters themselves.

Honey. Bobby Goldsboro's version of this iconic 1968 hit was one of those many songs that was played over and over again at parties and get-togethers during our college days. It topped the charts all over the world with its evocative lyrics set to a simple, hummable melody. The lyrics were mushy, demanding Kleenex tissues readily at hand. It was a time when people thronged to cinema halls to weep over *Love Story*. A sampler. *She was always young at heart / Kinda dumb and kinda smart / And I loved her so / And I surprised her with a puppy / Kept me up all Christmas Eve two years ago / And honey I miss you.*

Honeycomb. Jimmie Rodgers was a hugely popular American singer in the 1950s with a string of hits to his name, none more popular than *Honeycomb.* Never a Sunday passed during Calcutta's favourite radio programme, *Musical Band Box,* without this song being played. Again, a simple and singable song with the honeybee garnering all the attention. *Well it's a darn good life / And it's kinda funny / How the Lord made the bee / And the bee made the honey / And the honeybee lookin' for a home / And they called it honeycomb.*

Sugar Sugar. This 1969 teeny-bop hit had children and adults dancing to the tune of The Archies' bouncy track, based on an animated TV show inspired by the Archie comics. The lyrics, if you can call it that, does not exercise the mind, more the legs – *Sugar, ah honey, honey / You are my candy girl / And you got me wanting you.* As a stunning variant, the second line starts with *Honey, ah sugar, sugar.* Not exactly the Gettysburg Address, but the pop world loved it. What is more, the song was played in the command module of Apollo 12 on the way to the moon in November 1969!

Honey Pie. The Beatles again, in 1968, gave us this jaunty little ditty, a direct homage to the old-time, British music hall style. The lyrics, mawkish but nothing to write home about, suggests a hopeless admirer yearning for the company of a Hollywood starlet. *You became a legend of the silver screen / And now the thought of meeting you makes me weak in the knee / Oh, honey pie / You are driving me frantic / Sail across the Atlantic / To be where you belong / Honey pie come back to me.*

Tupelo Honey. One of Van Morrison's most beautiful songs, the Irish troubadour uses the theme of the unique brand of honey produced in the city of Tupelo (Elvis Presley's birthplace) in Mississippi, to describe the love of his life. *You can take all the tea in China / Put it in a big brown bag for me / Sail right round all the seven oceans / Drop it straight into the deep blue sea / She's as sweet as tupelo honey / She's an angel of the first degree / Just like honey, baby, from the bee.* The much-acclaimed 1997 film, Ulee's Gold, features Peter Fonda as a beekeeper who treasures the honeyed nectar from the tupelo tree. Van Morrison's title song was played over the end credits of the film.

Like Coleridge's Kubla Khan, on honey-dew have I fed in this piece, and it is all down to an unsung Slovenian beekeeper's pioneering efforts nearly 300 years ago. Happy birthday, Anton Janša.

Note: all the songs mentioned in this piece can be accessed on YouTube or Spotify. Just key in the song and artist name.

ABIDE WITH ME, WHILE I...

The beautiful lyrics for the hymn, *Abide with Me,* were written by Scottish Anglican Henry Francis Lyte in 1847 as he was dying from tuberculosis, the haunting melody for which was set by William Henry Monk. During my boarding school days in Bangalore, we often sang this paean during chapel service, along with other equally memorable hymns. *O God Our Help in Ages Past* and *Breathe on Me Breath of God* spring to mind. However, you would not be far wrong in saying that *Abide with Me* was, by some distance, at the top of the hymn charts. If you woke me up in the dead of night and demanded that I sing the first verse of this hymn, I could do it without batting a droopy eyelid. As most of you will surely be aware, this particular hymn has been hitting the headlines in India recently for all the wrong reasons. As India's 73rd Republic Day approached, it came to light that *Abide with Me,* traditionally played every year by one of the regimental bands at the Beating Retreat, alongside several Indian tunes that were redolent of valour, freedom and patriotism, will be conspicuous by its absence. Needless to say, this set the cat among the pigeons. Everyone and his uncle had something to say. I decided to clamber on to the bandwagon.

The powers-that-be who decide on such matters have clearly been mulling over this issue. A couple of years ago they took the decision to do away with *Abide with Me* at the Retreat, only to reinstate it, for reasons not clearly articulated. Perhaps somebody up there developed cold feet. This year, that same somebody decided enough is enough and the band stowed away the music sheet for this beautiful hymn in deep cold storage, with no prospect of thawing. Its place was taken by the uplifting tribute to India's martyrs, *Aye Mere Watan ke Logon* immortalised by the peerless Lata Mangeshkar. Lest we forget, there's always *Saare Jahaan se Achha* or *Vande Maataram* to fall back on.

Republic Day 2022, followed by the Retreat, has now come and gone without *Abide with Me*. For a few days, social and conventional media had nothing else to talk about. Musicians from various streams decided to put out their own versions of the hymn on Facebook, Twitter and Instagram in *simpatico* with those who felt hard done by at the omission. A few days later, all is forgotten as is the way with most 'hot topics' in our country, and life has returned to the usual humdrum normality about the assembly elections and the (hopefully) receding pandemic.

An interesting aside. During the rehearsals prior to the Republic Day parade, the band decided to let their hair down, shake a leg and play some popular Hindi film songs. The racy tune from the 1971 hit film *Caravan, Piya Tu Ab To Aaja (Monica my Darling),* drew a great deal of attention on social media and television news channels. Many thought this was actually going to be part of the R. Day official song list and went berserk, hurling invective at our officialdom for their gross lack of taste. Once the truth was known, the boot was on the other foot and our trigger-happy media socialites, to coin a term, had egg splattered on their faces.

Here's the thing. At the top of this column, I talked about attending chapel service in school and lustily singing those gems from the compact hymn book, *Hymns Ancient and Modern.* This was during the 1960s and the school in which I was a boarder, Bishop Cottons Bangalore, was run very much on Anglican Protestant lines. Church of England, if you must know. Now I come from an orthodox Tamil Brahmin family. I assure you they don't come more orthodox than that! There were many in my family circle who worried themselves sick over the possibility of our getting converted, if not in actuality, then perhaps through osmosis and 'sinister influences.'

Let me make it abundantly clear that nothing was further from the truth. If I enjoyed chapel service in school (I was even called upon to read the Lesson now and then), I equally revelled in learning Carnatic music and attending concerts by the great masters and exponents of the time. Though I was not of a particularly religious bent, I was quite happy to be a part of many of our family functions, especially weddings where classical music and sumptuous food were the order of the day. Music, be it a hymn by Henry Francis Lyte or Tyagaraja, or for that matter, Joan Baez (check out her incandescent *Amazing Grace*), the words were of scant significance. If I liked the tune, nothing else mattered; the lyrics were a bonus. If the music was unappealing, even the most profound lyrics had no impact. If words were all that mattered, we can always turn to poetry. I would recommend T.S. Eliot's *The Waste Land: Datta, Dayadhvam, Damyata / Shantih, shantih, shantih.*

What has all this got to do with the price of fish, I hear you ask. The government is of the view that vestiges of British imperialism, wherever possible, should be quietly done away with, though there is nothing quiet about it. This is a deliberate strategy not unique to the present dispensation. Ever since Independence, roads with English names have been gradually replaced with Indian equivalents. Mahatma Gandhi and Jawaharlal Nehru (and his descendants) have dominated our urban geography. Almost every other city in India has an M.G. Road or a Jawaharlal Nehru Road. I won't even get into the naming of stadiums. Calcutta's streets with British names were renamed not only with Indian equivalents, but with Communist icons like Lenin, Ho Chi Minh, Maxim Gorky and so on. They could not quite remove Queen Victoria's imposing statue in front of the Victoria Memorial, but the smaller plinths around the precincts have made way for Indian icons. This is not just a phenomenon unique to India. Most countries that were once colonized, would like to erase those painful memories over time. Let's face it, you are scarcely likely to hear the band strike up *Vaishnava Janato* or Mirabai's *Hari Tum Haro* at a royal procession in London. Both those lovely songs have been listed as among Gandhi's favourites, as has the present *cause célèbre, Abide with Me.* The Father of the Nation clearly had many favourites for us to be getting along with! In fact, the Mahatma specifically requested Nehru's 'Queen of Song', M. S. Subbulakshmi to render *Hari Tum Haro* at his last birthday celebrations. Speaking for myself, if the mood takes me, I am perfectly happy to listen to *Abide with Me* being performed by any decent choir with full throated ease. Truth to tell, the brass band version never quite worked for me. Too brassy.

Around the same time as the Republic Day furore, another controversy erupted, and I am not even touching on the annual Padma Awards hullabaloo. This time it was to do with the proposed installation of freedom fighter Netaji Subhas Chandra Bose's statue at India Gate in New Delhi, earlier occupied by King George V casting his imperious eye into the middle distance. In keeping with technological advancement, while Netaji's granite statue is being given the final touches, a hologram of the leader will be visible at night. Naturally, the ruling party and the opposition spokespersons were at each other's throats, the former justifying their decision while the latter saw it as little more than naked opportunism. If there is a grave somewhere containing Netaji's mortal remains (and that is an unsolved mystery), I am sure he is turning restlessly in it. While there are innumerable examples of statues and monuments being brought down all over the world for any number of reasons, leave alone statues that have been defaced, our politicians from all streams are only waiting for a chance to exercise their lung power when decisions are taken that go against their ideology. If history teaches us anything, it is that this will continue for as long as humans inhabit our planet earth.

The fact of the matter is, I have never been much of a one for parades of any kind. Floats and tableaux leave me largely untouched. I don't believe I have ever sat in front of my television set to watch the reverberating pomp and splendour, all the way through, during Republic Day parades. Snippets maybe, but no way are you going to catch me sitting through the entire shebang, even with jumbo bags of popcorn. That being the case, whether the band trumpeted *Abide with Me* or not makes no difference to me. Let the idealogues fight over the rights and wrongs of the alleged error of omission or commission. For myself, I can go to Spotify and select the venerated St. Albans Bach Choir rendering the divine *St. Mathew Passion* by, who else, but J.S. Bach. Come to that, a recording of T.N Rajaratnam's Pillai's mind-blowing *Todi* on the *nadaswaram* will work equally well. As for *Monica my Darling*, I shall give it a miss.

NO SEX PLEASE, WE'RE CUSTOMS

Sex toys hit city Customs barrier, end up in godown. The Times of India.

Honestly, I am fed up to the back teeth with our newspapers these days. All they ever talk about is the pandemic, border skirmishes, petrol prices, Modi and Putin bear-hugging, Sidhu, Channi and the Captain squaring off in Punjab, and some guy from Bollywood called Vicky getting hitched up to some gal named Kat, what the trousseau will consist of and who the lucky ones will be on their guest list. All right, so we thrashed New Zealand in a meaningless two-Test series at home. Big deal! In the midst of all this silliness, the tragic helicopter crash that took the life of India's CDS General Bipin Rawat, his wife and other officers, was an extremely shocking change from the everyday, anodyne script.

It's the same thing on television, only it's impossible to follow the storyline thanks to everyone on screen striving to break the sound barrier in disharmonious unison. Which is why I was startled to come across this extraordinary headline about sex toys being seized by Customs officials in Bangalore. Naturally, I ignored everything else in my daily paper and gave the full weight of my attention to this earth-shattering piece of news. Here's the gist of what this very enterprising reporter filed. Apparently, the pandemic has forced many of our denizens to look for diverting ways to take care of their claustrophobic idle hour. The Customs chappies were taken aback at the rapid increase in imports of a mind-boggling variety of titillating items, the primary aim of which was to satisfy man's basest instincts.

It occurred to me that if I am to obtain reliable information on the subject, I should go straight to the horse's mouth. I was certain the

Customs office in Bangalore would be having in their employ a Public Relations department who could fill me in on the details. Having got the helpline number from Google search, thither I rang. After the usual interminable wait, and having punched several digits to choose language, subject matter and 'if I wished to speak to one of our helpline officials,' and 'our lines are all very busy and we have limited staff owing to the pandemic, and we apologize for the long wait,' I finally reached a human voice. In between, I had to put up with some stultifying Kenny G type of music.

'Namaskar. This is Swati, how I can be of help?' Given the subject matter I was absorbed with, I would have preferred to speak with a man. No offence, I am a bit queasy that way, but I pressed on.

'Yes Swati, thank you. I am referring to a newspaper report this morning about which I wish to ask a few questions.'

'Are you from the media, Sir?'

'Not exactly. I am a columnist. Blogger, if you prefer. The news item I am referring to came from the media.'

'And what is this news item about, Sir?'

'Ah, well it's a bit delicate.' At this point, for some inexplicable reason, I dropped my voice to a barely audible whisper. 'Sex toys.'

'What? Sex boys? What are you saying, you dirty, old man. I shall complain to the higher...'

How could she have known I was old? No quaver in my voice. Anyhow, I interrupted her hastily. 'No, no. I was whispering, there were people about and you heard me wrong. Total misunderstanding. There was a news item about confiscation of some material at Customs, broadly classified as Sex Toys. Please forgive me if I was not clear. Blame it on the poor line.'

'Oh, sex toys. Why didn't you say so, loud and clear, in the first place?' She was quite blasé. 'Let me connect you to the concerned department. Please hold. It may take some time. Lines are jammed today with calls on that subject. Sorry for the inconvenience.' Gosh, they even have a dedicated department for this sort of thing! I was impressed.

After being put on hold for about seven minutes, while I was entertained to several recorded messages of the kind of punishment I could face if I brought in banned drugs, Chinese aphrodisiacs and pornographic videos, a tired sounding male voice finally answered.

'Yes? What is it that you want?' He sounded abrupt and vaguely threatening, as if daring me to bring up the subject of sex toys.

I decided to brave it out. 'Good morning, I wish to speak with you about these sex toys you have confiscated and are threatening to destroy. Can you give me some details?'

'What are you, a pervert, into kinky stuff? Don't you have anything better to do than to get cheap thrills first thing in the morning?'

'My dear Customs Manager or whatever your designation is, I am not seeking cheap thrills. I am not that kind of chap. I listen to Carnatic music. It is you who have proudly announced to the press about this haul of sex toys that you and your colleagues at Customs are sitting on, waiting for instructions to burn them. Like the cops do when they come across lethal arms, bombs, leopard skins, ivory tusks and the like. Usually, they pose proudly for photographs with the haul and the smugglers.'

'So, you want me to pose for the camera in front of a cache of inflatable dolls, S&M whips with thongs, floggers, vibrators, triple X videos and other such dubious items?'

He was clearly well-informed on the subject. 'Wearing a broad, triumphant smile, of course. And say "cheese." By the way, one thing about your statement to the press intrigued me. You said that after the pandemic struck, the import of such items has greatly increased. And that you have approached higher authorities for directions. Presumably to incinerate these degrading items of sexual gratification.'

'It has too. Increased after the pandemic, I mean. What is so intriguing about that? And your mocking, leering tone is not appreciated. We are doing a difficult job here. What do I go home and tell the wife and kids about how my day went at the office?'

'You have my sympathies, Sir. However, when you say imports have increased, it means, *ipso facto,* you have been allowing such items to come through in the past. Why get all cagey about it, now that more people are going in for such diversions? And you've been shouting from the rooftops about your capture, anyway.' I could see that he was beginning to get hot under the collar. Before he could respond, I came up with another salvo. 'With due respect Sir, my heart goes out to this bloke you have identified as Sid from Bangalore.'

'Who?'

'Sid. Not his real name, of course. He is heartbroken that, after paying 140 USD from an online Dutch portal for one of those thingummies I would rather not mention, you are now throwing the rule book at him. Have a heart, Sir. He is just a restless teenager with raging hormones. Just like Shirley (name changed) from Mathikere as well, who faced similar problems having imported some dicey stuff from the US. It's not just the boys, you see. They all have their needs, same as you.'

'Stop getting personal. You are skating on very thin ice. Look, I don't have to answer all these idiotic questions from a two-bit, deviant blogger like you. You don't even represent a third-rate, yellow-journalism rag. As it is, I have wasted too much time on you. As for this Sid and Shirley double-act, raging hormones, eh? Tough. They'll just have to do what all of us did.'

'And what is that, Sir?'

'That'll be all. End of.'

'Just one last thing,' I pleaded, ignoring all his insults. 'Do you actually burn all these items, or just claim that you do? My own sense is that they ultimately find their way into…'

At this point, the line went dead. After a week or so, I received a registered letter (with acknowledgment due) from the Customs Department, asking me to explain an online purchase of *Lolita* by Vladimir Nabokov and *Lady Chatterley's Lover* by D.H. Lawrence and would I appear at their offices the following week with both the books in question. I replied to them, through my lawyer, that they will be wasting their time poring through these great works of literature looking for cheap, salacious thrills. Much better if they can get hold of Shobhaa De's *Starry Nights* or *Sultry Days* to burn. Paperback editions, naturally. More combustible.

ROSENCRANTZ AND GUILDENSTERN ARE (NOT QUITE) DEAD

A one-act play (with apologies to Tom Stoppard)

The curtain rises and on stage are two beds in a nursing home. Lying on the beds are two very ill middle-aged males. At the foot of the beds hang two boards with the same bold legend on each, 'Rosencrantz – Nil by mouth, Guildenstern – Nil by mouth.' IV drips, tubes and clear, plastic bags carrying all manner of liquids into the patients and more tubes and bags conveying other liquids and semi-solids coming out of the patients, are visible. Flashing, beeping monitors overhead keep them constant company. It seems only a matter of time before they are carried away in body bags. However, they are able to speak, just about. For the benefit of our readers, it should be said their feebleness in speech is dramatically raised to what all theatre buffs call 'a stage whisper.' Loud enough for the audience to hear, and on the printed page, for us to visualize.

Rosencrantz – 'Good morning, Guildenstern. First off, is it morning, afternoon, evening or night? They keep the curtains drawn all day and all night.'

Guildenstern – 'I am going by my body clock. And in my present, enfeebled state, that is not ticking with Swiss precision. If push comes to shove, I'd hazard a guess and plump for late afternoon. Pre-dusk, kind of.'

Rosencrantz – 'You are not being very helpful. At least, if they wheeled in porridge, eggs and tea, I'd know it was breakfast time and I could keep tabs from thereon. This "nil by mouth" nonsense with all the tubes and everything, along with the drawn curtains, makes a mockery of time consciousness. Why don't they fix a clock on the wall, preferably one with a cuckoo?'

Guildenstern – 'A cuckoo clock. Nice idea. It will hourly jolt us awake if we drop off into a near coma. Actually, we should be grateful we are conscious at all. Why are you so obsessed with the time? It's not as if you have an appointment to keep. I mean, we are virtually strapped to these hospital beds for ever and anon. Me, I keep myself entertained, when I am not sleeping that is, watching these liquids racing up and down the tubes. Very soothing to the nerves. I have asked the duty nurse if she could see her way round to providing coloured liquids. Bit more psychedelic. Blue, red and orange sludge squelching around the tubes in tandem.'

Rosencrantz – 'You are a weird one, Guilders. And while you're about it, why don't we ask the nurse to place the beeping monitors somewhere in front us, instead of behind us where we can't see them. Not only would that be helpful in keeping tabs on our pulse, BP, heart rate and so on, but all those coloured flashing lights and metronomic sounds they produce, along with your multi-coloured liquids, would turn this place into a medical discotheque. Cheer us up no end. Why, even our playwright, Tom Stoppard worked it into our play, "The colours red, blue and green are real. The colour yellow is a mystical experience shared by everybody."'

Guildenstern – 'Good point, Ros. If they can play some bouncy, instrumental music along with all that, we may not actually be able to get up and shake a leg, but we can try and move side to side in rhythm. I'll speak to the nurse when she's here next with the bed pan. Music wise, what is your preference? Easy listening from the 60s like The Shadows, The Ventures or something more avant-garde like, say, Weather Report? It's all there on Spotify, so no problem.'

Rosencrantz – 'What on earth are you rabbiting on about? They can play our national anthem, for all I care. We can't stand up anyway. Or even sit down come to that. To get back to the point, Guilders, did it ever strike you that we can ask the nurse what time it is? Why did we not think of something so obvious? And why no television?'

Guildenstern – 'Your memory is shot to pieces, Ros. You did ask the nurse, last time round. And you know what she said. In fact, she didn't say it. She actually sang it, a snatch from that old Cyndi Lauper hit *Time after Time* - Lying in my bed I hear the clock tick and think of you / Caught up in circles confusion. Very cheerful, I don't think. And since you ask, television is too depressing, as they have only news channels.'

Rosencrantz – 'But very appropriate. The nurses here are quite strange. They don't give you a straight answer to any question. I once asked one of them if we will ever get out of here. Dead or alive. You know what her response was? And I am quoting verbatim. "Look on every exit as being an entrance somewhere else. Tom Stoppard." I could not make head nor tail of that. What did she mean "Tom Stoppard?"'

Guildenstern – 'Come on, Ros. Surely, you can't be that forgetful. Didn't you pop your memory pills this morning? Stoppard is the chap who wrote both of us into this play. You said it yourself just a short while ago. We might have been two minor players for old Shakespeare, recruited to stick our knives into Hamlet, and in the process, get our own heads chopped off, but this Stoppard chap detected hidden potential in the two of us and made us the heroes of this play. London's West End simply couldn't get enough of us. And I am sure we conquered New York as well.'

Rosencrantz – 'Of course, it's all coming back. "We're actors — we're the opposite of people!" What a line that was. The audience was rolling in the aisles. I am so glad you reminded me of who we actually are. Actors! So why am I getting so depressed. Is this a one-act play, a black comedy, or will there be an interval? I can't wait for the curtain call, then we can get in front of the screens, bow to the audience two or three times, and saunter off to the pub for a quick one, after the thundering applause dies down.'

Guildenstern – 'Look, let's not get carried away. I am still not absolutely certain if at this very moment of my speaking to you, we are in Tom Stoppard's play or if we are actually two terminally ill patients in a dank nursing home struggling to figure out what time of day or night it is with only colourful tubes and flashing monitors to keep us company. And not a cuckoo clock to be seen for miles around. And waiting for the Grim Reaper to claim us for his own. Then we *will* get carried away. Ha ha. As Mr. Stoppard wrote on our behalf, "We've travelled too far, and our momentum has taken over; we move idly towards eternity, without possibility of reprieve or hope of explanation." Let's just chew on this situation for a while. Perhaps it's all a dream.'

Rosencrantz – 'And here I was dreaming of retiring to our dressing rooms after the curtain call and sipping champagne with the rest of the cast, meaning those two nurses. The director would have been there, of course. Perhaps, even Tom Stoppard. Bouquets of red roses all over the place. Not forgetting the throng crammed outside the doors for selfies and autographs. I mean, if I am dreaming, I might as well go all the way. That line he gave one of us, I forget who, was a classic. "Life in a box is better than no life at all, I expect. You'd have a chance at least. You could lie there thinking: Well, at least I'm not dead." If you ask me, I am betting that we are just play acting. Don't you agree Guilders? Guilders? GUILDERS!'

(There's no sound from Guildenstern's bed. Not even the faintest comatose breathing. Rosencrantz looks up at his friend's monitor. Just flatlines.)

Rosencrantz – 'Maybe that's why they call it "theatre of the absurd." And why call it an existential drama, when I am not even sure of our ability to exist? What was that our celebrated quarry, the Prince of Denmark said, in the deft hands of the Bard - "I could be bounded in a nutshell, and count myself a king of infinite space, were it not that I have bad dreams." When the curtain rises, I'll know if all this was a bad dream, will my partner Guildenstern continue to remain inert and lifeless, or will he jump out of bad and break into song, *"Oh, what a beautiful mornin',*" from Oklahoma. Not that he has the slightest clue if it is morning, evening or night. For now, I can do no better than to end with Stoppard's own final line written for us, "We cross our bridges when we come to them and burn them behind us, with nothing to show for our progress except a memory of the smell of smoke, and a presumption that once our eyes watered."

(Stage lights off, curtain comes down, hall lights on)

SWEET DREAMS ARE MADE OF THIS

Of all sad words of tongue or pen, the saddest are these, 'It might have been.'
– John Greenleaf Whittier

As you age irrevocably, well into your dotage, you start to think more about things. All sorts of things. Could I have handled things differently, *should* I have handled things differently? Should I have considered a career in medicine, healing the sick and the lame, instead of landing up in an advertising agency helping to promote cigarettes, soaps, tea and tyres? I was a mean off-spinner as a teenager. Why did I not think of cricket as a potentially profitable livelihood? The answer to that question is not far to seek. There was no IPL when I was viciously turning those off-breaks. What I meant to say was that the off-breaks were vicious, not me. If you want me to be brutally frank, the god-honest truth is that my off-breaks never turned at all (just went straight on), and ironically that is how I deceived most batsmen who kept playing for the turn, poor saps. Cunning, I call it. Then again, I may not have made obscene sums of money thanks to there being no fat cat sponsorships those days, but look at Sunil Gavaskar. Same age as me. Extended his career brilliantly as a commentator and sports management consultant, and the best hair job in town as well. I could have done that, barring the hair job (I am quite happy with my shock of distinguished silver-grey hair, thank you). All else failing, I could have been a writer. If only I had started writing a novel around 50 years ago, who knows, by now I might have been the toast at various literary festivals, holding forth (and fifth) with great elan, my name being spoken of in the same breath as Salman

Rushdie. Look, if I am going to indulge in pipe dreams, I might as well go the whole hog. Instead, I write trite columns like this one, hoping a handful of staunch followers will actually read them and post a 'like' or 'thumbs up' on Facebook. That's pitiful, that is.

As that opening paragraph was becoming a tad too long, I must provide a separate segment for music, another passion. I was not a bad singer, even after my voice broke at the age of 15. Terrible thing this business of the voice breaking. For days on end, you are not sure if you are a soprano, an alto or a tenor, a kind of vocal schizophrenia, till it finally settles into a reedy tenor. Notwithstanding, I was an 'A' singer in the school choir, if you must know. At home, my mother forced Carnatic music down my throat, but in retrospect I am eternally grateful for her insistence. We are a family devoted to that arcane art form (my nephew is a top-flight Carnatic musician). I guess what I am trying to say is that, whether I crooned Paul McCartney's *Yesterday* at parties or Tyagaraja's *Entaninne sabari* in the raga *Mukhari* at family get-togethers, I drew generous applause from those two very different circles of audience, not forgetting the odd geometry box as a consolation prize at our local club. Not that I had the foggiest notion of what to do with set-squares, protractors and compasses. Actually, I am guilty of false modesty here. I did once take part in 'The Sound of Music' national talent contest and won third prize. One of the judges told me I could have won first prize, were it not for my ambitious attempt to reach an impossibly high octave in the girl's part in *You are sixteen going on seventeen.*, and coming a stunning cropper. Putting all that to one side, the final verdict was, 'He could have been a singer but didn't quite put in the hard yards.' Yet another instance of (sigh), 'if only...'

However, without getting all maudlin and soppy about it, I am quite happy with my lot. Advertising was an exciting profession to be in during the 70s and 80s, and a bit during the 90s as well. Earned my keep, met many interesting people, not the least of which was my wife. She was not my wife then, of course, but you know what I am getting at. All right,

I should have said 'my future wife,' thanks for nothing, you pedants. I could have also said 'alright' instead of 'all right' and the pedants would have been up in arms all over again. One has to be ever mindful of these sneaky devils who were once proof readers at publishing houses or ad agencies, and who take perverse delight in pointing out that you've got it all wrong with your apostrophes, colons and semi-colons. Ask me, I am a card-carrying member of that dubious and painful club.

All in all, while I am enjoying my early years of retirement, I think the verdict on my life could be summed up with a simple 'He has done all right.' (Here we go again!). That doesn't sound like much, I admit, but if doing all right was good enough for the Right Hon. James Hacker from the brilliant Yes Minister / Yes, Prime Minister television series, it's good enough for me. Not perhaps quite an Einstein, Fleming (the penicillin chap), Bradman or Dylan (Thomas or Bob, take your pick), but can't really complain. Sometimes, when our ad agency bagged an important client after days of blood, sweat, toil and tears, life got momentarily pretty exciting. Drinks all round and so on. The simple point I am striving to make is that you should be happy with your lot, if you have made a decent fist of it, and not worry too much about what might have been. Sure, who would not like to have been a Federer, but if the lord above gave you a backhand that was non-existent, you might as well just sit back and enjoy watching the balletic Swiss genius at work. A similar analogy can be applied to cricket. If you are incapable of dispatching a juicy full toss to the boundary, you are better off enjoying Geoff Boycott's classic description of that sorry state – 'Me grand mum would have hit that for four with a stick of rhubarb.' Get the picture?

In his celebrated essay, *The Superannuated Man,* the essayist, poet and antiquarian Charles Lamb, wrote this memorable sentence, *'I had grown to my desk, as it were; and the wood had entered into my soul.'* Had I heeded my father's advice and opted for a career in accountancy (he was a banker of some repute), I might very well have echoed Charles

Lamb's sentiments. He (Lamb that is, not my father) toiled for 36 years at the East India Company behind a desk, which explains his deeply felt cynicism.

Those of you, like myself who devoured the works of the Master, P.G. Wodehouse, will also be aware that he worked briefly at the Hong Kong & Shanghai Bank in London, a job he intensely disliked. Being a purveyor of humour and unlike Charles Lamb, he chose to put a mordant spin on it – 'If there was a moment in the course of my banking career when I had the remotest notion of what it was all about, I am unable to recall it. From Fixed Deposits I drifted to Inward Bills - no use asking me what Inward Bills are, I never found out….. My total inability to grasp what was going on made me something of a legend in the place.' Contrastingly, Nobel Laureate and poet extraordinaire, T.S. Eliot found his eight-year career at Lloyds Bank of London a soothing spur to his poetic pursuits. 'I am absorbed during the daytime by the balance sheets of foreign banks. It is a peaceful, but very interesting pursuit, and involves some use of reasoning powers.'

I can fully identify with the quandary in which Lamb and Wodehouse found themselves mired in. I manfully struggled through to obtain a university degree in Commerce when I would have been much better off taking Literature. Perhaps my dad had visions of his son following in his banking footsteps. Even today, if you asked me to analyse a bank reconciliation statement, you will find me gasping for air. All of which, of course, eminently qualified me to join the advertising profession, the primary *sine qua non* for which was to be in possession of a good English diction, an awareness of where the apostrophes were to be placed and above all, to be able to down three large rums (or whisky) straight up and be able to walk in a straight line or stand up erect and say, she sells sea shells on the sea shore. If you could play a bit of golf, you went straight to the top of the class. The rest you picked up as you went along. I may be accused of mild exaggeration, but as the saying goes, *in vino veritas*.

Seriously though, I guess the point I am driving at is not to look back regretfully at what might have been. Rather, grab whatever comes your way and make the best of it. If that sounds a wee bit preachy, so be it. As the late British comedian Peter Cook (alter ego to Dudley Moore) once said, 'I could have been a judge, but I never had the Latin for the judging.' Likewise, if only I could have actually turned my off-breaks, who knows what heights I might have scaled. Quite so, but having stumbled into advertising and now having become a maddeningly obsessive blogger, I am as happy as a lark. That does not stop me from day dreaming. In the words of the Bard of Avon, 'We are such stuff as dreams are made on, and our little life is rounded with a sleep.'

THE PM PHONES IN

Ihave been informed, by those in the know of these things, that the
Prime Minister is always ready to talk to the common man. Or
woman, come to think of it. One has to be ever so mindful of how you
employ these gender terms nowadays. If I had not hastily slipped in that
'Or woman, come to think of it,' I would have had to face an avalanche
of angry mails from the gentler sex. Always trusting to fate that they
have no violent objection to being described as 'gentle.' Sorry, haring off
at a tangent like that. I was reflecting on the Prime Minister's desire to
speak to India's common citizen at prescribed times on prescribed days.
I am excluding his weekly wireless fireside chat *Mann ki Baat* from the
purview of this discussion. This, if it is true, involves a person-to- person
chinwag over the phone with people like you and me, and it shows how
the leader of this impossibly vast and amorphous nation has his ear to
the ground and, evidently, to the phone as well. The common touch, to
borrow a phrase. The number given to me was obviously encrypted, this
for the PMO to be able to trace any crank calls that are bound to be made,
just for a lark. Like this one. 'Hullo, good morning Prime Minister, this
is Rahul Gandhi. I have underground connections in Sicily, through my
relatives in Italy. For your own sake, take me seriously. I strongly suggest
you had better watch your back. Say hello to my little friend. *Capice?*'

Any Mafia film buff would tell you that was a phony call. However,
the PMO was taking no chances. A trace was placed on Rahul Gandhi's
mobile number, but after a couple of days of snooping and listening in,
all they could get was, 'Mamma mia Mama, how many times have I told
you I hate Coco Pops? Where's my fluffy, cheese omelette? I WANY MY

FLUFFY CHEESE OMELETTE.' Every day it was the exact same line that was being repeated *ad nauseum,* and the PMO's telephone sleuths finally concluded that this was a recorded voice and that they had been had by the short and curlies. More likely it was a ring tone put in by some nutter with a corny sense of humour. Even Rahul Gandhi wouldn't stoop to something like that,

However, I am not one to throw in the towel that easily. I kept trying, those powerful words of Kipling ringing in my ears, *If at once you don't succeed, try, try again.* My perseverance paid off, eventually. And before any of you clever dicks jump out of your skins to tell me that it was not Kipling who said that but one T.H. Palmer, let me quickly assure you I am fully seized of the fact. At heart I am a bit of a tease and just wanted to have you on. Begging your pardon. Seriously though, this T.H. Palmer's name should have been up in lights for just that one memorable line he composed, but he was one of those poets who was born to blush unseen and waste his sweetness in the desert air. Thomas Gray. Once again, I am guilty of veering off from the subject on hand, but what the heck? Nobody ever told Shakespeare that he was using thirty words when seven would have served the purpose. My best friends keep telling me that my essays are too long. My philosophical response invariably is, 'How long is a piece of string? Go figure.'

In case you are wondering, I am having to indulge in all this meandering small talk mainly because getting through to the PMO was no simple task. I was placed at number 375 on the call waiting list. Then all of a sudden, before I could say, tongue-twistingly, Rashtriya Swayamsevak Sangh, my mobile started ringing in that familiar shrill ringtone.

'Good afternoon, are we speaking to Mr. Suresh Subrahmanyan?' intoned a strong male voice. Not to miss the royal 'we.'

'We are, we are,' I responded with an eagerness that was partly genuine and partly affected. 'Is that the Prime Minister? Sir,' I added as a respectful and precautionary afterthought.

"Not yet,' continued the voice. 'This is the Prime Minister's Office, and we have some questions for you before we can put you through to Him.'

I could sense the capital H. 'Does the Prime Minister's Office have a name?' I enquired somewhat cheekily. 'It is rather unfair that you know my name, I need to keep addressing you as an office. A bit weird, don't you think?'

'We do not appreciate your tone. The PMO does not take kindly to smart alecks who make tasteless wisecracks. One more remark like that and you will be taken off the list and your mobile number duly recorded for posterity and future reference.'

Gosh, now I had to worry about my posterior. This was going nowhere, and if it was going anywhere, I did not care for the destination. 'Sir, Mr. PMO, I did not intend to be smart. My apologies for the unintended solecism. Or gaffe, if you prefer. It's just that I am number 375 on the call waiting list, I have dropped every other normal household chore that I am expected to perform on a Sunday morning, blocked calls from my entire contact directory and have been sitting and staring at my mobile for "The Call." My eyes are hurting like blazes from the staring. I was merely anxious to know how much longer it's going to take before our leader comes on the line to exchange a few friendly words with me.'

'By and by, and if you keep on jabbering like this, it may never happen. Please answer these simple questions as briefly as you possibly can. How old are you?'

'That's a personal question. What's my age got to do with anything? Let's agree on 16. I know he likes to speak with youngsters.' I was bridling.

The PMO was beginning to sound irritated, but no more than I was. 'You do not sound like a teenager. If you are 16 going on 17, you know that you are naïve, in the words of that famous song from *The Sound of Music*. Once again, I must caution you. If you do not declare proper and correct information, there will be consequences. For the last time, what is your age?'

'99. Happy?'

'We need proof. Send me a scanned photo of you in standing position.'

'I am 99, I cannot stand. I have a picture of me in standing-erect position when I was 43, but what use would that be to you? Later on, I developed a bad case of scoliosis and my spine is bent. And if I sent you a photo of my grandfather standing in crouched position with a walking stick, how would you know the difference?'

The PMO was by now at the end of his tether. Exasperation was clearly evident in his voice. 'I have never come across such an ornery person. You wish to speak to the country's most powerful person and you behave like a juvenile delinquent. I am afraid I cannot waste any more Government time, when there are 625 others waiting in the queue. So kindly…'

Just then a sonorous, authoritative voice chimed in. 'Secretary Saheb, I have been listening in to your conversation with Mr. Subrahmanyan on the hotline. Please keep the line free. I will speak to him now.'

'Yes Sir, Yes Prime Minister. Right away, Prime Minister. I am connecting you Sir.'

Next thing I know, I was on the line with none other than the PM himself. 'Hullo,' he said, very friendly and everything. What do you say after someone says hullo? Not just someone, but India's leader extraordinaire.

'Hullo ji,' I responded, my voice barely above a croaking whisper.

'My office will allow me to entertain just two questions from each caller, because there are so many on the waiting list, so please ask both your questions one after the other and I will try to answer them to your satisfaction.' He was ever so courteous and polite. He didn't say "Shoot" but I was ready with my two questions.'

'Prime Minister Sirji, whom do you consider your greatest opponent on the Indian political scene? Second question. Who will take over from you as your party's leader once you decide to retire? Thank you, Sir.'

'Very good questions, Subrahmanyan ji. My greatest opponent is myself. I am fighting myself everyday to be a better leader for my people. Other opponents from all parties are also fighting – amongst themselves. I hope that is a good answer.'

'Brilliant answer, Sir. *Jawaab nahin.* What about my second question, Sir? Who are you grooming to be your successor? And Sir, please don't call me Subrahmanyan ji. I am underserving.'

'You are 99. That demands respect. Recently I honoured someone who was 125. As to your second question, I will follow our veteran cricket captain, M.S. Dhoni's footsteps. No unnecessary talking in advance. In our party, anyone can become the leader, but not till I retire.'

'But Sir…'

The PM was now off the air. The PMO was back, 'Your two questions are over, which is more than you deserved. Your time is up.'

Needless insult from the officious PMO. The PM was nice, but I still nursed doubts. Was this real or fake? He sounded like the PM but his English was faultless. Hmmm…

I'll check later with number 376 on the call waiting list.

HOW ABOUT SOME STRICKEN BORN POOP?

There are things that happen to us at various points in our lives on a consistent basis, simple and apparently inconsequential things, that we never give a second thought to. On reflection, however, and with the passage of time, these little happenings begin to acquire a somewhat deeper, philosophical tinge. Things that are sent to try us. In case you are wondering what this orotund introduction is all about, let me quickly cut to the chase. Take for instance, an everyday matter of ordering food at a restaurant. There you are, seated comfortably, along with your wife (or partner) and another couple, oblivious to some gormless fusion music playing in the background. A happy foursome, enjoying the liberty of post-pandemia, to coin a term. While you are still giving the menu the once-over, the waiter hoves into view with a cheery, 'And how can I help you with the menu this evening, Sir? Some wine to start with, perhaps? I could recommend the Burgundy red. Or the Sauvignon blanc, if white is your preferred tipple.' A vintner in the making, our waiter. Fact of the matter is while you've been intently studying the menu, you haven't actually been paying any attention to the items. It is possible that the obscene amounts mentioned on the right-hand column, particularly the wine section, have distracted your attention from the actual offerings on the menu. You then turn to the waiter with a 'We are still studying the menu, please come back in ten minutes, thanks.' And the waiter vanishes, like he was never there.

Before I get to the actual ordering, a quick word about the menu itself. Barring a few sensible eateries, most restaurants have now decided they will not waste good money designing and printing lavish menus, where frequent, blotchy redactions have to be made for items currently unavailable for some reason or the other, as well as to incorporate frequent price changes owing to cost escalations, GST and unbridled greed. 'Sorry Madam, we are fresh out of avocado, but might I recommend the Waldorf salad?' Shades of Basil Fawlty!

Instead, what they do now is to digitize the menu. So, when you ask for the outsize printed thing, the waiter points to a glass-encased card prominently displaying a squiggly design, like a QR Scan. In fact, I am informed it *is* a QR Scan, silly old me. Then you go through the elaborate and embarrassing process of holding your mobile phone in front of the display. When nothing happens, the ubiquitous waiter, reappears miraculously. He obligingly takes the mobile from you, ever so gently, turns the phone round the other way and says in an unctuously superior tone, 'This way, Sir.' You are tempted to tell him tersely that you were not dropped on the head as a child, but hey presto, the menu, all 125 pages of it, is in the palm of your hands in a type font and size that is barely readable. Let me rephrase that, it is completely unreadable. You now enter the rarefied world of scrolling – up and down. The process is repeated for all the four of us, and we are now ready to order, our mobile phones just a click away. Sadly, the establishment does not provide a magnifying glass to enable easier reading. One can, of course, expand the type by the simple expedient of the employment of your thumb and forefinger, but then half the text goes out of the screen and you are back to square one!

Given that we are not enjoying the first flush of youth, the digital menu is the cause for much squinting and removal and replacement of spectacles. If you ask me, we end up making quite a spectacle of ourselves. The waiter is still hovering obsequiously.

I clear my throat and announce, 'I think I will have the *Stricken Born Poop* for starters,' thus setting the ball rolling for the others to follow.

The waiter, looking puzzled, says that there is no such item on the menu. I give him a stern look. 'Look, my friend, it clearly says *Stricken*

Born Poop on your digital menu. Under *Soups and Starters.* I have no idea what it is but I am feeling adventurous, so let's have some steaming hot poop, pronto.'

'Sir, what you have ordered is *Chicken Corn Soup.* Perhaps the lettering was not very clear on your mobile. Try increasing the brightness, Sir.' Tactful chap.

'Ah, I see. Right then, *Chicken Corn Soup* it is. Pity. I was so looking forward to some stricken poop, just born.' The waiter smiles patronizingly and turns to the others, who he hopes would be blessed with keener eyesight.

'No starters for me,' declares my wife. 'I'll go straight to the mains. *Chicken a la Kiev* sounds good, if I've read that right. And by the way, should that not be spelt Kyiv, or are my eyes also deceiving me? I read about Kyiv every day in the papers.'

'Sorry Madam, that item is banned ever since war broke out between Russia and Ukraine. The management is sensitive to the feelings of our Russian and Ukrainian clients. Never mind how you spell Kiev. Or Kyiv.' And cheeky, as they come.

My friend pipes up, 'That's taken care of my Molotov cocktail, I guess. And my Russian salad goes up the spout as well. Why did we choose this place, anyway? How is it you haven't banned *falafel, shawarma, hummus* and all those Middle Eastern dishes? They are forever at war in that part of the world, aren't they?'

Before the harried waiter can frame a suitable response, my wife rejoins the discussion with a curt 'I take it you can manage the *Shepherd's Pie* on digital page 79? Please place the order immediately before Britain declares war on Russia. And don't spare the mashed potatoes.'

The waiter scribbles something on his pad and looks expectantly at my friend's wife, who has remained silent thus far. She, fortunately, does not seem unduly fussed about the political ramifications on the restaurant's food menu. Easy come, easy go was her motto in life. She then places the mobile phone very close to her eyes, adjusts her spectacles and pronounces gaily, "I'll settle for, to start with, *Honey Chirri Flied Potatoes* followed by that old-time classic, *Chicken Flied Lice.*' Let me quickly add that it was a multi-cuisine eatery.

The waiter then gets into the spirit of things and responds with a smart 'I am afraid we are fresh out of lice madam, flied or otherwise, but I can get the chef to do you a plate of delicious *Chicken Fried Rice.* But if you insist on lice, there's that louse of a street dog sitting outside the gates that might be willing to delouse himself in exchange for a marrow bone.' And we all have a good chuckle, though I felt he was overstepping the limits for a waiter. I told myself I should tip him handsomely for the unsolicited entertainment. One rarely comes across hotel waiters with an ironic sense of humour.

That said, cuisine life in a touchy-feely-menu-less world is nothing to write home about. It has its uses if you are ordering food from home online. Seductive photographs of various dishes in all their lip-smacking splendour serve a purpose, enabling us to tap our fingers on the chosen item. Notwithstanding the fact that more often than not, the pictures flatter the actual items that arrive an hour later, often cold and unappetizing. However, when you are seated comfortably in a restaurant, the last thing you want is to bury your head in your mobile phone, squinting tightly, asking the waiter if *Camel Custard under* 'Just Desserts' on digital page 124 is veg or non-veg, not counting the eggs. Even the poor waiter stops seeing the funny side of things.

Thus, I return to my original premise. Apparently insignificant things in life happen for a purpose. It may not be immediately clear what that purpose is, but some unseen power that directs our destiny, moves in a mysterious way its wonders to perform. Today it is menu cards in restaurants that gradually disappear from our lives. The anticipated death of the newspaper has been greatly exaggerated, though environmentalists may ensure that eventuality in the not-too-distant future. Thanks to the internet of things, the ominous signs are already there. Cassette tapes, vinyl records and CDs are fast becoming one with the dinosaur, the rarity only adding to their false snob value. Hullo Spotify. In the meanwhile, menu or no menu, I am making a beeline for quality restaurants in the company of close friends, before food as we know it and conviviality, disappear altogether. We could be swallowing 'food pills' three times a day that provide all the vitamins and nutrients our bodies need. Like our astronauts in space. Convenience foods will acquire a completely new meaning. I hope by then, I will be one with the dinosaur.

THE LAW IS NOT AN ASS

The sitting judge at the Delhi High Court (take a bow, you wigged worthy) has just ruled that a woman is perfectly within her rights to donate any organ from her body to a cause she deems fit *without* seeking prior permission from her husband. In the legal argot so favoured by judges, it was noted that applicable rules did not mandate any 'spousal consent' in case of organ donation to a close relative. Adding, quite tersely, that 'she is not a chattel, it is her body.' Hear, hear. All you husbands out there contemplating sympathy from our justice system, you are duly warned. If your wife comes home one of these evenings and announces that she has just divested herself of one of her body parts in a good and noble cause, you cannot fly into a mad rage and start flinging the crockery around and haring off to courts. In this particular case, the body part concerned was one of the woman's kidneys which she decided to donate to her father. *Her* kidney, *her* father, she may do as she pleases. No prior consent from her hubby required. As any student of medicine will tell you, a human being can lead a perfectly normal life with just one kidney, so what is all the fuss about? Two kidneys are not entirely surplus to requirements (they were placed there for a purpose) but push comes to shove, one is enough, 'twill serve.

That appeared to be the broad view of the honourable judge of the Delhi High Court. Not sure if the estimable purveyor of justice, while pronouncing the verdict recalled Hamlet's memorable line, *'There are more things in heaven and earth, Horatio, than are dreamt of in your philosophy.'* Had he done so, he would have been moved to paraphrase Shakespeare while admonishing the husband, 'there are more things to worry about than your ego. Your wife donated her kidney to her dad. The matter ends there, the law does not require her to obtain an NOC from you, so let's have less of your chauvinistic protests. Mr. Bumble from *Oliver Twist* might think "the law is an ass," but we beg to differ. Take her to a nice movie, and dine out afterwards. That's the least you can do to show your appreciation to a noble gesture.' Well said, m'lud. A judge after my own heart. Knows his Dickens as well.

This unambiguous ruling clearly puts the husband in a bit of a quandary. Taken as a precedent, as all judicial rulings generally are, husbands across the land will be fretting every time their wives come home late in the evening, wondering if they are in possession of all their anatomical parts with which they were born, or have they been scattering parts of their body to the winds, unmindful of domestic consequences? Enough to put any husband off his dinner. The following exchange could be a typical conversation at a couple's home, after the husband returns late from work to an empty home, his wife yet to return from work. She is normally back earlier than her beau. He has just helped himself to a drink when their merry cocker spaniel lets out a piercing, happy yelp indicating that the good wife has just driven in. Dogs know these things. She lets herself in quietly.

The husband opens the proceedings. 'Hullo darling, long day? You are never this late. You look a bit bushed. Everything all right?'

The wife, after dealing with the customary passionate greeting from the spaniel, responds. 'Why do you ask? Why should everything not be all right?'

'No, no, simply asking. Another tiring day at the office, eh? You normally get home by six, it's half past eight now. Just wondered, that's all. Are you sure you are feeling fine?' The husband was obviously fishing and his better half could sense that.

'You seem to be wondering about things a great deal. I come late one evening and you seem to be imagining all kinds of things. Precisely what is it that you are concerned about? I am not having an affair, if that's what is bothering you.' She was clearly a bit tetchy, and it showed.

'That is uncalled for and beneath you. Look, any responsible husband would be concerned if his wife comes home unexpectedly late. You should be happy, not become irritable simply because I asked after your welfare. But since your brought it up, why have you covered your left ear with the end of your sari?'

'*What?*' The lady of the house was beginning to lose it.

'Just curious, that's all,' replied the hubby trying to sound calm. 'I mean, you normally never cover your head with the *pallu,* and yet here you are, only your left ear covered whereas the right ear is fully exposed and looks as normal as any right ear should. What gives?'

'My dear husband of fifteen years, can you please explain what is behind this incoherent jabbering. Is that your first, or seventh large peg? You are not making any sense. Are your sodium levels dropping again? Should I call the GP?'

As she was making these inquiries after her husband's health, the offending sari end dropped to her shoulder and it was plain that her left ear was fully in place. No bandage, no Van Gogh syndrome visible. While that brought him some relief, he now started worrying about other parts of her body. He muttered to himself, 'thank heavens for that.'

She was beside herself. 'Thank heavens for what? Look, I am going batty here. What is your problem, exactly? I've had a difficult day at the office, and I come home to this. Will you kindly explain what's biting you? Perhaps we should drive you to the hospital and get a quick check up done.'

He calmed down. 'Look my dear, let me come clean. I have been reading about how a judge in Delhi ruled that a wife need not seek her husband's clearance to donate any part of her body to someone, especially her close relative, if she so desires. If you have any such intention, you will talk to me first, won't you? Don't think of it as seeking permission or anything like that, but just to let me know. A second opinion is always useful, if you wish to go through life without one of your big toes. Albeit in a good cause, of course.'

'You really have gone bonkers. And you thought I might have donated my left ear to someone? I know where you are getting all this from. I too read the papers. That was a case of a woman who donated her kidney to help her father's critical medical condition. The judge was merely emphasising that her husband's permission was not mandated by law. End of. Tomorrow, God forbid, if you needed a kidney, would I not come forward, even without your permission?'

'Thank you, light of my life. That is most comforting. I simply wanted to make sure you don't suddenly turn up and go, "ta da, look ma, no hands."'

'I honestly think you are suffering from an acute case of paranoia. Every time I return late from work, you will start imagining me with something missing from my body. Lung perhaps? Eye, people do donate eyes, don't they? You've already lopped off my left ear. Dread to think what else you've been chopping off. I would suggest you stop reading the papers. TV news is much better. You won't follow anything for all the cacophony and you might even go to sleep.'

And so, in hundreds of thousands of households in India, similar heated exchanges are taking place even as this piece is being put to bed. The Delhi High Court ruling has set the cat among the pigeons and husbands are lying awake in their beds, tossing and turning restlessly, unable to sleep and wondering if their wives are levelling with them or is there something missing and they are in the dark? Last we heard on the subject many males of the species were examining their bodies closely to see if they can get rid of some unwanted parts without their wives knowing. After all, they now have a precedent. And judges love precedents.

DEAR DIARY

The nicest part is being able to write down all my thoughts and feelings; otherwise, I'd absolutely suffocate. Anne Frank, 16 March 1944.

Anne Frank's diaries are now part of literature's legend and song. The young Jewish Dutch girl, who was gifted a diary in 1942 when she was barely 13 years old, poured her heart out in those invitingly blank pages. Over the next couple of years, hiding in a secret attic in Amsterdam to keep away from the depredations of Nazi occupation, she wrote prodigiously; about her growing up in such forbidding conditions, about her sense of self and above all, about the ever-present danger of capture and the dreaded concentration camps. In spite of all that, she constantly exuded positivity in her pages and thought nothing but good in the human soul and spirit. The best-selling book, *The diary of Anne Frank* ends on a high note of optimism. Describing herself as a 'bundle of contradictions,' Anne Frank had this to say about her general outlook on life. 'As I've told you many times, I'm split in two. One side contains my exuberant cheerfulness, my flippancy, my joy in life and, above all, my ability to appreciate the lighter side of things.' She could have been speaking for me as far as 'appreciating the lighter side of things' is concerned. I can barely bring myself to imagine what the darker side of things must have been for Anne.

My thoughts, however, are concerned more with the humdrum aspects of life that we used to post in our own diaries many moons ago. If that suggests going from the sublime to the ridiculous, so be it. Question: do people maintain personal diaries nowadays? I have met the odd person who does, odd being the operative word, and chances are that these oddities were born during the forties and fifties or perhaps even earlier. This is not to say that stationers, book sellers and some organizations do not print diaries (and calendars) which are avidly sought after, particularly during the dawn of a new calendar year. These specimens are essentially meant for those who are not quite *au fait* with the digital versions on their mobile phones or personal computers. I have also been amazed at how, when November and December came around, so many people would be seen running helter-skelter looking for diaries or calendars to cadge from wherever they could lay their hands on. It was almost as if diaries were about to become extinct. And that is almost true.

For the most part these diaries are the exhaustive repositories of laundry lists, provisions purchased, sundry expenses, not to mention birthdays and other milestones that one needs to be reminded of in order to send flowers or make that courtesy phone call. It carries infinitely more weight than being reminded by Facebook. My father, who passed on in his late eighties about twenty years ago, was a stellar example of a man who jotted down all manner of details about his family and close friends in a tattered and torn diary that was well past its sell- by-date. His diary would also contain faded newspaper clippings of anything that he thought might be of interest for future reference. If I was lost in trying to hunt down some old news item about somebody in the family, all I needed to do was ask him. Why his personal diary was considered a safe haven for these snippets, which also worked as bookmarks, was a closed book to me. That said, I know many people who acquired several diaries and simply stowed them away in a safe place, never having even opened them! However, try prising one of these moth-eaten items out of them and they will get all cagey and evasive.

During our boarding school days, and here I am harking back to the swinging 60s, some of us boys maintained little pocket diaries, or just a plain exercise book which worked just as well. Only we had to write in the date on which we were entering our profound thoughts.

The school administration encouraged this activity during our spare time and holidays, as they felt it would improve our writing skills. That was a laugh. Most of the boys would vent their spleen on other boys, or even on the masters, in ways hardly calculated to improve their knowledge of the language. If the school honchos got their grubby hands on these incriminating tomes, there was hell to pay but that was a risk the boys were willing to take. Here are some samplers, drawn from varying imaginary dates. I have randomly chosen the year 1963 for no reason other than the fact that President John Kennedy was assassinated that year, Martin Luther King made his famous 'I have a dream' speech and not to put too fine a point on it, I discovered The Beatles. These milestones leave a lasting impact.

25th July, 1963 – Acted in our school play, 'The Language Shop.' Was cast as the Weak Verb. Hell's bells! Why couldn't the director give me the role of the Proper Noun or something. I got awful stick from the Transferred Epithet and the Definite Article. The Indefinite Article, like the Weak Verb, was considered a pariah. Enough to drive anyone up the wall. I was the laughing stock of the school.

Actually, the play was pretty smart. Plenty of puns and humour and calculated to enable us boys to appreciate the language better. But Weak Verb? I deserved better. I could have been the Strong Verb, if there is such a one. Wren & Martin, what say you?

17th August 1963 – Somebody has torn a huge hole in my mosquito net. I think I know who it is. It has to be that cowardly cur, Charlie the Chump. You've got it coming Charlie boy. Where is that old bottle of ink?

Not the finest example of the language of Shakespeare, but more on the lines of Enid Blyton's *Famous Five.* Always remembering that we were in our early teens. As to what the chronicler proposed doing with 'that old bottle of ink' is anybody's guess.

21st August 1963 – I got just 27 marks for my geometry paper. I first thought it was out of 50, until I was told by our maths teacher Mr. Caleb, *that it was out of 100! Meaning I plugged! Shit -o! What am I going to tell my pop when I write to him this weekend? Bloody Pythagoras!**

That was a typical entry. 'Plugged' by the way, was schoolboy slang for failed. I don't know what it is, but we always came out of our exam halls exuding disproportionate confidence. 'I think I maxed it,' was the standard, hubristic response to being asked how we fared. We might have cried into our pillows after lights out at night, but no one noticed. Matron had to deal with plenty of moist pillows in the dormitory next morning.

*As this blog is being put to bed, news has just filtered through, that educationists in India have questioned Pythagoras' theorem and Newton's apple gravity theories as being possibly fake and that they have most likely taken their posits from ancient Indian texts. Mera Bharat Mahaan!

29th August 1963 – I told the skip not to place that fat slob Ganga at first slip, but does he listen? He goes and does just that, and a dolly catch spilled off my bowling. Butter fingers! Screwed up my bowling analysis. I shall make sure to grass the next catch that comes my way. You wait and watch.

Ah, school cricket politics. It was worse than what we witness now at the BCCI. The fight for a place in the school eleven for any representative game was fiercely intense. Those who missed out made no bones about what they thought of the selector, namely, the poor games master. Invective was hurled, behind closed doors; or closed pages, naturally.

2nd September 1963 – How the hell did he pick Yousuf ahead of me? And why Ranjit, for God's sake? Neither of them can hold a bat straight and they are the biggest, what's the word, ah yes, liabilities on the field. Something very fishy going on here. I shall send an anonymous letter to the Warden.

22nd November 1963 – One of the house prefects comes barging into our dormitory early in the morning shouting, 'John Kennedy is dead. Shot by some crazy lunatic.' Big deal. What was John Kennedy to me? I was much more interested and excited by the news that The Beatles have released their second album 'With The Beatles' on that very day. Their debut album, 'Please, Please Me' was also released earlier in 1963. I mean, for a 14-year-old in the early 60s, given John Kennedy vs The Beatles, who will win? Go figure.

There you go. Most of us boys were not precocious beyond our years to grapple with deep, contemplative thoughts about the world, the theory of evolution or delve into theocratic or philosophical thoughts. Cricket, comics, classroom capers and pop music tended to fill our waking thoughts. Oh yes, girls did occupy our thoughts now and then and a typical diary entry would go something like this:

November 26ᵗʰ – Four of the boys went to visit their sasses today. They came back with autograph books for some of us boys to sign on the 'Wall of Friendship.' Guess what, I am on the list of three of them. What do I write on them other than signing the damn things? And why was I not on the fourth list? Woe is me! I shan't sleep tonight.

In case you were wondering, 'sasses' was school shorthand for sisters. Anyhow, such was the childish silliness that our diaries were filled with. If you ask me why we were not inspired by the likes of Anne Frank, the answer is simple. We were not even aware of her till many decades later, and then too only because of her diaries. If there are those in 2022 who maintain diaries and jot down their thoughts and activities, I doff my metaphorical hat to them. I would like to maintain a diary again but the moment has long since passed. I write blogs instead. Oscar Wilde, who always had something memorable to say about anything at all said, 'I never travel without my diary. One should always have something sensational to read in the train.' Most of us don't lead the kind of sensational life Mr. Wilde did. Which is just as well.

ADD TO CART. EVERYTHING MUST GO.

'C ause we're goin' out of business / Everything must go.
– Steely Dan

A few years ago, I wouldn't have known the first thing about booking or ordering stuff online. You know what I am talking about – airline tickets and hotel rooms, to name just two. And I am not even getting into Amazon, Swiggy, Zomato, Big Basket, Dunzo, Ola, Uber and the like. The whole world seems to be waiting to open up for your sole pleasure, between the tips of your fingers and that magic touch screen on your mobile phone. It is by now a well-established fact that most of us keep ordering things online we would normally never even have remotely thought of, simply because it is so infernally convenient to do so. Ironically, we now do everything remotely.

The fact that you are not actually shelling out hard currency from your wallet, and that the expenditure is being debited to some invisible, bottomless pit of an account in your bank, only to surface a month or so later in your bank or credit card statement gives you a cushy, if false, sense of well-being. Long live UPI. It is almost as if you have just helped, or rather, gifted yourself to that pair of ankle weights you would never have dreamt of buying a few hours earlier. Of course, when you actually study that bank or credit card statement, you do wince and go, 'did I actually order that?' *Ankle weights?* All you have to do is tap on the 'Add to Cart' or 'Buy Now' tab and a couple of days later the ankle weights duly arrive courtesy Amazon. You admire the item in question and put it away somewhere safe. So safe that you forget all about it until you guiltily discover its forlorn presence six months later. At which point you push it further back into the loft so no one can spot it, including yourself.

Like everything else, these online marketers or aggregators as some of them are fancifully called, have allowed success to go to their heads. They are now beginning to show those tell-tale signs of slackness, the result of extreme hubris. I guess that was inevitable. If you aggregate so much you don't know what to do with it! In recent times, many items that you would like to order are out of stock. Of course, items you don't particularly need, like ankle weights, are plentiful in supply. I would have thought these smart chaps, who are supposedly wizards at forward planning would have been able to analyse their customers' needs based on past buying behaviour and so on. But no. Pepsodent G, my regular toothpaste brand, not available (my gums will start bleeding again). Heinz ketchup, try again next week. Heinz baked beans, you must be kidding. Heinz Means Beanz, but not here. Kellogg's Almond and Honey cornflakes, try the plain ones. Coca Cola, we can give you Diet but not Regular. Cadbury's Silk Plain, sorry we have Hazelnut or Fruit and Nut and in small 250 gm packs only. As for Ching's noodles, velly solly prease. I think you get the idea.

I can hear some of my patriotic, tricolour-waving friends going, 'you buy only American and Chinese brands? Shame on you. Why don't you try Mohun's cornflakes or Amul Chocolates or Kissan ketchup?' Yes, point taken, but those American and Chinese brands are being made in India and sold through Amazon India. So, put that in your pipe and smoke it.

Bottom line, what with no one talking of Covid any more, we drive to our nearest departmental store, suitably masked, and get those very items the aggregators said 'no' to. As far as I can tell, more and more people are visiting brick and mortar stores to do their shopping. This is as much because of the supply problems online I spoke about, but also to once again experience the pleasure of walking around a departmental store, browsing, touching and feeling the products. Something by definition and inherently not experienced with Amazon. Or Big Basket, come to that. This is further accentuated by a nameless dread. 'What if Covid comes back with a vengeance? Let us enjoy going out while the going is good,' about sums up the general view.

Since the Amazons of the world do have a window to talk to one of their representatives over phone in case of some intractable problem, I felt I must let off some well-worded steam and let them know that their standards are clearly slipping. Press 2 for English and you will get someone greeting you in Tamil, *'Vanakkam.'* Wiser to press 5 for Tamil, and you will be put through to an English-speaking representative. On no account should you press 8, unless you are fluent in Swahili. Always pre-supposing that in order to be able to have this conversation, you need to first get across to them, which involves navigating through several options and hoping fervently that the line does not suddenly go on the blink. If that happens, God forbid, you will have to go through the whole painful process once again. However, if at first you don't succeed and you try, try again, ultimately your perseverance will pay off and you will win through to an almost human voice, as I did.

Almost Human Voice (AHV) – 'Good morning Sir and how can I be of help to you?

Yours Truly (YT) – 'I shall dispense with the courtesies and get straight to the point. No chocolates, no baked beans, no toothpaste, no noodles, no cornflakes, no Coke, what the hell is going on? You call yourself Amazon? You should be renamed Lilliput.'

AHV – 'Lilliput Sir? I do not understand.'

YT – 'I didn't think you would. Go and read *Gulliver's Travels.* What about all those items I listed that you are stocked out of? All pretty much standard items.'

AHV – 'We do have other toothpaste brands, Sir. Likewise for chocolates, noodles and so on. You should patronise some desi brands,

Sir. Baba Ramdev's Patanjali range of ayurvedic products is highly recommended.'

YT – 'Baba Ramdev, eh? Next, you'll be telling me to stand on my head for 20 minutes! I don't need a lecture on patriotism from you, young lady. It's not good enough. Always assuming you are a young lady, and not a 14-year-old boy whose voice has not yet broken, in which case I shall complain to the authorities about employing underage children. Anyhow, I am a very brand loyal person. You, of all people, must know that, since you keep quoting from my past purchase records.'

AHV – 'Sir, it is very difficult to follow what you are saying. But Sir, we do have ankle weights and you have purchased them from us. I can see it on our records. I hope you are happy with them.'

YT – 'I am sorry if you cannot follow proper English. Look, I can't brush my teeth with ankle weights now, can I? Nor can I have them for breakfast. What good is ankle weights when I am starving at breakfast time?'

AHV – 'I can help you there, Sir. Why don't you try our MTR idli or upma mix? Easy to prepare, the instructions are on the pack. Even a child can do it. And we are well stocked up on these items.'

YT – 'I am sure you are. All the things I am not interested in, you will have abundant supply. Right now, I am not in the mood for idlis or upmas. Or, for that matter, Mohun's cornflakes.'

AHV – 'How about porridge or oats, Sir. Very English. You sound very English, and we have plenty of brands like the world-famous Quaker Oats.'

YT – 'All right, maybe I'll give it a try. My apologies if I have been somewhat abrupt with you. Not your fault of course, but you should play this recording to your bosses. A disembodied voice did say at the start of this dialogue that this conversation is being recorded for "training purposes." So there, I shall cry off for now and hope you will be better stocked next time round.'

AHV – 'Thank you, Sir, and I hope the ankle weights are serving your ankles well.'

At which point, I disconnected. I thought she was being a tad cheeky with that ankle weight send off, but I had to appreciate her tongue-in-cheek gumption. However, the conversation had gone on long enough and it was time to terminate. My final view on the subject is that, taking it for all in all, warts and all, I would greatly welcome being able to shop once more at physical stores without let or hindrance. Good exercise too, walking round and round those aisles. The Amazons, Big Baskets and their ilk will continue to rule our lives, but at least, if I do not find my favourite brand of sliced cheese at the shop, I can gently vent my spleen at another human face, and not at some telephonic, faceless juvenile delinquent who will remind me of the availability of ankle weights when I am desperately hunting for my favourite shampoo brand, in addition to those cheese slices.

KING FEDERER I

Ever since Roger Federer announced that he is hanging up his racket for good, there has been an avalanche of goodwill messages from all over the world wishing the maestro well. Copious tears have been shed. That was only to be expected, given all that the great man has achieved in the world of tennis. Nadal and Djokovic, Federer's greatest rivals, have been leading the charge with their emotion-filled missives on social media, followed by any number of other tennis personalities, both from the men's and the distaff side of the game singing hosannas to the player who defined elegance, style and class on a tennis court. We saw it coming, his exit that is, over the last couple of years (he *is* 41 years old) but when the announcement actually arrived, most tennis aficionados felt that this was a vacuum that may never be filled. Nadal and the Djoker are still there, not for long one suspects, and brilliant, young upstarts like Alcaraz and Sinner are putting down a marker on the world stage. The moot question is, can anyone capture the public imagination like the genius from Basel did? Time, and it will be a very long time, will tell. The GOAT debate has raged for a while and depending on whether you are from Spain, Serbia or Switzerland, the accolade for the greatest will vary. If the vote was not based on sheer numbers and only on emotion, the Fed will win hands down. For when the dust has settled and the fat lady has sung, that is how Roger Federer will be remembered - an Emotion. As our magnificent Lone Ranger rides off into the sunset on his white steed, swinging for one last time his Wilson Pro Staff RF 97 Autograph racket, we can hear a distant 'Hi-yo, Silver! Away!'

I have been asked by some of those who read my blogs (about five of them when I last checked) why I have not yet joined the clamorous bandwagon of gushing fans penning an appreciative paean on arguably the greatest tennis player ever to whip a single-handed, backhand cross court winner past a bemused opponent. I have succumbed to pressure as you can see, if you are reading this. My initial hesitancy was due to the fact that I could hardly add anything of value to the reams of copy already circulating around the globe, across media, telling us why we are all going to miss this icon of the game. Not that we needed any telling. Furthermore, Federer's timing of his retirement coincided with the passing of a much-loved British monarch, give or take a few days. That meant the King of tennis had to vie with the Queen of Great Britain and Northern Ireland for public attention. For all that Federer is an adored superstar, Her Majesty, regally holding nothing more than her Sceptre for some 70 years, now interred at Windsor, was going to win that particular contest hands down. Queen Elizabeth II could not do much about when she was going to pass on and join her royal ancestors at the great palace in the sky, but the sultan of the tennis court could have deferred his announcement by a couple of weeks. That may sound facetious (I speak as a tennis buff) but Federer certainly deserved to be given a proper send-off without high-profile and protracted royal obsequies raining on his parade.

Roger Federer may not be a royal in the sense in which members of the Windsor family are, but anyone who understands the difference between a second serve and a double fault will tell you that the balletic Swiss is regal. Regal in a way no tennis player before him has been, certainly not on a tennis court. Federer's racket skills can only be compared to Zubin Mehta's baton waving while conducting the Los Angeles Philharmonic. His personality off court was as winning as his achievements on court. Measured purely on the scale of fan following, he reigns supreme. All he needed was the Ermine cape, the Orb, the Sceptre and the Crown and he could have walked into Buckingham Palace, no questions asked, though King Charles III might have thrown a hissy-fit like he did recently when his fountain pen leaked. However, Federer is certainly the King of Wimbledon measured by the number of singles titles won, unless Djokovic goes past him in the near future. However, let us not get completely carried away. Roger Federer was and is human. Almost. As a callow youth, he had to deal with anger management issues and was known to throw temper tantrums like you wouldn't believe. The broken rackets at the Federer homestead would have kept the family warm at the fireplace during the chill winters of his home country.

Fortunately, unlike some other famous tennis stars I could name, Federer quickly learnt how to disport himself on the world stage, particularly when he started winning the biggies on the circuit. All the world was, indeed, a stage for him. He smiled a lot when he won, cried a lot when he won, and lost. A lachrymose chap, our Roger. I had mentioned earlier that Federer was an Emotion with a capital E, but he was also emotional on court and wore his heart on his sleeve. And didn't his fans love him for it. It's not that they loved Nadal less, it's just that they loved Federer more. As for Djoko, even he knows nobody loves him (his compatriots aside), and the feisty Serb draws strength from that. When the crowd yells 'C'mon Roger,' Novak hears 'C'mon Novak.' But that's another story. Incidentally, I am glad Roger got rid of that pony tail he flaunted in his initial days on the circuit.

Federer's retirement has also unleashed the dreaded punning epidemic amongst headline writers in the print and social media. A rash of puns, some clever, some plain asinine, mostly overwrought has assailed readers this past week. 'End of the FED-ERA' screamed one, 'PeRFection' was not bad, 'Roger and Out' went another, 'Roger that!' blared a third. War comics cliches are clearly still an inspiration. The transportation major, FedEx lapped up a lot of cheap publicity every time Roger won somewhere with copywriters falling over each other to come up with lines like 'Fedex delivers on time.' In slightly cruder, impolite usage, we have also heard the phrase, 'So-and-so was Rogered in straight sets.' I need hardly elaborate on that. One headline in the French newspaper

L'Equipe puzzled me slightly. The paper dedicated its front page to Federer with the phrasing 'God Save The King.' Apparently, the tribute to the tennis legend is a reference to the accession of King Charles III in the United Kingdom but as an attempt at the telling *double entendre* it was a bit of a stretch and did not quite make sense. That is the problem with punning for its own sake. You can miss the wood for the trees.

It is axiomatic that you cannot compare players of one generation with that of another, purely on the basis of numbers. By any reckoning, Australia's finest sportsman (a photo finish with Don Bradman) would be Rod Laver, the tennis colossus who won, back-to-back, all the four Grand Slam singles titles in the same calendar year, and he did it twice with a 7-year gap in 1962 and 1969. Djokovic came within a whisker of achieving that feat in 2019 but fell at the last hurdle at the US Open. The ongoing Laver Cup, pitting Team Europe against Team World being played in London, featuring the present-day giants of the game, including for one last time Federer, is a fitting tribute to 'The Rockhampton Rocket.' As I put this piece to bed, I have just seen Roger's final match partnering Rafa at the Laver Cup, post which the tears flowed freely. Roger, as is his wont, choked up while trying to speak, Rafa was almost inconsolable as was the sobbing full-house at the magnificent London 02 Arena. Rumours that a super-sopper had to be employed to mop up and dry the court for the next game was a tad exaggerated.

Over the last century many changes have been wrought in court conditions, quality of equipment, physical fitness and so on. Then there's the money. Enough said. Even taking all those changes into consideration, for three players to win, between them over roughly the same period, 63 Grand Slam singles titles (and counting) is staggering. Longevity is being redefined. Novak and Rafa will enjoy superiority in numbers over Federer and that is not to be pooh-poohed in our unabashed adulation of Federer. I would only like to end by throwing one challenge, the ultimate acid test. Just walk out onto the street and buttonhole one hundred people at random, and ask them who their favourite tennis player in the world is. If Roger Federer does not overwhelmingly win that statistically valid dip-stick survey, I will eat my non-existent and metaphorical hat. *Vox populi!* King Federer has retired. Long live the King!

Now then, where's my box of Kleenex tissues?

TELL ME ABOUT IT

There might be some debate as to exactly what percentage of the world's population speak the English language, but there can be little doubt that it covers a very large swathe of the globe. After all, not for nothing did the Brits sail around the world a couple of centuries ago, seeking whom they may devour. While their avarice to conquer and stay on as uninvited guests for long periods has been resented by the colonised, and rightly so, we need to graciously acknowledge their sagacious contribution in leaving behind a language that binds many nations and keeps the wheels of commerce well oiled. Else we might have been bumbling our way through with French, Dutch or perhaps, Portuguese. It is true that in each geographical region, the English language has been suitably adapted to cater to its own vernacular needs, resulting in uniquely different accents and emphases on words and phrases. Why, in India the way a typical Bengali speaks English is vastly different from how his compatriot in Chennai would hold forth in the same lingo. The native mother tongue influences the English pronunciation and phraseology. In that respect we Indians laugh at ourselves all the time, good-naturedly mocking our fellow countrymen and women.

The rapid spread of English has been, by and large, helpful though it has provided much comic relief when people attempt to mimic the way English is spoken in different tongues. All those years ago, British comic actors Peter Sellers and Spike Milligan, through their immensely popular Goon Show, attempted to create a 'one-size-fits all' Indian accent and had their admirers from all over the world helplessly rolling in the aisles. Listen to the song *Goodness, Gracious Me!* featuring Peter Sellers and

Sophia Loren, recorded as a promo for the film *The Millionairess* (though excluded from the main film) and you will know what I mean. A more recent reprise of the same song, enacted by Rowan Atkinson (whom I otherwise admire) falls way short of the original.

My own preoccupation for some years now, has had to do with the wonder that is the way English is spoken in the United States of America. Notwithstanding allowances made for marginal differences in the way a Texan would drawl as opposed to a New Yorker's staccato, rapid-fire way of communicating, one can safely club American English into one unique slot. In India, for obvious reasons, most of us have been more used to the British way of speaking and writing English when it comes to spellings, idioms, phrases, aphorisms and so on. Bernard Shaw's fictional Professor Henry Higgins *(Pygmalion* and *My Fair Lady)* famously complained that 'in America, they haven't used it (English) for years.' The reason American English intrigues me is that, while they seem to be speaking English, there are many phrases and expressions they employ that continue to baffle me. The Australians too speak English in their own, unique way. Listen to former Australian cricket captain Ricky Ponting or eccentric tennis star Nick Kyrgios, speak. You will need an interpreter to translate what they are saying into decipherable English, but that is simply the accent. The Americans appear to have a vocabulary all their own. That said, now that we have cable television and any number of American TV serials and films readily available at our finger tips, English as she is spoke, particularly by the younger generation in India, is slowly but surely morphing from the Union Jack to the Stars and Stripes. And who are we fuddy-duddies to complain?

Several years ago, on my first visit to New York City, I called my hotel from the airport where I held a reservation. The conversation went something like this.

'Good morning, my name is Subrahmanyan. Not Submarine. No, no, I am not from Suriname. My *name* is Subrahmanyan, and you are holding a single room for me. Could you kindly confirm the same? I should be arriving in about an hour.'

'Can you spell that for me, please? I didn't quite catch that. Just the first five letters should do it,' replied the chap at the reception.

'Right, here goes. S U B R A...'

'Got it. Pretty long name, huh?'

'Sub-rah-man-yan. Just four syllables. No longer or more unpronounceable than Zbigniew Brzezinski.'

'How much?'

'Never mind. The name, for the last time, is Subrahmanyan, Suresh.' I was beginning to get just a little peeved.

'Check. Copy that.'

'How do you mean check, and copy what? Anyhow, you can copy it wherever you like. Just wanted to be sure of my booking. And by the way, Zbigniew Brzezinski was a former National Security Advisor of your great country. Just so you know.'

'Whatever,' he responded, laconically. I also suspect he was chewing gum.

I was to learn later that *copy that* means 'noted and understood.' We hear that often enough now in American movies. Back home in India, we were entertaining an NRI family from New Jersey. The husband and wife were to land up at our place for high tea along with their teenage son, who was finishing his schooling in the US. The couple arrived bang on time, the youngster was coming from elsewhere. While we were chit-chatting, the time flew by and their darling boy was yet to put in an appearance. The mother became quite agitated and called the tardy scion on the mobile and spoke in an exaggerated Yank accent. 'Where are you, Raja? You were supposed to join us an hour ago, da. Will you drop whatever you are doing and come here already?'

Come here already? Never heard the word 'already' used that way before. Sounded like a contradiction in terms. In more recent times, particularly on streaming video, this phrase has become increasingly commonplace, and Indian kids, be they from the US or from India's urban elite, are quick to latch on. To complete that high tea story, when the errant boy did arrive, he examined the generous fare on the dining table and exclaimed, 'Goody, goody gumdrops! Am I going to *pig out.'* Ah well, each to his own, I suppose. Speaking for myself, immense hunger would have driven me to venture, metaphorically, that 'I could eat a horse.' As for G.G. Gumdrops, the Americans and the British have been squabbling for long over who owns the copyright. Let me quickly add here that phrases like *I don't care* in place of 'I don't mind' and *my bad* in place of 'I am sorry' have already become *passé,* a cringe-worthy part and parcel of our daily lexicon, such that I shan't elaborate on them. Suffice it to say that, so far, so bad.

Let's move along to *behind the eight ball.* The phrase, drawn from the game of billiards or pool, is meant to indicate that you are falling behind the competition in whichever subject is under discussion. 'My friend, let me caution you that in the matter of winning the confidence of your boss, you are clearly behind the eight ball as compared to that greaseball, Jack. You had better buck up.' I actually like this phrase, but if used indiscriminately, you will just come across as a boor and a show off.

I first came across the word *period,* when I joined school; 9 am to 10 am was Geography period, 10 am to 11 am was History period and so on. To say nothing of the British Period, the Mughal Period, the Chola Period, *et al.* We now know that this word has very many different meanings and shades, and I shan't go through all of them here. (If she is having her period, show some understanding.) It is a common enough word. Period can also mean 'full stop,' and in the bygone days when we dictated letters, we would use the word frequently. 'Dear Sir, Thank you for your kind enquiry about our tyres for animal-drawn vehicles period.' Your smart secretary would automatically translate that to full stop. In the more trendy, conversational style of the present day, one is apt to say something like, 'I do not wish to dwell on this subject anymore. *Period.*' This, to indicate firmly, that the topic is irrevocably closed.

Here's one that has not quite gained currency in India, but it will only be a matter of time. 'Hey look, I have no time for late night parties. I am *working the graveyard shift.*' Those swotting away in India's IT and services sector speaking to clients all over the world, who start work at around 11pm and slog all night till the sun comes up, *work the graveyard shift.* It won't be long before some of your friends start mouthing this phrase, if they aren't already at it. I was also struck by yet another unheard-of beauty. 'Wow! Where did you get your hair done? It's absolutely *on fleek!*' I have it on good authority that the expression denotes appreciation for a job perfectly done.

I end this far from comprehensive rumination on spoken or written expressions one comes across from 'the land of the free and home of the brave,' spreading like a rash to other parts of the world. If you have come this far with this piece, lolling back and going out of your way to find nasty things to say about it, you are nothing more than a mean, old *Monday morning quarter-back.* The phrase is obviously derived from American football, which is not football at all. At least, not as we know it. Why this hyper-critical quarter-back chooses Monday mornings to vent his spleen on his colleagues is an even greater mystery. I will now need to scour Wisden's cricket almanac to find a suitable local riposte. At that I may not even get to *first base.* I think I'll just *take a raincheck, ride shotgun* with my friend in his Audi and *shoot the breeze.*

American English. Some may say *it sucks.* Will my English masters in school have approved? Not on your nelly (that's British), and they are unlikely to have said, *no can do.* My 21-year-old nephew just called me from Chennai. As we were ending our brief chat, he said, 'I'll ring off now. *Peaceful.*' This, for a change, may be a recent Indian coinage but puzzling, all the same.

Tell me about it.

DREAM A LITTLE DREAM OF ME

I had a strange dream last night. I dreamt that I was dreaming. What did I dream that I was dreaming about? I will come to that in just a moment. The moot point is, why could I simply not have had a dream? That is what most normal people have, when they hit the pillows and count to twenty or count sheep, if that is their preference. Just a simple dream. Unless it was a nightmare. Applying the same logic you could also, I suppose, have a nightmare that you were having a nightmare. Why did I have to *dream* that I was having a dream? All very complex and rather Freudian. Which is hardly surprising because that was exactly what I was dreaming that I was dreaming about - having a conversation with the much-celebrated shrink, Sigmund Freud. When I finally woke up from the dream, I realized that I was still dreaming that I had woken up from the first dream. So, I went back to the land of Nod, when my mobile phone alarm finally woke me up, and I rubbed my eyes, relieved that I was no longer dreaming, or indeed, dreaming that I was dreaming. So complicated.

Let me back up a bit here. As most normal people who sleep and dream know only too well, it is an extremely rare case where one can recall precisely what one was dreaming about. Once the mists of sleep dissolve, you can only have a bare-bones recollection of what your mind-at-rest was going through while you slept fitfully. Sometimes the dream disappears altogether only to play back much later, while you are fully awake, leaving you in a state of torpid unease – a sort of *déjà vu* that I cannot quite put my finger on. I take a cynical view of people who have a tendency to chunter on endlessly about how they dreamt they had scored 500 not out in a Test Match, won the Wimbledon final thrashing Djokovic in straight sets, played the lead violin to rapturous applause at the New York Philharmonic under the baton of Zubin Mehta, split the atom, found a cure for cancer or had a *tête-à-tête* with the Prime Minister over tea and *dhoklas* and what a lovely man he was, contrary to how a handful of cynics perceived him. Some of my mean-spirited friends might aver that being invited to tea by the PM should be classified as a nightmare, but I shall dismiss these ne'er-do-wells with the contempt they deserve. If nothing else, the *dhoklas* would have been scrumptious. To say nothing of the *khandvis*.

Let me get back to my dream. Or the dream within a dream. I am not sure which is which. Anyhow, there I was, minding my own business, lying comfortably on a leather couch in a luxuriously fitted-out, oak-paneled room somewhere in the Austrian capital, Vienna. I could vaguely hear a sonorous voice counting down from 10. Ending with 4,3,2,1 and a sharp snap of the fingers. I woke up with a start, eyes wide open, and spoke those three immortal words, 'Where am I?' I could have added, 'And who the devil are you?' but the bearded visage got ahead of me.

'Good morning. I am Sigmund Freud, your psycho-analyst. You have just woken up from your second dream. As we speak, you have moved to your first dream, but you do not know that. You are still fast asleep and dreaming that you are being interviewed by the world-famous neurologist and founder of psychoanalysis. I shall be asking you a few questions, after which I shall release you from your first dream and you will be home and dry.'

At this point, I found utterance. 'Look here, old man. All this is rather Freudian. Ha ha,' I chuckled at my own weak joke. 'But seriously, how the heck did I get here, even in a dream, first or second? And clearly Mr. Freud, modesty is not your middle name. *World-famous neurologist and founder of psychoanalysis?* Even though you say so yourself?'

'I say so myself because it is what it is. Anyhow, you are not here to talk about me. Tell me about yourself. What seems to be the trouble? Time to unburden.' The shrink sounded a bit shirty. A shirty shrink!

'The trouble Sir, is that I went to sleep with nary a care in the world. When I woke up, or thought I had woken up, it appears I was still sleeping and dreaming. That was in my cozy home in Bangalore. India, in case you are not aware. Next thing I know, I have woken up again in a strange room in Vienna, travelled back in time and am being quizzed by an Austrian loony doctor.'

'Not just any Austrian shrink, I'll trouble you, and less of the loony doctor stuff, if you please. Let's have some respect. I am here to help you. Don't worry your pretty little head over first dreams and second dreams. They are all the same. The function of dreams is to preserve sleep by representing as fulfilled wishes, that which would otherwise awaken the dreamer.' He might have been Austrian but he was talking double Dutch.

'Yeah, I follow you completely. Do you think you can call Starbucks and order a skinny latte for me. That's coffee. I really could do with a pick-me-up. Get one for yourself, if you like.'

The psycho-analyst looked befuddled. 'My friend, I cannot understand a word of what you are saying.'

'That makes two of us,' I retorted.

Freud went on. 'You are still in a dream state. Once you wake up, your life will return to normal. For now, just imagine you are drinking skinny whatever-it-is and your thirst will be slaked.'

'Gosh, you speak funny as well. I can't wait to wake up. By the way Doc, what year is this that I have woken up in but in restful slumber on my second dream, or first dream?'

'1930, and Hitler and his Nazi Huns are swarming all over Austria. My own life is in peril. I am a Jew, you see.'

'I am sorry about all that, but why are you filling my head with your troubles? I am supposed to be the patient. Anyway, it was all such a long time ago, and you were rescued and shipped off to England where you died a couple of years later. I am talking to a ghost. In my dreams. God almighty!'

Sigmund looked distraught. Bad memories. 'I am sorry about that. Shouldn't have taken you back to my terrible past. Most unprofessional. Bit of a slip.'

'A Freudian slip, eh?'

He guffawed good-humouredly. 'Good one. Look, all this has given me a thirst. I am also feeling somewhat pooped. Need some caffeine. Cup of coffee do you nicely?'

'Good call, Doc. Not too much milk, and don't spare the sugar. Can you stretch it to a croissant?' In my dream state, I looked forward to the coffee. 'Shall we carry on with the session, Sigmund? Hope you don't mind my calling you Sigmund. We are now practically on first name terms.'

'No issues, my friend. As time is running out and I have more patients waiting, I have to gradually conclude this session, stimulating though it has been. Now let me wrap this up by asking you again. What is it exactly about your dreams that is troubling you.'

'It is not the dream itself, or the dreams themselves, that bother me. Like you as I am sure, I have had all kinds of dreams, and I have learnt to live with them. As I told you earlier, it is the fact that I am dreaming that I am having another dream that I am unable to cope with. There I am, telling off the Income Tax johnnies who are crawling all over my apartment, that I have nothing to hide, and just as their chief honcho is about to gyve my wrists and haul me off to an unknown destination, I wake up in a sweat, but immensely relieved. "Thank God it was only a dream," I tell myself, only to realise that I have lapsed into another dream involving my landing in Bangalore from London and promptly being hauled off by customs officials into the red channel and being administered the third degree. Can't take it anymore, Doc. One bad dream, *theek hai.* Par for the course. I can handle that. Two bad dreams is pushing the envelope, and not in a nice way. Capiche?'

'My, my, Italian and everything. These are anxiety dreams, my friend.'

'Tell me something I don't know, Doc,' I riposted.

'You may be worrying about something altogether different but it manifests itself allegorically in your dreams as troubling touch points. I know a patient who frequently dreams that he is in the middle of a fancy, stylish party. *With no clothes on.* Not a stitch.'

'What, starkers?'

'Absolutely. In the buff, as we say at our annual psychoanalysts' ball.'

'Thank heavens I haven't reached that stage yet. Maybe if a third dream intrudes on the first two, a fate worse than death may also eventuate.'

'Now, now. Let us not get melodramatic. Yours is a simple condition. My diagnosis is clear. There are too many things going on in your life. These daily occurrences and thoughts of everyday life is what I have coined as "dream-work," which are nothing but "secondary-process" thoughts which become subject to the "primary process" of unconscious thought. These, in turn, are governed by the pleasure principle, wish gratification and the repressed sexual scenarios of childhood. In sum, it is all about dream distortion, displacement and condensation of the repressed thoughts to preserve sleep. You have nothing to be concerned about. That's it for now. The bill's in the mail by dream post.'

At which point, my alarm went off. Again. Alarm bells, more like, contemplating Freud's bill in the post. I sat up in my own bed. My wife was fast asleep and everything appeared to be kosher. I let out a stifled yowl of relief. Thus awakened, my wife asked me what the matter was. I skipped the whole Freudian episode and replied that I had just dreamt

I had solved The Times Crossword Puzzle inside a world record three minutes.

'In your dreams,' she mumbled and turned back to sleep.

Exactly.

ARE WE READY FOR RISHI?

When Joe Biden assumed office as President of the United States on January 20, 2021, here in India there was much excitement. Not because anyone in India gave a toss about Joe Biden. The appeal of American Presidents to the Indian public, both domestic as well as the diaspora, depends largely on whether they are good looking or so ridiculous that you have to pay close attention. On that score both John Kennedy and Donald Trump, for those very reasons (you can work out which applied to whom), merited our keen interest. In the case of Biden, our curiosity in India had much more to do with his vice-presidential candidate, Kamala Harris because of her Indian antecedents. That she was also part West Indian on her father's side did not seem to matter. Perhaps some sections of the Indian public interpreted West Indian to mean Mumbai and not Jamaica. However, for a few, brief shining moments, those of us from south India, particularly Chennai and its environs, went ballistic with joy. Reams were written in Indian newspapers about Kamala's maternal family background from a conservative Tamil Brahmin household. Unknown relatives crawled out of the woodwork. Which also meant that her love of the cuisine from that part of India, including idli, vada, dosa and curd rice received as much billing as her untested political nous. If she also enjoyed spare ribs and beef steak, we did not mention it.

All very droll. That was over a year ago, when Kamala Harris was sworn in. In that period, even if she was not being publicly sworn at, it was a near thing. At any rate, she appears to have gone clean off the radar. Not even a blip. No one talks about 'our Kamala' any more. Not even in suburban Chennai. Lotus (Kamala in Sanskrit) is unlikely to become POTUS, unless Biden decides to throw in the towel before his term ends. I have heard tell that a soothsayer has predicted the lady could get the top job before Biden's term ends! Such is the fickle, ephemeral nature of fame.

That preliminary introduction about Kamala was prompted by the current hullabaloo we are witnessing over the possible ascension of an Indian-origin candidate, Rishi Sunak, as a potential successor to the ousted Prime Minister of the United Kingdom, Boris Johnson. The Indian media, social circles, our neighbours, friends, relatives and possibly their pet dogs, are all waiting with bated breath to see if young Rishi (he is only 42) can become the first non-white Prime Minister of Great Britain, albeit a tad wet behind the ears. Incidentally, my friends who are clued up on these things, assure me that the terms United Kingdom and Great Britain (and by inference, even England) are freely interchangeable. The golden rule appears to be that if they win the football World Cup, which they did against West Germany 4 – 2, in 1966 at Wembley (aided by a controversial third goal), or an Olympic gold, the cry will ring out, 'another triumph for Great Britain.' Whereas if they lose, it will change to 'England loses again.' It's complicated but it is what it is. Scotland, Wales and Northern Ireland don't count.

Let's get back to the bright-eyed and bushy-tailed Rishi Sunak. Straight off the bat, let us recognize that the aspiring PM is no more Indian than Boris Johnson is Punjabi. Sunak's parents came over to the UK from East Africa in the 1960s, as did thousands of others of their ilk, thanks to the tender ministrations of Idi Amin, and ran a successful if modest pharmacy, which may or may not have been a traditional corner shop. Sunak was born in Southampton and the rest of his meteoric academic and political career has been well documented. I shan't go over them again. My preoccupation is more to do with why we in India are going all gaga over someone who is attempting to become the Prime Minister of a nation that ruled India for close to 200 years. Is it the

Indian origin thing? I haven't even heard of a family in India called Sunak! Nasser Hussain captained England's cricket team and worked overtime to convince his countrymen that he was English, and not just a fair-complexioned lad from Madras with a posh public-school accent. Is it the pigmentation? Could be, but if you walk around Central London and hurl a brick randomly into the middle distance, you are more likely to bean someone of an Asian, African or Middle Eastern descent. Let's cut to the chase. I'll tell you why we in India are getting super excited about Rishi. He is married to a true-blue Indian girl. That's why! He is our son-in-law; Daamaad, Jamai babu or Maapillai, depending on which part of India you hail from.

There's more. Rishi's father-in-law, N.R. Narayana Murthy can safely be described as one of the fathers of India's IT revolution. A highly principled, self-made man, he is one of the many poster boys in India's rise as an economic power house, thanks to the company he founded, Infosys. Not that Mr. Murthy would himself care to be described as a poster boy, he being of a somewhat modest and self-effacing disposition. His educationist and philanthropist wife Sudha Murty (she drops the 'h' in her surname, insists her husband's name is spelt incorrectly!), is a woman of substance in her own right, seen as a role model for the betterment and upliftment of women, children and the downtrodden. She is a prolific writer having authored many books, in particular for children, and is ever ready to reach out to the needy with a helping hand. And their daughter Akshata it was who said 'Yes' to Rishi Sunak when he popped the question to her on bended knee in the sylvan surrounds of Stanford. And now, dear reader, can you at all be surprised that in India, it is a completely different kind of rishi all the way from the UK who is hogging the headlines as opposed to the ones we are so accustomed to seeing? This one is suited, booted and clean-shaven, and speaks with an Oxbridge accent. Not a tinge of saffron anywhere.

The rishi double entendre is even more apt when you consider the fact that Rishi Sunak is reportedly a practicing Hindu, and that he took his oath as Chancellor of the Exchequer with his hand placed firmly on the Bhagavad Gita. Should he ascend to the exalted office of Prime Minister and take that short hop from No.11 to No.10 Downing Street, Britons will be counting many 'firsts' in their rich political history. This also raises a pertinent question. When push comes to shove, is a predominantly Christian nation such as the United Kingdom ready to entertain a devout Hindu (one assumes he is devout) as their chief executive? In order for that to happen, Sunak has to take on some stiff headwinds from his shortlisted colleague, Liz Truss, who is fond of saying, 'we'll hit the ground running.' While the lawmakers from Britain's Conservative party have selected these two worthies, the complex voting process will take place through a balloting system involving some 200,000 party members in early September. Notwithstanding Sunak receiving more votes than his rivals in the initial phase, Liz Truss could well be holding all the aces. She could be following in the footsteps of Margaret Thatcher and Theresa May as the third woman Prime Minister of 'this sceptered isle.' There's everything to play for. At some point during these proceedings, erstwhile Prime Minister Boris Johnson will quietly make his way out of what can surely be described, in his case, as '10 Drowning Street.' If you read that gag in one of the British tabloids, remember you saw it here first!

Meanwhile, not to be outdone, we in India are witnessing our own history in the making. The ruling dispensation's candidate, Droupadi Murmu, is all set to take the oath as India's 15th President, and the second woman to do so. The uniqueness is derived from the fact that President Murmu (get used to that name) hails from a tribal community in the state of Orissa. The BJP has once again caught everyone, particularly the opposition parties, completely off guard. The move is seen as being far-reaching, statesmanlike and above all, a sure-fire vote catcher — depending on whether one is a supporter or a cynic of the government in power. India's Prime Minister, meanwhile, sits back comfortably and smiles beatifically. Like the cat that's had its cream. A final thought on what it could mean for India if Rishi Sunak does, indeed, make it to 10 Downing Street, provided he can get past Liz Truss.

Not very much, I don't think. Rather like Kamala Harris, Rishi will need to keep an arm's length distance from his ancestral nation, lest his countrymen come down on him like a ton of bricks. The British press are already pooh-poohing his 'humble-humble' background claims. His wealth and their sources are being closely examined with a fine toothcomb. In other words, he will have enough problems running the country without pointedly cosying up to India. This may create some domestic unrest at the Sunak household at No.10, but that's the way the cookie crumbles when you sit on the hot seat. However, let us not get ahead of ourselves. As I put this piece to bed, the smart money has Liz Truss with her nose in front as the odds-on bookies' favourite. She may well pip Sunak to the post in this two-horse race, in what could be a photo finish. Sunak's nick name to some of his close friends is 'Hedgie,' derived from the fact that he had earlier worked in the hedge fund business. He will certainly be hedging his bets now. But just in case Sunak defies the odds and pulls through, is India, in the words of his campaign plank, 'Ready for Rishi?' Maybe, maybe not. Either way, I shan't be holding my breath.

Postscript: This could be apocryphal, but a group of Indian tourists to the UK, visiting Winston Churchill's burial site at St. Martin's Church, just outside Blenheim Palace grounds, swore they felt something turning in his grave!

TO BE PERFECTLY HONEST

I am always deeply suspicious of anyone who starts a sentence, particularly in answer to a question, any question, with the words, 'To be perfectly honest with you...' It matters not a whit what the question is. I have watched several eminent personalities resort to this reflex induced, often irrelevant, for the most part dishonest, kick-off to their response. I suppose it is slightly better than the patronizing 'I am so glad you asked me that question.' Then there is the present-day abomination where almost anyone on television starts a sentence with the monosyllabic *So*. 'Do you think inflation will be a problem in the near future?' 'So, let me be perfectly honest with you.' You get the picture. This does not include Indian politicians at the very highest echelons because most of them prefer to converse in Hindi or some other vernacular of their preference. The local lingo does not quite possess an equivalent to 'To be perfectly honest...' Not literally, but metaphorically. Furthermore, most of our political top guns are never unduly worried about whether they are going to be scrupulously honest (ha ha) or, as some prefer to describe it, 'economical with the truth.' There are exceptions of course, even in political circles, but finding such gems of purest ray serene would be akin to hunting for a needle in a haystack.

Take Shashi Tharoor for instance, the silver-tongued Congressman, who speaks English as to the manner born, Oxbridge accent *et al.* Not that he went to Oxford or Cambridge, but he somehow developed his plummy, English accent while studying, debating and treading the boards in Calcutta. That helped him enormously at the United Nations and other august international bodies where doors opened for him the moment he sonorously intoned, 'Good morning, Mr. Kofi Annan.' He even gave a lecture at the Oxford Union (so he did go to Oxford after all, in a manner of speaking) and told the Brits off in no uncertain terms for their 200 odd years of misrule in India. However, if I have heard him say this once, I must have heard him several times. To the question, 'Mr. Tharoor, how did you come to speak English with a pluperfect accent and in such an orotund a manner that even the English are floored?' His answer? 'I am so glad you asked me that question. To be perfectly honest with you, your question incorporating words like "orotund" and "pluperfect" leads me to the inescapable conclusion that you are having a spot of risible fun at my expense.' That may not be a verbatim reproduction of the hypothetical question posed or the imagined answer proffered by the loquacious parliamentarian, but near enough. I'll say this in his favour, he does not start his sentences with the semi-literate *So.*

One last, if contentious issue about our eloquent MP from Trivandrum (or Thiruvananthapuram, if you want to be pedantic). I recently watched him on YouTube trying his hand at stand-up comedy and my sincere advice to him is to cease and desist. Just not his bag. I found his jokes contrived, flat and very unfunny. That he was reading these one-liners off handwritten notes made it only that much worse. He is much better off taking the strips off his political rivals with his Shakespearean flourishes and Wildean wit as his potent weapons. For one thing, his opponents don't know what on earth he is saying which in itself is half the battle won. Only that they are being vaguely put down. Stick to your strengths, Shashi. As an incidental aside, dear reader, try saying Thiruvananthapuram slowly, provided you are sober, without tripping up around the fourth or fifth syllable. It is not easy if you do not belong to Kerala or the south of the Vindhyas. BJP's cherubic and feisty spokesperson Sambit Patra tried it several times recently on television and came a cropper. He kept saying Thiruvanthpuram on numerous occasions without hitting the bull's eye. I invite readers, even while ploughing through this blog, to closely compare Thiruvanthpuram with Thiruvananthapuram to spot the difference. The doughty Sambit Patra struggled manfully, unaware of his dysarthria. In similar fashion most of our news readers and north Indian politicians can never pronounce Karnataka. For inexplicable reasons, they will insist on pronouncing the name of the state as Karnatak. Ditto Keral for Kerala. Are they dyslexic or something? How would they take it if I pronounced Haryana as Haryaan?

To be perfectly honest, our Prime Minister set the ball rolling to send out friendly smoke signals to his fellow brethren in south India, Tamil Nadu in particular, when he quoted a line from poet and freedom fighter Subramanya Bharati, *in Tamil,* during the newly named Kartavya Path inauguration and the Netaji Subhas Chandra Bose statue unveiling in New Delhi. As a Tamilian myself, I would give the PM full marks for effort and displaying great courage. However, as the complex Tamil syllables (for a Gujarati, that is) *Parukulle nalla nadu, engal Bharata nadu (India is the greatest nation in the world)* hesitantly escaped the PM's lips, many of us might have been excused for feeling that discretion could have been the better part of valour. Aren't there any great Gujarati poets? I can do no better than seek recourse in Hamlet's words, *Speak the speech, I pray you, as I pronounc'd it to you, trippingly on the tongue; but if you mouth it, as many of our players do, I had as lief the town-crier spoke my lines.* The Bard of Avon was the master of the *mot juste.*

My point being, what is there to be 'perfectly honest' about while making a simple and logical point. Let me now take another example, this from the world of management and business. 'You must learn to think outside the box,' is a phrase much favoured by business school students and their bosses in the corporate world, most of whom are also products of the same hallowed portals of management academia. As I had not graduated from a business school, I had problems with some of my better qualified colleagues and superiors in corporate life, who had the wood on me and kept asking me to think outside the box. Or square, if they wanted a bit of jargon variety. When this particular cliché was first thrown at me, my immediate response was, 'To be perfectly honest, I am not sure I follow you. How do you mean outside the box? What box, which box?' I was quite pungent with my reaction, which endeared me not one bit with my toffee-nosed colleagues. It was suggested to me that I might not climb very high in the corporate ladder, if I insisted on being 'too clever by half.' There's another one, I thought. My response was a real zinger. I replied vaguely, 'Ah well, what you lose on the swings, you make up on the roundabouts.' The recipient of this remark had no clue what I was talking about, as I flounced out of the room in high dudgeon.

Clichés, when used sparingly, can help one make a telling point. However, more often than not, we tend to scatter them around like confetti, more to impress than to advance a serious case for its usage. I was once scolded by my history teacher in school for 'taking one step forward and two steps back,' and that I will not make much progress in class. At the time, I was happy just to put one foot in front of the other. I was 12 years old and I used to walk around the school grounds taking one step forward and retreating two steps back, wondering if that would throw some light on what my teacher meant by that strange admonition. In so doing, I discovered that I was standing at the same place and not making any progress in terms of moving forward. Then the meaning of the phrase hit me. *Voila!*

At the end of the day (that's another favourite), my heart is heavy with whatever hearts are heavy with. To be perfectly honest, I concur with the homily that a bird in the hand is worth two in the bush and that you can't go through life with your head buried in the sand. What's more, no man is an island, necessity is the mother of invention and one should always let the shipwrecks of others be your seamark, so long as you remember that for things unknown there is no desire. Always bearing in mind that there are horses for courses so long as you don't look a gift horse in the mouth, and never forget that you can take a horse to the water trough but you can't make the stubborn equine drink.

To be perfectly honest, I don't know what on earth I am talking about any more, my head is all abuzz with aphorisms and other sayings we tend to come across and employ in our daily lives, oftentimes without even knowing what they mean. Nevertheless, nothing ventured, nothing gained. I take refuge once again in Shakespeare from 'Measure for Measure,' *Our doubts are traitors and make us lose the good we oft might win by fearing to attempt.*

C'est tout.

'HELLO, THIS IS VANDE MATARAM'

Those of you who follow current affairs in India will doubtless have heard that a recent pronouncement by the big nobs in the Maharashtra Government has declared that, henceforth all telephone calls to government offices or officials will be greeted by a cheery *Vande Mataram,* presumably spoken and not sung. In other words, it's goodbye to hello. Or as The Beatles so presciently and harmoniously put it all those years ago, *Hello, Goodbye.* This edict will need to be strictly followed by all government and quasi-government officials. In due course, it is hoped the habit will spread to all sections of the society in that state. While I have yet to read the small print in the form of an official circular, if there be one, presumably it would have been written in Marathi for starters, a language I am not familiar with, then translated into Hindi, thence to English, by which time the trial run of greeting all and sundry in the corridors of Government establishments in Maharashtra with a *Vande Mataram,* will have run its course. Or run out of gas, with any luck. This is not unlike forcibly thrusting the National Anthem down our throats in cinema halls at the start or at the end of watching three hours of *Ben-Hur* or *Gone with the Wind.* Doesn't quite gel, if you get my meaning. Thankfully, wiser councils prevailed, the courts took a dim view of it and we are now spared the ignominy of watching people rushing to the exits to get to the loos first, while the anthem is just about gathering up a nice head of steam.

Loosely translated, *Vande Mataram* means 'salutations to the motherland.' Written by Bankim Chandra Chattopadhyay in 1875, it is officially designated the national song of India, not to be confused with India's national anthem which, of course, is Rabindranath Tagore's *Jana Gana Mana.* One should be mindful of how one employs those two terms – anthem and song. Why we need to have a national anthem as well as a national song is beyond all understanding. There was much heated debate in our media on the subject, but as with so many such controversies, it all came to nought and we are back to the comfortable status quo. What is more, *Vande Mataram* has so many musical variants that its real personality gets obfuscated. From the 1952 *Anand Math* film version, based on Bankim Chandra's story of the same name, down to A.R. Rahman's latter-day, much-loved rendition *(Maa tujhe salaam),* the song has gone through several gears – lyrically and musically. What is more, in south India over the decades, Carnatic musicians have rendered in a garland of ragas (ragamalika), the Devi shloka *'Vande Mataram Ambikaam Bhagavatim'* an essential part of a Carnatic music concert repertoire.

That said, the thought of tinkering around with two anthems is not without precedent. When the great British mystic poet, William Blake wrote his rousingly patriotic poem *Jerusalem* in 1804, little did he know that it would be set to music a century later and dubbed Britain's national song, as opposed to their anthem *God Save the Queen / King.* Musically, *Jerusalem* is more melodic and rousing than the preferred anthem, but these are matters for the denizens of Great Britain to mull over. Even now, Britishers constantly debate if *Jerusalem* would make for a better choice as their anthem. As we in India usually tend to follow our erstwhile masters in many respects, it was refreshing to see the present dispensation in Delhi take the road less travelled and replace the hymn *Abide with Me* with Kavi Pradeep's seminal poem, *Aye mere watan ke logon* (immortalised by Lata Mangeshkar) at our Republic Day parade. This has not gone down very well with the many who go misty-eyed and nostalgic for all things past. That Mahatma Gandhi too was reportedly extremely fond of *Abide with me* only added to the contentious confusion.

For myself, I love the movingly composed Biblical hymn. We sang it often during chapel service in school, but I can see where the government is coming from. We are making moves, whenever an opportunity presents itself, to divest ourselves of long-time symbols of colonial subjugation. Thankfully, this patriotic logic has not been extended to great monuments and the like (Ye Gods!), though replacing British royalty with Indian stalwarts on existing plinths and canopies is perfectly acceptable. Netaji Subhas Chandra Bose in place of King George V at India Gate was widely welcomed, and the current political masters in New Delhi milked it for all it's worth. However, being a contrarian fellow, I would hate to see the magnificent statue of Queen Victoria sitting on the throne at the entrance to the grand Victoria Memorial Hall in Calcutta, being replaced by someone like, say, Ashoka the Great. Not that I have anything against the great Mauryan Emperor. It is simply an artistic genuflection, nothing to do with patriotism. Meanwhile, cities and street names all over the country are constantly renamed such that the Post Master General is tearing his hair out trying to keep abreast.

While on the subject of British relics, there is an interesting, and somewhat saucy, footnote pertaining to the Queen's recent funeral ceremonies. On television many Indian viewers were pleasantly taken aback when they were shown a group of British children reciting, most proficiently, a well-known Sanskrit *vedic shloka* from the Upanishads. It was wrongly assumed this was performed specially as part of the dedication obsequies for the late Queen Elizabeth II. Now here comes the twist. It turns out that the video, which dates back to 2009, showed the children reciting the *shloka* at the Commonwealth Games, The Queen's Baton Relay 2010, which was held on 29 October 2009 at Buckingham Palace, London. Whether this was stated upfront by those responsible for the telecast or not is unclear. To give the organisers of the funeral telecast the benefit of the doubt, they probably meant well and most of us were impressed with the recitation.

Little wonder that some states in India like Karnataka have arranged to have their own state anthem in the local language, in this case Kannada. There has been much argy-bargy over this issue and I am not sure if a final decision on the matter has been taken. Depending on the length of these anthems, the start of an international cricket match, say between India and Sri Lanka in Bangalore could be a long-drawn affair. The Indian team will have to mouth the national anthem and keep their eyes closed during the Kannada anthem, since the players will not know the lyrics or the tune, followed by the Sri Lankan anthem which, I happen to know, goes on forever. The toss will, literally and metaphorically, go for a toss.

To get back to the *raison d'etre* of this piece, it would be fascinating to speculate on what prompted the Government of Maharashtra to come up with this knee-jerk decision to disband the familiar 'hello' salutation with part of the first line of our national song, not to be confused with the anthem. One assumes the Chief Minister and his colleagues have more pressing issues on their plate, including the vexed question of which of the two warring factions of the Shiv Sena has the right to take legal possession of their brand name and symbol. The courts are still chewing the cud over that matter.

There must be so many other everyday problems to be tackled by the ruling coalition in Maharashtra. The problematic question of which faction of the Shiv Sena can address their multitudes at the legendary Shivaji Park in Mumbai during the Dussehra celebrations has been settled by the courts, and they have many more issues to fight over. Yet with all these distractions, out of nowhere the Chief Minister walks into his morning meeting with his cabinet and declares, 'From this moment on, we stop using anglicized words like "hello" to greet one another. It is going to be *Vande Mataram*. Got it? Please pass this message down the line to every single government servant. Thank you. *Vande Mataram.*' Caused quite a shindig, did CM Shinde. All that would have, naturally, been said in Marathi. I take it that 'thank you' will pass muster for the time being till an acceptable vernacular alternative can be agreed upon.

I shudder to think what would happen if this initiative from Mumbai's Mantralaya becomes a national movement! Tamil Nadu's *Vanakkam* some of us are already familiar with, though not enforced officially and Bengal could have the time of their lives and go the whole hog with *Nomoshkar.*

This naming and nomenclature sickness, not to speak of language politics, always on the boil, has reached endemic proportions in our country. It keeps happening in dribs and drabs but, like the proverbial canary in a coal mine, could presage a major linguistic fracas in the making - a Tower of Babel we can well do without in polyglot India.

IT'S TOO LATE TO STOP NOW

If you can't annoy somebody, there's little point in writing.
– Kingsley Amis

For close to twenty years, give or take a few this way or that, I have been writing a weekly column or blog (call it what you will) purely for my own pleasure. Some newspapers and online sites have been good enough to publish my material on a regular basis, others less frequently, still others have given me the old heave-ho. Short shrift. However, for the most part I let myself go, high, wide and handsome, once a week in the verdant, unfettered pastures of my own blog. Of more pertinence, a handful of readers has been kind enough to read my offerings off and on while providing critical feedback. The advantage in managing my own blog is that there's no word limit to constrain me, no junior sub 'correcting' my apostrophes and punctuations wrongly, which can drive you up the wall. Worse still, an entire line, at times, goes inexplicably missing making a hash of the sentence or paragraph. I am quite punctilious that way, and if an error does creep in, I am fine with it as long as it is my own. That way I can take full responsibility, be master of my own fate. It's when I key in "O. Henry" and someone else converts the great American storyteller into an Irishman "O'Henry," that sets my jangled nerves on edge. Over a period of twenty years, at an average of a column a week, that works out to a number, not to be sneezed at. Quantitatively, I can point to a modicum of accomplishment. Qualitatively, the jury will always be out, a constant assessment in progress. I could, of course, put all that on the calculator and come up with a daunting figure. Then again, I am superstitious and have no wish to tempt the fates. I am the sort of chap, who will fret ceaselessly for seven years if I inadvertently break a mirror at home, worrying about the ill omens that are likely to visit me.

A close friend of mine recently asked me what keeps me going and did I ever consider taking a break. You know, get away from it all for a few weeks and come back refreshed and raring to go. I had to hum and haw before answering. I thought I detected a veiled hint that perhaps I *should* take a break as my pieces were beginning to show signs of fraying at the edges, but then writing is a bit like being a performing musician, even one from the top echelons. It enjoins upon you an unwritten commitment to keep at it unceasingly. A vocalist has to keep singing if he or she wishes to uphold high performance standards. If one stops singing or practising even for a week, it will almost certainly show. As to why I keep writing without giving myself pause, the only answer I could come up with was, 'Sheer bloody-mindedness.' It was just something I had to do. It's rather like responding to your early morning alarm. You don't want to get up but you do just that, grumbling the while and getting down to that 30-minute constitutional and those recommended exercises. It's the boarding school boy in me. Oftentimes, you have to push yourself to come up with an idea, when you are gazing at your computer screen with a glazed look. All said and done, writing has become an ingrained habit and as troubadour Van Morrison said, "It's too late to stop now."

The late Miles Kington (one of my many inspirations), an effortlessly funny writer who was literary editor of the defunct and celebrated humour magazine Punch, then went on to write for The Times and The Independent, had this to say about *writing a column a day spanning thirty years!* Allow me to repeat that – *a column a day.* I puff and pant to complete one a week. One every single day is really pushing the envelope. Kington wrote over thirty-thousand newspaper columns in his lifetime. Mind you, he never wrote a full-length novel. 'From an early age, I knew I wanted to be a humorous writer and a jazz musician… and when I went to Oxford University, I spent most of the time playing the double bass in jazz groups and writing undergraduate humour. Thus, when I left university, I was almost entirely unfitted for life, and consequently went to London to try my luck as a freelance humorous writer, where I nearly starved to death.' That's another thing about achieving great success in certain fields. You need to go through much suffering. It's almost a *sine qua non*. Ask Kafka, Camus or Dostoevsky. They made a good living writing about other people's suffering. I am not implying *schadenfreude* as they probably suffered themselves. Considering I have taken up writing purely as a hobby and relatively late in life, I can safely opt out of the suffering phase. I had enough of that in my professional career in the corporate world, so I'll pass up the dubious agony and vainly aim for the illusory ecstasy.

The late Bernard Levin (forgive me for drawing upon the wisdom of eminent columnists no longer amongst those present) who wrote a column for many years for the venerable The Times of London, was a writer of coruscating brilliance. Like Miles Kington, Levin never wrote a novel and never wished to. His frequent observations drew more readers that many authors could aspire to, only in their dreams. Fortunately, we have his prodigious compilation of writings in several of his published books for our undiluted enjoyment. If I were to select just one of Levin's many purple passages, I will go for this one, where he uses the genius of Shakespeare in a unique way to demonstrate how much we owe the Bard of Avon. In our everyday conversation, we casually toss familiar phrases and aphorisms at random, with nary a thought being given to the original source. The quote is long, but I would not dream of paring it down even a jot. Enjoy this Bernard Levin gem: of purest ray serene, I might add. 'If you cannot understand my argument, and declare "It's Greek to me," you are quoting Shakespeare; if you claim to be more sinned against than sinning, you are quoting Shakespeare; if you recall your salad days, you are quoting Shakespeare; if you act more in sorrow than in anger; if your wish is father to the thought; if your lost property has vanished into thin air, you are quoting Shakespeare; if you have ever refused to budge an inch or suffered from green-eyed jealousy, if you have played fast and loose, if you have been tongue-tied, a tower of strength, hoodwinked or in a pickle, if you have knitted your brows, made a virtue of necessity, insisted on fair play, slept not one wink, stood on ceremony, danced attendance (on your lord and master), laughed yourself into stitches, had short shrift, cold comfort or too much of a good thing, if you have seen better days or lived in a fool's paradise -why, be that as it may, the more fool you, for it is a foregone conclusion that you are (as good luck would have it) quoting Shakespeare; if you think it is early days and clear out bag and baggage, if you think it is high time and that that is the long and short of it, if you believe that the game is up and that truth will out even if it involves your own flesh and blood, if you lie low till the crack of doom because you suspect foul play, if you have your teeth set on edge (at one fell swoop) without rhyme or reason, then - to give the devil his due - if the truth were known (for surely you have a tongue in your head) you are quoting Shakespeare; even if you bid me good riddance and send me packing, if you wish I was dead as a door-nail, if you think I am an eyesore, a laughing stock, the devil incarnate, a stony-hearted villain, bloody-minded or a blinking idiot, then - by Jove! O Lord! Tut tut! For goodness' sake! What the dickens! But me no buts! - it is all one to me, for you are quoting Shakespeare.'

Phew! Elsewhere in this column I had talked about being bloody-minded and given short shrift, having no idea that I might have been quoting Shakespeare. Mr. Levin set the record straight on that one. That goes for 'Tut-tut' and 'By Jove!' as well. However, I take perverse delight in being able to correct Mr. Levin when he attributes the expression 'but me no buts' to Shakespeare. I researched this thoroughly owing to a nagging doubt I harboured. Sure enough, the quote (it is authoritatively drawn from several unimpeachable sources) was coined by one Susanna Centilivre in the play, *The Busie Body* in 1709. That was centuries before Bernard Levin was even a twinkle in his great-grandparents' eyes! Incidentally, that's the way 'Busie' is actually spelt, in case you are about to shoot off a tart mail to me. Probably archaic, given the year of the play's introduction. In the event, Bernard Levin is not around to take up cudgels with me, in case he was right in the first place. That said, if there are a bunch of keen Shakespeare Wallahs out there hiding in the woodwork, who wish to come out in high dudgeon and set the record straight yet again (with papers to prove it), they are most welcome.

There you are, you see. I am stuck with writing columns and may never write a full-length novel in my lifetime. I have no regrets on that score, even if I should never say never. If you must know why, I am delighted to quote one of my favourite authors, P.G. Wodehouse, 'It was one of the dullest speeches I ever heard. The Agee woman told us for three quarters of an hour how she came to write her beastly book, when a simple apology was all that was required.'

THE PRESSURE TO PERFORM

During my carefree days in boarding school, and here I hark back to the swinging sixties, I did not really feel all that carefree. There were all kinds of pressures that beset us students, pressures that our school masters and teachers, dormitory matrons as well as our parents unwittingly placed on our young, impressionable minds. Not all the problems we had to deal with were necessarily of earth-shattering importance. At least, not in in the generally accepted sense, but for us kids it was the be-all and end-all of human existence. For instance, we could have been part of an inter-house elocution competition. Having qualified for the finals, I had to rehearse Henry V's famous St. Crispin's Day speech. Will I remember all the lines or am I going to fluff? That alone was cause enough to find me tossing and turning restlessly through the night. Try this on for size. *If we are mark'd to die, we are enow / To do our country loss; and if to live / The fewer men, the greater share of honour / God's will! I pray thee, wish not one man more.* And that's only for starters. Tongue-twisting lines upon lines that only Shakespeare could have gleefully wrought for a 14-year-old, pimply, adolescent school boy to struggle through. By the time I got to *We few, we happy few, we band of brothers,* I could see the finishing line, tongue hanging out, puffing and panting. The same held true if we were acting in a play or being part of the soprano section in the school choir.

Other pressures that confronted us could have been an inter-school cricket final with the trophy on the line. Everybody from the games master to the pantry sergeant fell over each other, offering gratuitous advice. 'Keep your eye on the ball and your head still,' 'Do not bowl outside the leg-stump,' 'Anything outside the off-stump, shoulder arms and leave severely alone,' 'If the umpire says you're out, you're out, don't stand statuesquely at the crease looking sorry for yourself,' 'Keep your knees bent while fielding, else the ball will slip through your legs.' It was like the Ten Commandments, barring that bit about committing adultery. Don't ask me how we confidently stepped on to the field of play and actually strutted our stuff. Similar words of encouragement were always provided to us in a kindly spirit whether we were representing the school in hockey, football or athletics. Boxing was a particular favourite. 'Always lead with your left hand, unless you're a southpaw, and mind you don't hit below the belt.' What about stopping a vicious left hook and getting my maxillary bone dislocated? Pressure, pressure, pressure.

Then there were the end-of-term exams that set our nerves on extreme edge, or in the memorable expression employed by our English master, 'the collywobbles.' I speak for myself but there are many of my colleagues who will echo my sentiments. There were three term exams during the academic year, the final term deciding on our promotion to the next, higher class. Failing which, we were faced with the dark ignominy of being retained for another year in the same class, a fate worse than death. In schoolboy patois, 'He plugged in his 6th standard and in every other year so that he became everybody's classmate!' In my case, my report card after each term turned up a 'just above average' performance. 'Scraped through' would have been the *mot juste*. The master who would sign off on our reports loved the phrase 'Could do better.' My report card was littered with 'Could do better' at the end of almost every term. I had a horrid time explaining this to my parents. What exactly did it mean? That I did not try hard enough, or that I was actually pretty good but was meant for higher attainments? Who knows? It was a mystery that stayed with me forever. Another perennial favourite on my report would read, 'His marks do not adequately reflect his true ability.' Again, that could either be an encouraging comment, or conversely, to indicate that I should not get carried away simply because I did well in that particular term. I could have been less than met the eye! Given that some of our teachers were on secondment from the United Kingdom, we applied the old Hollywood Apache lingo, 'White man, he speak with forked tongue.' These were mysteries beyond our ken. Our report cards were notoriously opaque. In that famous Churchillian phrase, 'a riddle, wrapped in a mystery, inside an enigma.'

Another engaging trait amongst us during exams was to find unique ways to impress the other boys, all swotting away, furiously erasing and rewriting. Craning your neck to take a quick peek at your colleague's paper will be quickly put down by the master with a stentorian, 'Do not copy your neighbour's mistakes.' It goes without saying that all of us had ink stains smudging our hands, shirt fronts and even at the end of our noses. They were not really stains, they were symbols of great courage and honour. Remember we used fountain pens those days, with a handy bottle of Parker or Quink Royal Blue by our side for refills. One sure fire way to make others envious was to keep putting your hand up and asking the supervising master on duty for an extra sheet of writing paper every ten minutes or so. The rest of the class would glance at you with awe, wondering how this guy can write reams when they themselves are still struggling to fill up their first sheet. You, naturally, will look smug and scribble away furiously. That you are filling your sheets with absolute nonsense, putting up a brave front, will not be plain to the rest of the class. That is, until the results are announced later, by which time you are home alone for your summer holidays, safe from prying eyes.

As the time runs out for the allotted two hours and the master gravely intones, 'Five minutes more boys, then I will come round and collect your papers.' At this, all of us are turbo-charged with a second wind of furious energy. Scribble, scribble. Scratch, scratch. Rub, rub. By now, most of the boys have submitted their papers. You keep writing rubbish till the master snatches the answer paper away. As you drag yourself unwillingly from the class, some of your classmates gather round with eager questions. 'What were you writing endlessly for so long, I say? My god, you will probably max your paper.' You respond mock modestly, 'Listen chaps, you can't max a paper on English Language. I wanted to finish with a long quote from T.S. Eliot's poem, *The love song of J. Alfred Prufrock,* but master grabbed my paper crying "Time." I still had eleven lines to go, but I think the examiner will be impressed.' That would have effectively ruined the rest of the day for my classmates. As to their valid query that Eliot was not even on our syllabus, I merely wipe the ink stain off my nose in a marked manner and walk away and in my wake, leave my mates non-plussed. The truth of the matter is that I was struggling to remember a few lines from S.T. Coleridge's *Christabel,* which was part of our syllabus but T.S. Eliot sounded far more impressive; more snob value. *In the room the women come and go / Talking of Michelangelo.* We were quite insufferable as kids.

Bearing in mind all the mental agony we boys had to go through, particularly in our senior years, the Warden of our school, an ordained priest and a wise, thoughtful Welshman, would invite us to his cottage over the weekend for an evening of lemonade, cookies and some popular records of the day on the turntable. Elvis Presley, Ricky Nelson, Pat Boone, Cliff Richard and later on The Beatles, being particular favourites. He was broad-minded enough to say, 'I am sure you've all had enough of hymns and psalms during chapel service.' Some parlour games which included boys being picked out at random to sing a song or recite something of their choice was always on the cards. *Antakshari* was unknown, thank heavens! Some of us would try and hide behind the settee and play with the two Siamese cats that were the Warden's popular house pets. However, nemesis would invariably catch up, leaving none of us unscathed. 'Next your turn, Suresh, don't hide behind the rubber plant. You are not the Invisible Man.' So, you sidle in awkwardly from behind the rubber plant, drawing awkward patterns on the carpet with the toe-end of your left shoe, clear your throat, and start warbling Andy Williams' hit song, *Number 54, the House with the Bamboo Door.* Some of the boys join in, the others hold their stomachs. The Warden is pleased as punch, the Siamese feline twins purr contentedly. It was meant to be an evening of relaxation. For some of us boys, however, it was more crushing pressure to perform.

FIRESTARTER

Denied loan, man sets bank on fire.
– News reports

Spare a thought for Wasim Hazaratsab Mulla, 33, a resident of Rattihalli town in Haveri district, Karnataka. He had applied for a loan for an undisclosed sum from his friendly (or so he thought) neighbourhood branch of a nationalized bank. As is the way with bureaucracy the world over, the boffins at the bank processed his application, took their own sweet time over it, and finally informed the wretched man that his loan application had been rejected. And the reason given? The applicant, the above Mr. W.H. Mulla returned a low CIBIL score. As the press report blithely assumed all its readers knew exactly what CIBIL's expanded term was, I tried to look it up. While the expansion of the acronym remains unrevealed, I was able to conclude that it related to a person's credit rating. We are in the dark as to the criteria applied to determine a loan applicant's creditworthiness, but we can safely assume that our friend Wasim didn't quite make the cut.

That appears to be, in a nutshell, what transpired between the bank and its customer. Now most people I know, who are in dire need of some cash at less than extortionate rates of interest, lean on their banks to cough up generously from their swelling coffers. Provided, of course, the loan is to be used for some genuine workaday purpose – buying property, purchasing a car or a two-wheeler in easy instalments, sending your child abroad for higher education, a medical emergency – that kind of thing. The bank, in turn, wants to be sure you are not squandering the loan betting on the horses or going on a wild bender at the local bar. Hence, they ask about 150 questions, in very small, illegible print, to make sure you are on the level and have more than an even chance of returning the principle and meeting your interest obligations. Not to speak of painful issues like lien and mortgage. All this information is analyzed till the customer is blue in the face, to determine that the money will be returned in God's good time. If the results indicate that the would-be borrower is not a risk worth taking, he is politely shown the door. At times, not very politely.

Which is precisely what happened in the case of Wasim Mulla. Since I am not privy to the precise nature of the reasons ascribed for rejecting his application, one will have to assume they were sound. Most people, on facing such a rejection, would have merely shrugged their shoulders philosophically as if to say, 'Ah well, that's the way the cookie crumbles.' They may then have approached some shady-looking money lender sitting just outside the bank, who can recognize a loser when he sees one. Which would have led to a successful deal where the interest burden alone would have led the borrower to take his own life at some future date. Mr. Mulla, however, was not having any of this nonsense. He was made of sterner stuff. He had, in his opinion, clearly done everything he could to satisfy the skinflint pen pushers behind their desks at the bank. Just the paper work involved would have driven most customers to distraction. 'Vengeance is mine,' cried the stricken man rather biblically. Deuteronomy 32:35. Romans 12:19. Those may not have been his exact words, but close enough.

Wasim Mulla went home in a dark mood and pushed away, untasted, the plate of chicken biryani his wife had lovingly prepared for him. This should have aroused her suspicion as to what had upset him and what might follow, but she knew better than to question her husband. The hour was late while Mulla planned and plotted. 'That bank must be torched,' he muttered grimly to himself. He then took with him a tin of petrol and a box of matches and stole out of the house at the dead of night, while his wife slept dreamlessly. He then crept up to the bank premises, broke open one of the windows, sprayed the petrol as far as his arm and wrist work would allow him, struck a match and threw it into the highly combustible gas. We have to assume no security guard was posted to challenge nocturnal marauders. The resultant conflagration caused extensive damage to furniture, equipment and sensitive files and documents. It would have provided ironic satisfaction to Wasim, as he scarpered from the scene of the crime, that his own rejection papers would have been amongst the records that were charred beyond recognition.

In attempting to make good his escape, the avenging arsonist was soon chased down, apprehended and brought to book by the local PC Plod. As I type these words out, he is doubtless being given the third degree, rubber truncheons *et al,* to understand what led him to resort to such extremes. On reflection, he could have gone back to the bank, sat down with the manager over a nice cup of tea, discussed cricket for a while and tried to sort things out. The manager might have even taken pity on him, after listening to his tale of woe, called his assistant who processed his file and asked him to take a relook. I realize that he might have been hoping against hope, but he should recall that unattributed quote 'If at first you don't succeed, try, try again.' Then again, given his choleric temper, patience might not have been one of Wasim's virtues. Anyhow, he did what he did and is now behind bars. I have no idea how the interrogation went, but if I happened to be an inquisitive fly on the wall at the dank police station, I might have been witness to a fascinating conversation. Naturally the exchanges would have been in the flavourful local lingo, but I have to necessarily imagine it in my brand of English.

Police Inspector (PI) – 'Right Mr. Mulla, I take it you have been read your rights and you know exactly why you are here at my station.'

Wasim Mulla (WM) – 'Because I was not sanctioned a loan by the bank.'

PI – 'No, no, that is why you set fire to the bank and was arrested. I am asking you, Mr. Wasim Hazaratsab Mulla, why you decided to flood the bank premises with petrol and throw a lighted match into the building, thereby causing great damage to public property.'

WM – 'Because I did not have bombs or any other explosive materials.'

PI – 'I am sorry?'

WM – 'I should be sorry for not doing a more thorough job. I am only answering your question. I am a poor man and at my home, I could only lay my hands on a can of petrol along with a box of matches. I could not afford anything more lethal. I will try to be better equipped next time.'

PI – 'Smarty-pants. Mr. Mulla, I am trying to be patient and polite with you, but you are trying me. This is no time to be funny. You are in big trouble already.'

WM – 'Funny? Who is trying to be funny? I was not laughing when my loan application was rejected. What would you have done Sir, if you had been turned down like me?'

PI – 'God give me strength, again with the loan application. That is a matter between you and the bank. Look, for the last time, arson is a serious crime and you could be put away for a very long time. You are lucky no one died.'

WM – 'Lucky, lucky? Ha, ha. You are the funny man, Sir. I am crying here. I asked the bank for a small loan for my daughter's wedding expenses, for which I had to fill 35 pages of a highly complicated form. I spent Rs.500 on a human shark sitting outside the bank to help me fill the form. Then they sit on it for four months and tell me I did not score enough points with CIBIL'

PI – 'You were trying to score with Sybil? Who is she? This is interesting. A bit of excitement and forbidden romance. And why is the bank interested in your love life?'

WM – 'Now who is being the smarty-pants? What love life? Are you trying to confuse me? I know all these slimy police methods of interrogation. By the way, if you are the good cop, where's the bad one?'

PI – 'I am the bad cop. There's no good cop. You said you failed to score with Sybil? She could be an important witness.'

WM – 'CIBIL is not a girl's name, Sir. C-I-B-I-L. I don't know what it stands for. Something to do with credit, of which I have been declared unworthy.'

PI – 'Oh, I see. Now I get it. And you get this Mr. Mulla. You are not worthy of my spending so much time on you, either. I will draft out a confessional statement and you can sign it. In triplicate. End of interview.'

As Mulla was taken back to the lock-up he asked the constable for a light. The cop handed him a matchbox, which the accused casually slipped into his trousers pocket after lighting his fag. There was a wicked gleam in his eye. Now if he could only find a way to smuggle in a can of kerosene.

REDISCOVERING THE JOYS OF SHOPPING

I went window shopping today. I bought four windows.
– British comedian Tommy Cooper

A few weeks ago, I had sounded off on the unintended perils of online shopping, regretting our inability to actually shop at shops, if you get my drift. All that is fast changing. What with the pandemic and everything, for the past couple of years or so, we have hardly ever stepped out of hearth and home to do a bit of shopping. The operative phrase there is 'stepped out.' Shopping, as in finding a place to park the car, wheeling around the premises pushing a cart, looking at packs and bottles, squinting at the almost unreadable expiry dates and price tags, going through that touchy, feely, tactile experience that real-life shopping entails. The other kind of shopping we have done aplenty, all of it online from the comfort of our drawing room or study or wherever the mood took us. Highly impersonal of course, but the convenience cannot be denied. Press a few keys on your smartphone, select the items, approve the amount, tap in the OTP and literally in the blink of an eye, 4 tetra packs of mixed-fruit juice and 2 packets of salt have arrived in place of the 6 cans of Coke and 2 packets of sugar you had ordered. No problem. The complaints procedure online is smooth, somebody will rush round to your place by the evening to collect the erroneous deliveries, but you will have to re-order the original items you wanted. No, the amount will not be refunded, but will be held in suspense and adjusted against the fresh order, which will be delivered the following day provided said items are in stock. Which is often not the case. Some of them agree to send the money back to your credit card account, but tracking the credit to see if Rs.153.40p has actually been returned is tedious in the extreme. The only hassle with this arrangement is that we might have invited guests over that very evening. Woe is me. Let me try another portal.

I should not be too harsh. Fair's fair. Most of the time the online giants get it right, but until we have actually opened the delivery bags, we will have no clue what surprises and shocks are in store for us. That said, now that the pandemic appears to be behind us, more or less, most of us have ventured out to enjoy the real, and at times dubious, pleasures of real-life shopping, something we had almost forgotten about. Virtual shopping will be there till the cows come home but now we have an alternative option, one that we are accustomed to. I am, of course, referring to those of us who were born before the new millennium.

The nearest departmental store is just a stone's throw away from where we live, so thither we repaired in good spirits, the wife and I, suitably masked up. Parking was not an issue as we set out fairly early. As we approached the entrance, we observed, to our dismay, that the shutters were three-quarters of the way down, and there were a handful of other customers waiting to get in. I turned to the nearest gentleman and inquired of him what the problem was. 'The uniformed chap at the entrance says they are taking an audit of the inventory, and that the sales boys and girls are being given a quick briefing. All this could take some time and we will have to wait.'

'Was the shop burgled overnight or something?' I asked. 'It's 10.30 in the morning. Surely audits and stuff take place during the small hours of the morning.' The equally miffed customer merely shrugged his shoulders.

Anyhow, after another 20 minutes or so of idling and goggling (and Googling) at our mobile phones, the shutters clattered up. Open sesame. We all rushed in like there's no tomorrow. An assortment of smells assailed our olfactory senses. Fishy from the meat corner, heady perfumes wafting from a nearby shelf and spices catching our throats and nostrils from the condiments and provisions space further down. A strange, smelly concoction this, one that I was quite happy to experience though they could have spared us the fishy pong. It was time to hurry along and not waste time tarrying. The poet might have said, '*What is this life if, full of care / We have no time to stand and stare.*' Unless we were standing and staring at our mobile phones, naturally. The adrenalin was now coursing through my veins as I looked forward to that touchy, feely experience I was talking about. While my wife traipsed off to some section specialising in branded astringents and cleaning agents, I made tracks for the food section. I was looking for some interesting salad dressing and dips for our cocktail snacks. My intense searches having revealed zilch, I cast around for a shop assistant. There were not more than three in the entire shop, so I walked across and cleared my throat behind a slender, uniformed girl, who looked not more than 17 years old and who was bending down inspecting some nameless bottles in a cardboard carton. She turned round, startled, on hearing my catarrhal throat-clearing.

'Yes Sir?'

'I need some help. Can you please point me to where I might find dips and salad dressing?' That was plain enough but the adolescent looked out of her depth.

'Fruit salad, Sir? This way, please.'

'No. no, not fruit salad. I am looking for salad dressing. As well as some interesting dips.'

'Dips?'

'Yes, got it first time, well done. And salad dressing.'

The girl scrunched her nose, raised her eyebrows and said, 'Sir, we have got chips. Also clips in that section,' she pointed vaguely towards the middle-distance behind her back. Why she would word-associate chips or clips with dips and salad dressing was a mystery, but I let it pass.

I felt like giving her a clip round the ear, but wiser counsels prevailed. I decided to put her out of her misery. 'Why don't you call your supervisor?'

Relieved of the inquisition, she rushed off to some back office. After another ten minutes had passed, a tall, not-so-young man presented himself - an authority figure. I felt reassured.

'Good morning, Sir. I understand you are looking for drips. Saline, would that be? Sorry Sir, we do not have a pharmacy section here. There's one just across the road.'

What was wrong with this place? Was everyone hard of hearing? 'Thank you,' I replied not hiding my irritation very well. 'How about salad dressing? Are you going to send me into the waiting arms of a nearby Italian restaurant?' He didn't quite catch my bitingly sarcastic dressing down.

'Salad dressing,' he repeated thoughtfully spelling the syllables out, like he had never heard of it, which he probably hadn't, 'you mean like that gooey liquid they mix all those leaves and vegetables with?'

Now we were getting somewhere. I had wronged the man. I knew how to leap on the back of dawning intelligence and make it gallop, as I once heard someone describe it. 'Exactly. Gooey liquid. I couldn't have put it better myself. I am talking about Vinaigrette, Thousand Islands, Honey and Mustard, Bleu Cheese, that sort of thing.'

The dawning intelligence took three steps back towards fading dusk. We were back to square one. He whipped out his mobile phone and called up someone, presumably another colleague sitting in that mysterious back office. He moved further away from me so I couldn't follow the conversation. After five minutes or so, he stuffed the mobile into his shirt pocket and returned with a half-smile.

'Sir, we can do some imported olive oil and vinegar dressing, nuts and seeds, beans and legumes as well as a variety of dried fruits. Not to mention baked tortilla, pita chips, shredded hard cheeses and fresh fruit. I am told you can make an excellent salad from these ingredients. We are well stocked with all these items.' I was irresistibly reminded of the Waldorf Salad incident in that hilarious television comedy, *Fawlty Towers*.

I was on the verge of stealing Clint Eastwood's *Dirty Harry* copyright with a threatening *'Go ahead, make my day,'* but by now, in a strange turn of mood, I started feeling sorry for the staff of this establishment. I mean, they have also been suffering without a single customer walking in for over two years. This sudden deluge of walk-ins had left them unprepared and caught off-guard. Fresh, wet-behind-the-ears trainees were being put through the mill. Inventories were out of whack. It was a mess. Still and all, actually interacting with another human being made for a refreshing change. I was *simpatico*.

'I fully understand, my old Supervisor. We have to give you all time to differentiate between dips and drips and salad dressings can be tricky. Tell you what, I'll take 250 gms of all that stuff you just listed and we'll see how it goes.' The supervisor beamed and the adolescent was all smiles, 32 pearly teeth in good order. I had made their day!

As I was proceeding to the check-out counter, I saw my wife approaching with what looked like a fancy, stainless steel pedal trash can and a roll of black, perforated rubbish bags. 'What happened to the branded astringent and cleaning agent?' I asked. 'Not in stock, but they helpfully gave me these' she replied, not without a touch of irony. We paid for the items, after some drama with the recalcitrant credit card machine and reached home, tired but happy. Settled in my favourite reclining arm-chair, I got my mobile out and logged on to my Amazon account.

'WE HAVE A BLACKOUT. CALL THE DOCTOR.'

Unconfirmed reports indicate many doctors in the country are looking for alternative jobs.

All of a sudden, everybody and his uncle is talking about the unemployment situation in our country. Let me rephrase that. All those who are opposed to the present ruling dispensation are spewing venom on the government for allegedly turning a blind eye to the plight of the huddled masses who cannot find work and could well be on the verge of starvation, if not extinction. On the other hand, those favourably disposed towards Prime Minister Modi and his policies, aka *bhakts,* point to the sterling work his government is putting in, not only to get the economy kick-started after the pandemic ('which we have tackled better than any other country in the world'), but to generate employment on a pan-India basis. Employment and unemployment are the two key words in this political binary that we are going to get a lot of in the coming months, what with several key state elections in the offing. To say nothing of the blockbuster General Elections in 2024.

As matters reach fever pitch at the hustings, the populace will be inundated with mind-numbing statistics on the entire employment scenario. Without a shadow of doubt the jungle of figures will be suitably massaged and finessed by all the stakeholders at the elections in a manner to suit their own argument, given that employment is a highly emotive issue. As a matter of policy, I pay scant attention to these numbers, a) because I am numerically challenged and b) its all lies, damned lies and statistics anyway, as Mark Twain so pithily put it. Let all the economists, financial and political pundits make what they will of the verbal diarrhoea soon to be unleashed on an unsuspecting populace. I am much more intrigued by something else I heard recently. It may just be an irresponsible rumour, but there is some talk that the medical profession is worried about losing jobs in large numbers because the coronavirus is in swift recession, while hospitalisations and visits to doctors are almost back to pre-pandemic days. Into each life, a little rain must fall. I am then contemplating a situation where doctors, for want of adequate work in their chosen area of medical expertise, are offering themselves to undertake other jobs, even in relatively uncharted waters, just to keep the wolf from the door.

The scene opens in an upper middle-class family home in one of India's urban cities. The husband has gone to work. The wife has just called one of those 24 x 7 service companies, who can take on any task from fixing a gas leak, checking on the plumbing system, cleaning the carpets, fumigating the house, and taking the little doggie out for 'walkies.' In this particular case, the power supply system at their semi-detached villa has collapsed. The wife is desperate, she rings her husband at the office and brings him up to speed. The hubby, taking no chances, also calls the service chappies, and the next thing you know, the doorbell rings and the harried, but now relieved wife rushes to open the door. Quick correction. The doorbell does not actually ring because there is no power. The wife runs to the door on hearing the horse-shoe, brass metal door knocker going ballistic. She is confronted by a pleasant looking young man displaying a stethoscope sticking out of the pocket of his large, white waistcoat.

The Service Chap – 'Good morning, I understand you called for an electrician. Perhaps you could let me in and tell me exactly what the symptoms are.'

The Wife – 'Symptoms? I am sorry, I am a bit confused. You look more like a doctor than an electrician. What is that rubber tube thing sticking out of your pocket?'

The Service Chap – 'Don't worry about that. Just tell me exactly where the pain is?'

The Wife – 'Pain? You mean the electrical problem. Yes, for a moment there I thought you said pain.'

The Service Chap – 'It's this howling wind. Storm brewing. Plays tricks with one's ears. Right, let's get down to brass tacks, shall we? Are we talking about a complete power failure, or just partial blockage?'

The Wife – 'Blockage? Look, there's power in all the neighbouring homes. I called many of them and checked. So, it is not the electricity company's problem. What? Of course, we have paid our monthly electricity bills. It's one of those auto-debit things with our bank. ECS or something. It could be our back-up UPS system that has gone kaput or some kind of undetected electrical fault. That is what we want you to check and, hopefully, rectify, if you are up to it. The food is beginning to get rancid in the fridge. So could you kindly get a move on?'

The Service Chap – 'Madam, we cannot just rush these things. This is a serious case. I would go so far as to describe it as critical. I need to conduct a battery of tests before arriving at the correct diagnosis. Only then can a proper course of treatment be recommended.'

The Wife – 'What on earth are you chuntering on about diagnosis and treatment? Next you will be recommending surgery. Are you sure you are not a visiting doctor accidentally come to the wrong address? You certainly look like one. Some poor patient might be at death's door even while you are wasting your time at my place. I'll call the company again.'

The Service Chap – 'No, no. Ha, ha. Madam, don't be so hasty. I read a lot of medical thrillers in my spare time. You know, A.J. Cronin,

Robin Cook, Michael Crichton, that kind of stuff. It's a passion. So, I tend to use medical terms at times. Metaphorically. Take no notice. Just point me to your generator room.'

The Wife – 'Follow me. It's part of our garage, actually. There, that's where the UPS system is. I checked the batteries, and they have all been properly serviced just a week ago. We have an AMC with the company.'

The Service Chap – 'AMC, UPS, ECS, we only speak in acronyms these days. Now then, Madam, may I request you to leave me alone with the patient for a while. I need to concentrate fully without any distraction.'

The Wife – 'Patient? Did I hear you say patient?'

The Service Chap – 'Did I, I mean did you? Gosh, must have been a slip of the tongue. Force of habit. Sorry. Allow me to continue with my investigation.'

The wife thought she heard this strange chap mutter under his breath, 'and I don't even have a nurse to assist me,' but she let it pass. At least, he didn't blurt out, 'scalpel.' Instead, she went back to her room and called her husband on the mobile.

'Listen dear, sorry if I disturbed you at a meeting or something, but this so-called electrician that the service company sent down appears to be a complete nincompoop. Non compos mentis. He keeps talking about symptoms, tests, patients and so on. I am at my wit's end. He might burn the entire place down.'

My husband went into a controlled spasm of laughter. 'My dear light of my life, I think I know what the entire confusion is in aid of. Didn't you read in the papers that a large number of doctors could be out on the dole, looking for employment in other fields? I am sure this bright spark, whom you fear might be a potential arsonist, is one of those. I wouldn't worry. They have been properly trained. I am sure he knows what he is doing. Even I could have managed it, if I had had the time.'

'You! Please. Last time you tried to change a light bulb, you brought the entire crystal glass chandelier crashing down on our dining table. And don't even get me started on your changing the fuse. I am on a short fuse here, myself. Thanks for nothing. I'll take care of this lunatic.'

The wife went anxiously back to the garage and found the ex-doctor fiddling furiously with some wires. He even carefully placed his stethoscope on one of the batteries and listened attentively! And hey presto, next thing you knew, the house was awash with blazing lights and whirring fans. Even the refrigerator was purring contentedly.

The Wife – 'My God, you did it! It'll probably go off again in a few minutes, but well done. For a moment there, you really had me worried sick. I feared that we will all be sitting on a mound of ash and rubble. For an ex-doctor, you do seem to know something about electricity. What was the problem?'

The Service Chap – 'Thank you Madam. Who told you I was a doctor?'

The Wife – 'Oh, I don't know. That stethoscope sticking out of your white coat pocket was a dead giveaway. Then all those references to diagnoses, symptoms and so on. I smelt a rat. Anyhow, thank you. I'll go and make us a nice cup of tea. We've both earned that.'

The Service Chap – 'Thank you Madam. Most kind. I also notice that you are suffering from a hacking cough, and your eyes are watering. If you wish, I can do a quick check up of your pulse and BP, give you the once over and prescribe some medication. And that will be on the house.'

The Wife – 'Wow, a two-in-one pro. Would you check me out? Terrific! You still haven't told me how you fixed the electrical problem. I need to know. It could happen again as soon as you leave.'

The Service Chap – (enigmatically) 'Ask me no questions and I'll tell you no lies. Trial and error, more error than trial.'

They both laughed heartily and enjoyed their cups of tea and cheese and tomato sandwiches. As the service chap-cum-doctor took his leave and drove away on his battered-up van, he thought he heard a loud blast coming from very close to the villa he had just left, along with a muffled scream from a woman. From his rear-view mirror, he could see a thick black cloud of smoke rising in the receding distance. He jammed his foot on the accelerator pedal right down to the floor and sped off as fast as his rickety vehicle would take him.

WARDLE'S WORDLE

Some things just creep up on you. One minute you are strolling along merrily, whistling a happy tune like Anna in *The King and I*. Next thing you know, you feel a slight crick somewhere in your lower back, possibly between your third (L3) and fifth (L5) vertebrae, think nothing of it and before you can say slipped disc, you are instructed to lie in bed for a fortnight, with orthopaedic weights straightening you out. That may not be the best parallel to introduce the subject of my column this week, namely, the word game Wordle, that is now the rage and spreading like a rash all over the social media world, but 'tis enough, 'twill serve. For me, at any rate, it crept up quite suddenly. A Welsh-born, Brooklyn-based techie by the name of, wait for it, Josh Wardle is responsible for inventing or discovering this game. Evidently, he dedicated it to his techie Indian girlfriend, collaborator and Spelling Bee addict, Palak Shah. These techies tend to stick together. Wordle by Wardle. There's a nice ring to it. A fortuitous serendipity, I call that, to be able to name a word game that sounds so very like the name of the game's discoverer. Of and by itself Wordle (the name, not the game) is just a jumble of letters, amalgamating Word and Wardle. You might even be excused for feverishly seeking an anagrammatic solution. However, if the inventor of the game is called Wardle, you have to cut the man some slack while indulging in a spot of rhyming slang.

A couple of weeks ago, I had not even heard of Wordle. For that matter, even the name Wardle meant nothing to me. The only Wardle I had ever heard of was Johnny Wardle, a miserly left-arm spin bowler who turned out in English colours during the late 40s and early 50s. My research does not indicate that the two Wardles are related. However, if someone feverishly goes through details of the family tree with a fine toothcomb and deduces that Josh is the twice-removed grand-nephew of Johnny, I shan't quibble. Live and let live, that's my motto.

While I am still trying to get my head around the intricacies of this deceptively simple word puzzle, there are some side issues that provide for interesting reading. Apparently, the app for Wordle (where will we be without apps?) started off modestly with less than 100 users in November 2021, a figure that burgeoned to 300,000 users by mid-January 2022, and as we go to press, those numbers have exploded exponentially to hundreds of millions, who play the game daily. Even Omicron's superfast version BA.2 will struggle to keep up! Most of you who have started dabbling in Wordle know that it's a once-a-day online game that gives a player six chances to figure out a five-letter word, using the least number of guesses. Sounds like a bit of a lottery, if you ask me. A guessing game with minimal skill sets involved, interspersed with a smidgen of logic, but then again, I have been wrong before on such matters and will therefore suspend judgement. There could be more to it than meets the eye. Meanwhile, one has to bear with the Facebook and Twitter maniacs who are going, 'Guess what, I got it in 2 guesses.' Followed by 125 appreciative likes / memes / emojis and a few 'got it in one.' To which my only response is, 'Go tell that to the Marines.' Even our Congress Party's first family scion and leader Rahul Gandhi took to Twitter, sailing close to the wind with a not-so-veiled Wordle swipe at the ruling BJP. His opening five-letter salvo? JUMLA, followed by highly suggestive, if somewhat contrived, efforts like TAXES, SNOOP and ending anti-climactically with the correct Wordle answer, a *non sequitur* – PHOTO.

Like any decent Welshman, Josh Wardle was quite satisfied with his efforts at introducing a new challenge to excite the minds of those who are sitting at home and fretting about the pandemic. And he, with no small help from Palak, did it all for free! His occasional visits for a beer and pub lunch with Welsh rarebit (cheese on toast being the common or garden term) on the menu in Brooklyn was probably all that he craved. A man of simple pleasures. However, he was on an unbelievably lucky streak, and next thing he knew, some slick suit from that media monolith, The New York Times buttonholed him on one of the high streets in Brooklyn, offering him a seven-figure payoff to buy out all the rights to Wordle. 'Gosh, this is your lucky day, Josh,' he exclaimed to himself. A closet poet, our Wardle. 'I am so relieved,' he sighed, 'not overcome with joy or anything. Just a sense of relief.'

That understatement of the year may not be an exact quote, but pretty damn close, from what I could glean from various media reports. Rumours that he promptly fainted and needed a dose of smelling salts to revive him appear to be apocryphal. As is the word going round that when he came to, he said somewhat theatrically, 'Where am I?' Even if that has been romanticized, Wardle could have been subconsciously thinking of fellow Welsh celebrity and poet, Dylan Thomas who, in his famous poem *Do Not Go Gentle Into That Good Night* penned these memorable lines, Good men, the last wave by, crying how bright / Their frail deeds might have danced in a green bay. If a green bay had been conveniently to hand, our Josh would have certainly danced in it. On the other hand, it is more than likely that another famous Welshman, pop superstar Tom Jones resonated with Wardle belting out those two mega hit songs, It's Not Unusual and Help Yourself. One day in the distant future, Josh and Palak will put all this aside and settle luxuriously in their Green, Green Grass of Home.

Till Wordle came along to divert my attention, I was quite happy unjumbling jumbled letters to form a simple word and feeling good about myself. PAPEL was comfortably rearranged to read APPLE. If you are partial to Roman Catholicism, you can also struggle briefly with LAPPA and come up with PAPAL, which will earn you a few brownie points with the Pope. Slightly more challenging would be INKDEL, which I would triumphantly convert to KINDLE. If push came to shove and the degree of difficulty was stretched to breaking point, I would snap a pencil or two, scream a familiar four-letter expletive (ending with the letter K) but finally emerge victorious translating EGLTA into AGLET. Time for a celebratory drink. And if you wish to add to your vocabulary, 'Aglet' is a metal or plastic tube fixed tightly round each end of a shoelace. 'Damn and blast, where's the aglet on my left shoe lace?' We live and learn.

Those of us who started out playing Snakes & Ladders, Ludo, Draughts aka Checkers and later on, took halting steps towards Chess while struggling with Crosswords, were feeling reasonably comfortable in our own skins. Bridge was still a far cry. Then along came Sudoku for the numerically proficient, which put the kybosh on chaps like me who managed to barely scrape through his arithmetic paper in school. Sitting next to a Sudoku-mad passenger on a flight is a painful experience. 'If you don't mind, could I take page 9 of your newspaper please, if you are not doing the Sudoku?' I do mind, as *Charlie Brown* and *Hagar the Horrible* were on the same page, but what the hell. One has to be civil to one's fellow passenger. It did not help to elevate my mood when, after solving the Sudoku puzzle, my neighbour passes the crumpled, folded page back to me with a smug 'Today was plain sailing. You should have tried last Sunday's. Absolute nightmare. Devised by a sadist. Took me nearly 12 minutes to solve.' I buried my face in page 9 and took refuge in Charlie Brown.

As for Wordle, I am getting the hang of it. Very slowly. I DRUNEL (NURDLE), do not allow my mood to RUDLEC (CURDLE). *Au contraire*, I BWRLAE (WARBLE) like Keats' blithe Spirit, the skylark. To those who tell me the game is a LUHRDE (HURDLE), I draw myself up to my full height and EDIRLB (BRIDLE). Come to think of it, some of those jumbled-up non-words could easily pass for names of some unpronounceable Welsh towns! All right, I can see you all going 'Those words are all six-letter words. Wordle is a five-letter word game, you dolt! And it's not a jumble game.' As if I didn't know. Gimme a break and pin your ears back, folks. I have got the drop on this Johnny-come-lately, Wardle J. This is Wordle 2.0, this is. My own version. The new, improved six-letter word game. I am getting frantic calls from The New York Times and The Times of London. As soon as I get my eight-figure payoff from either one of them (I am not fussy), I shall settle up promptly with Wardle on his well-deserved royalties. I shall not DDLWAE (DAWDLE). Fair play to you, Josh. If we ever do meet in Brooklyn or Bangalore, I'd like a quick Wordle in your shell-like ear.

THE RUSSIANS ARE COMING, THE RUSSIANS ARE COMING

The Third World War will be fought with the most sophisticated and destructive weaponry imaginable. The Fourth World War, if there be one, will be fought with sticks and stones.
– Anon

In the year 1966, when I had just started my university education, and Hollywood films were very much a part of our entertainment and distraction, a film titled *The Russians Are Coming, the Russians Are Coming* had just been released. A fictional war comedy, it dealt with a Russian submarine that is inadvertently stuck in a sandbar just off the coast of New England in the United States of America. The resultant capers involving Russian soldiers getting entangled with the local island citizenry (pop. 200) provided much cause for cinematic merriment. Those were the days when Russia was America's public enemy number one and vice-versa, long after Hitler's Germany was laid to rest. Sounds familiar? Being a Hollywood production, I offer no prizes for guessing who the good guys were. It set me thinking. Things are no different in 2022. The Russians are coming, have come, with a vengeance to Ukraine while the United States and the rest of world do not seem to have the foggiest notion of what to do about it. Plenty of collective head-shaking and hand-wringing but little else. What's more, this is no flippant war comedy on celluloid. This is the real thing with state-of-the-art fighter jets, bombs, T-14 armoured tanks, AK 47s and hundreds of thousands of foot soldiers; to say nothing of the ever-present danger of a nuclear attack looming. Whatever else it may be, *it is not funny.*

However, the purpose of this piece is not to delve deeply into the whys and wherefores of the present conflict in Eastern Europe, its global ramifications, the subdued role of NATO, trying to second guess canny China's likely response, where India fits in, if at all, in this axis of meaningless and bloody conflict. Our television screens and newspapers are so full of the Ukraine-Russia battle that we have actually become inured to it. If it were not for India's young students being unfortunately caught up in Ukraine and our government's efforts to ferry them safely home, our thoughts could have so easily turned elsewhere. State elections and the Covid situation, which so occupied our media space, are all but forgotten. I daresay they will resurface again when poll results start coming in shortly, along with the clamour over the steep hike in fuel prices, which is as certain as night follows day. Hopefully, a forlorn hope at that, the Russian aggression by then would have started receding and the warring factions will sit across the table and start talking to each other, even if they will be talking from the side of their mouths. Hope springs eternal.

So much for serious stuff. Let me get back to what prompted me to write this column in the first place. It was a movie title of over five decades ago that spurred me to think of the present imbroglio. Or perhaps the other way round. More to the point, I thought it might be an interesting idea to look at other movie or book titles and examine what relevance they have for us today. Writers and movie producers have no idea when they launch into their creative efforts that, several years down the road those selfsame books, songs and films would strongly resonate with a public, most of whom may not have even been born when these magnum opuses were first released for public consumption.

A popular song by The Beatles during the late sixties that instantly springs to mind, in the present scenario is *Back in the U.S.S.R,* a jaunty number with a resonating chorus line that goes like this – *The Ukraine girls really knock me out / They leave the West behind / And Moscow girls make me sing and shout / That Georgia's always on my-my-my-my-my-my mind.* Well, I guess when The Beatles wrote that song way back when, things were quite hunky-dory and oojah-cum-spiff, to pinch a Wodehouse copyright, between Ukraine and Russia, as they were all part of the homogenous Soviet Union bloc. And speaking of songs, how can we forget Sting's feelingly sung ode *Russians,* in which he says, *We share the same biology / Regardless of ideology / What might save us me and you / Is that the Russians love their children too.* Prescient.

Still staying with the 60s, which was probably a decade that made the greatest impact on me for a variety of reasons, director Stanley Kubrick's black comedy classic from 1964, *Dr. Strangelove or: How I Learned to Stop Worrying and Love the Bomb,* made a deep impression. Shot in evocative black and white and starring Peter Sellers and George C. Scott (of *Patton* fame), the storyline deals with an unhinged U.S. general who orders a first strike nuclear attack on the Soviet Union, and how the best brains of the American and British defence establishment try and prevent the crew of a B-52 bomber from unloading its deadly arsenal on the Soviet Union and start a disastrous nuclear war. The film was widely considered to be one of the best satirical films of its genre ever made. If you, dear reader, are a film buff and have not seen *Dr. Strangelove,* you could do worse than search your cable networks and reel it in. It will be time well spent.

Then there was Russia's venerated writer Lev Tolstoy, whose first name was conveniently changed by the English-speaking world to Leo Tolstoy. Now what is so dashed difficult about pronouncing Lev that it needed to be changed to Leo, even if the anglicised equivalent is justified? Beats me. It's the same baffling non-reasoning behind why Chennai became Madras, and reverted to the original name later. I have Google-searched and spoken to a couple of notable historians, but to no avail. Some say the city was named after a fishing village called Madraspatnam, but no rigorous, historical facts of substance are adduced to support the claim. Even Wikipedia is stumped. I am open to being corrected by superior minds on this subject. But I meander. Tolstoy wrote *War and Peace,* a novel of such prodigious length that you were better off watching the film version, of which there are many. Even then, I got the distinct impression that there was much more war than peace in the narrative. At the risk of being cynical, one must conclude that the blood, gore and pumped-up, rah-rah patriotism makes war a far more saleable concept than somnolent peace. What is it with the Russians that at the least pretext they decide to take up arms and go to war? Vladimir Putin is merely keeping the hoary traditions of Lenin, Stalin and Khrushchev alive. Remember Cuba? One can quickly add that their arch rival, the United States is no different. The world is their theatre of conflict.

To continue with my random thoughts on war as a mode of entertainment, what about those handy, little illustrated war comics that were freely available during our school days? In tune with Hollywood war movies, these comics invariably celebrated the bravado and brilliance of the allied forces during the Second World War, making the Germans look like grotesque, villainous caricatures of themselves. We kids lapped it up because we were well and truly brainwashed. 'Take that, you nasty Krauts. BLAM, BLAM, KA-BOOM and KAPUT.' Not to mention the German commander threatening a captured allied soldier with a pair of live electrical cables, 'Ve haf vays to make you tok, you Yankee pig / English dog. ACHTUNG! ACHTUNG! SCHNELL! SCHNELL!' Naturally, the brave American or British soldier is daringly rescued, more BLAM, BLAM leaving behind a pile of dead German corpses. KAPUT. Didn't we just love it! I have little doubt that Russian muscle-flexing and aggression will soon become the hottest theme for a slew of forthcoming Hollywood releases. Step forward, Steven Spielberg.

Lest we forget, that brilliant satire that lit up the 80s on the British government machinery, *Yes Minister* and *Yes Prime Minister,* in one of the episodes, did a rib-tickling send up of the possibility of a hypothetical nuclear confrontation between Britain and Russia. Fictional Prime Minister James Hacker's utter confusion on being questioned on how he views the concept of a nuclear deterrent involving Russia, or even Germany and when would be the right moment 'to press the button' makes for arguably some of the funniest scenes one can wish to witness, superbly scripted and acted, as only the British can. Speaking of which, one also recalls with fondness BBC's hilarious *Dad's Army* television series, loosely based on the UK's Home Guard during the Second World War, that so captivated audiences during the late 60s and 70s. The present-day Ukrainian common man and woman taking up arms against the mighty Russian invaders put me in mind of *Dad's Army's* doddering village folk who attempt to stave off the invading Germans with hilarious results.

I guess what I am trying to really get at is this. Rather than watch our dreary television news channels gloating about flying out a slew of correspondents with a camera and telling all of India how brave they are to be right there in the thick of things, and how each one claims to be the first to reach the scene of action, you are better off reading the newspapers and getting a more informed view. There's simply too much sound, fury and noise on the TV channels, such that the viewing becomes painful in the extreme. Instead, divert your attention during the long evenings by watching some great war films like *Saving Private Ryan*, *The Longest Day*, *Bridge on the River Kwai*, *Merry Christmas Mr. Lawrence*, *The Hurt Locker*, *The Dirty Dozen* and so many more. Not to be outdone, the Russians recently produced a hagiographic biopic on Mikhail Kalashnikov, the man who designed and developed the iconic AK-47 assault rifle, and after whose name the weapon is sanctified. It is now an accepted axiom that war benefits not only the armaments and allied industries but the film world has also done very well by conflicts that have occurred since time immemorial. If American singer-songwriter Edwin Starr is known for nothing else, he will be remembered for his 1970 hit, *War / What is it good for / Absolutely nothing.*

I think we can all sing along with that. Altogether now...

GET MARRIED, BE GAY

In recent months, I have been shadowing two of my senior-citizen, nodding acquaintances (they are no more than that), as they take the air of a pleasant morning at a nearby park in our leafy Bangalore suburb. Their conversations, while they go about their lung-filling, oxygenated perambulation, oftentimes can be quite riveting. When I am privileged to be a serendipitously unseen auditor to such a free and frank exchange of views, I have seen fit to report the same to my band of readers. Not all that big a band mind you, more of a sextet or an octet, but as the great man said, ''tis enough, 'twill serve.'

By sheer dint of observation, I have placed the age of our two protagonists as being somewhere in the vicinity of 75 to 80 years of age. As is their usual routine, three gently ambled rounds of the periphery of the park, suitably accoutred with walking sticks, earns them a well-deserved rest on one of the comfortable park benches. It is here that they are able to give vent to their pent-up views on the state of the nation, nearly always based on news reports gleaned from their morning daily. While they are not averse to watching television, they appear to give more credence to the news purveyed through their broadsheet. You can put that down to decades of the reading habit ingrained in them. And a very good thing too.

The subject that appeared to be animatedly engaging them on this particular morning was somewhat unusual. As always, I took my place comfortably in a neighbouring bench, pretending to be thoroughly engrossed in P.G. Wodehouse's classic, *Psmith in the City.* In the normal course of events, I do not need to pretend to be involved in that great work by the Master of humour, but on this occasion, I was all ears for the approaching feast of reason and flow of soul. I have been in this situation before and looked forward to the upcoming treat, one that provides occasional grist to my writing mill. As I was saying, the unusual topic of discussion this morning was 'Same Sex Marriage.' The Government of India and our Supreme Court have been giving this rather delicate matter the full weight of their combined intellect, resulting in some well-mannered, verbal fisticuffs as is now the norm between the judiciary and the executive.

As the two septuagenarians were chewing the cud over the respective merits and demerits of the case, a final resolution of the bone of contention is still a work in progress, and it may take a while before the apex court delivers its verdict. We take up the conversation of my senior citizens in the park. Let us call them Bhatia and Rao, the better to monitor who is saying what.

Bhatia it was, who decided to take first strike, if one might be pardoned a cricketing metaphor. 'I say Rao, what is all this hullabaloo about same sex marriage and related subjects that seems to be engaging the attention of our Supreme Court and the government?'

Rao appeared a bit preoccupied. 'Look Bhatia, before I answer that question, do you see that chap sitting on the next bench? I think he is trying to spy on us. Better watch what you are saying.'

'Spy on us?' Bhatia was puzzled. He was vaguely aware of his friend's creeping senility and paranoia, but this was a bit much. 'Why should anyone spy on two old farts discussing matters of public interest? Your imagination is running away with you. Actually, if you look carefully through your powerful bifocals, you will observe that he is reading good old Wodehouse's *Psmith in the City*. A young man with excellent taste, I'll wager. And he is laughing, which is hardly surprising if you have read the Master.'

'Sniggering, more like. He is holding the book upside down, or haven't you noticed? What does that tell you?' Rao was getting quite agitated.

'It tells me, Rao, that he has read the book umpteen times and is challenging himself to read it upside down. Happens all the time with us literary folks. Bit like doing Sudoku in double quick time.'

Rao was not convinced. 'Literary folks? Us? Pull the other one. I suggest we keep our voices down. You never know these days. He might be a plant from RAW. Anything is possible.'

'If that is true, I have to say the chaps at RAW have a fine sense of humour. Listen, my friend, forget about your Kim Philby, Anthony Blunt or Guy Burgess. I think you've been reading too many John le Carré novels. Wodehouse is an infinitely better option. Let's get back to our subject. What is your view on two individuals of the same gender taking wedding vows?'

Rao stole one more nervous glance at the Wodehouse fan and turned to Bhatia. 'As I have understood the situation, our laws now recognise the legitimate existence of gay couples. Decriminalised, as the legal boffins have it. The government's problem is with them gaily, excuse the unintended pun, tying the knot and pronouncing themselves man and wife, or man and man or wife and wife, or whatever. That is where the government wishes to draw the line. And, between you, me and the gatepost, I think they might have a point.'

Bhatia looked at his friend scornfully. 'Come on Rao, which world are you living in? Grow up. I never thought I would say that to a 77-year-old man. However, there is one thing that startled me during these court proceedings. Out of nowhere, the judges and the lawyers started throwing the G-word around.'

Rao looked lost. 'What G-word? You speak in riddles, Bhatia. Explain yourself.'

'You have obviously not been reading the papers carefully. The word they kept repeating in court,' and here Bhatia stage-whispered loudly enough for me, exaggeratedly buried in my Wodehouse, to hear the word *'Genitals.'* At which point, I dropped the book and went into an uncontrollable spasm of laughter.

Rao was aghast. 'I told you that fellow was spying on us. He is very clever, you know. Reading Wodehouse is an excellent cover. We don't know if he is laughing at our conversation or at something hilarious Psmith said in the city.'

Bhatia was not having any. 'Look Rao, forget about your spy. What is your take on our judicial beaks and civil servants throwing words like 'genitals' around like confetti?'

'Why do you keep repeating that obnoxious word? And I don't mean confetti. Walls have ears or didn't you know?'

'What walls?' Bhatia riposted. 'Which walls? We are sitting in a park, open to sky, birds chirping all around us, and people walking their dogs. Or just jogging. Unless you meant trees have ears.'

'Don't be so literal, Bhatia. It's just that I do not want this spy sitting there with his, ha ha, upside-down Wodehouse, thinking the worst of two old men using words like that. He will think we are sick. He might even think we are *that* way inclined.'

'No wonder that chap is laughing. Words like what? Genitals? The Times of India's front page was littered with it this morning, and it was quoting the judges and the solicitors and other legal luminaries. What is your problem?'

Rao was still uneasy, if not actually squirming in his park bench. 'Why couldn't they just say PP?'

'PP? Now I am really foxed. Please expand PP.'

Rao went close to his friend and hoarsely whispered, 'Private parts.'

This time, I lost it. *Psmith in the City* went flying out of my feeble grasp, the cover went one way and the inside pages the other way, while I held my stomach for fear of collapsing with helpless mirth.

Rao could take this no longer. He strode aggressively up to his imagined Kim Philby, namely, *moi*.

'Listen, young man. I don't know what your name is, but I'd watch it, if I were you. Why can't you go and sit somewhere else instead of eavesdropping on us and mockingly laughing at us. Where's your manners? Left it at home?'

I must confess I was totally taken aback by this unexpected onslaught from Rao, but I had to politely defend myself.

'My dear Sir, I am equally at a disadvantage in that I too do not know your name. Nevertheless, let me put your mind at rest. My laughter has nothing to do with whatever conversation you and your friend were having,' I lied. 'I am reading Wodehouse, and if you are familiar with his works, you will know that people who read him in public are often embarrassed by not being able to control their emotions. The man is a genius. You should read him sometime, Sir. He will instantly lift your mood from 'dark and gloomy' to 'bright and sunny.'

Rao was not sure if he should be offended by this upstart's gratuitous advice or take him at face value. He seemed to possess an honest face. He decided to climb down from his high horse.

'All right, I am sorry if I was a bit peremptory. It's just that one never knows these days who is who and what is what, if you get my drift. Here is your book, or whatever is left of it.'

At this point, Rao's friend Bhatia joined us. 'Everything all right? We should be on our way home, Rao, before our wives start calling the police and the hospitals. Nice book, by the way, young man. Seen better days, I daresay. Seeing as you are a Plum *bhakt,* I would also recommend highly, *Leave it to Psmith.* Bye for now.'

As the two senior citizens strolled away, they passed by another couple laughing their heads off while scanning a newspaper. What is more, they distinctly heard one of them say, *'Genitals,* for God's sake!'

'I am never coming to this park again,' exclaimed Rao. 'Wild horses won't drag me here, ever again.' Bhatia merely sighed resignedly and added, 'And stop reading newspapers.'

THAT DREADED DOUBLE NEGATIVE

A few days ago, I was watching a programme on television, a talk show pretentiously titled 'Whither English education in India?' Or words to that effect. The anchor of the programme was talking to three teachers of English language and literature from major Indian cities. One of the participants, a lady of some standing amongst the teaching fraternity, was asked what she thought of the standard of English in our country today. Sounding quite haughty and full of herself, she replied, 'I have always told the children in my school that until and unless they don't read Shakespeare, they will never be successful in mastering English.' That rumble you may have just heard is Shakespeare turning in his grave. Now here's the thing. Without so much as batting an eyelid, this guardian of the colonial language that we have come to adopt as our own, fell straight into one of the most common hidden traps we are prey to, the inadvertent employment of the double negative, which reverses the meaning originally intended. This is a common affliction endemic to our country. On hearing this I asked myself, if this teacher has not realised the folly of her grammatical ways what earthly chance did the children have?

I do not have a problem with the man on the street speaking informally, spreading double negatives all over the place like a rash. After all, to him English is an acquired habit and one should be grateful, in a polyglot country such as ours, that taxi drivers and bus conductors make a spirited attempt to speak in a common lingo to get across to people from different geographies. Kudos to them, and one should refrain from sticking on dog and correcting their grammar. My problem is more to do with the so-called upper crust class of people who hold forth on just about any subject under the sun, with nary a care about merrily stepping into syntactic pitfalls. If you ask me, the television programme I referred to earlier should have been called 'Wither English education in India.' I trust, dear reader, your hawk-eye spotted the difference.

Our television anchors, news readers and those political representatives who constantly infest our small screens, are notoriously guilty of committing the crime of the double negative. Only the other day, an oft-seen lady of obstreperous temperament with a preternatural sulk, from one of the leading political parties had this to say to the anchor, and I am paraphrasing, 'Until you don't apologise for that remark, I won't walk out of this programme this instant.' Naturally, the anchor man, who came from a better finishing school, heeded her instruction and declined to proffer an apology! There is comic irony in this exchange, and how a word or expression out of place can create confusion and misunderstanding. However, for the most part, our conversations tend to sprinkle double negatives like largesse and no one is any the wiser. We have learnt to live with them. During my professional working days in marketing and advertising, I would often chide a junior colleague for saying things like, 'until you don't call me, I won't come.' My riposte to the puzzled colleague was, 'I won't call you, and you need not come.'

I will freely grant you that I must have been a bit of a pain in the posterior, forever looking out for errors to correct in other people. It comes from having spent much time in dark, dank printing houses in the dark, dank days of incessant power cuts in Calcutta during the 70s, reading galley proofs in 6 pt Helvetica or Garamond typeface for annual reports and corporate brochures, with only a kerosene lamp to throw some light. We were not aided by Word software telling us where we have gone wrong and to correct same. M/s Microsoft have some cheek telling me to correct 'realise' to 'realize!' And they don't oblige if I ask for the British spelling option in favour of American. I can't even tell them to sod off with a terse, 'Until you don't give me the British option, I won't use Microsoft Word.' You won't get much change out of Apple, either.

At this point, I shall abruptly change the subject to Pink Floyd, the much revered and massively followed British rock band. To be honest and strictly speaking it is not really such a big change of subject, just a change of protagonist from English teachers and TV anchors in India to a band of British musicians. One of Pink Floyd's most famous songs, *Another Brick in the Wall* opens with the lines, *We don't need no education / We don't need no thought control.* Now here is an English band, as English as Fish and Chips or Shepherd's Pie, resorting to an American abomination, viz., the use of the double negative. That said, I think there are extenuating circumstances here that one must contend with. The world of pop music allows its own liberties with the language which the lofty world of the spoken or written word frowns upon. If Pink Floyd had sung the song pedantically correctly as *We don't need any education / We don't need any thought control,* it just would not have sounded right, certainly not to the younger generation, and the metre would have been all wrong. Pink Floyd's equally celebrated compatriots, The Rolling Stones rocked the world with *I Can't Get No (Satisfaction),* and The Beatles, in their song *Oh! Darling,* pleaded, *I'll never do you no harm.* Enough said.

There are many more such examples but to cite three of the United Kingdom's most legendary pop groups and their minor grammatical *faux pas* (not that they really are) would suffice for the present to make a point. Elvis Presley did complain that *You Ain't Nothin' But A Hound Dog,* but then, Elvis was as American as Mom and Apple Pie so we must make allowances.

Lest you should harbour a false notion that only famous pop musicians and semi-literate Indian television personalities frequently come under the spell of the double negative, take heart. No less than William Shakespeare was once found guilty of using a triple negative in his play Richard III, when he wrote, 'I never was *nor never* will be.' Hell's bells! The italics are not the Bard's. It goes without saying that had

I challenged Shakespeare on his excessive use of the negative, he would have fobbed me off with a 'More of your conversation would infect my brain.' (Coriolanus Act 2, Scene 1). I doubt if anyone had the gall to tell old William that most of his conversations, as gleaned from his plays, gave many of his readers some level of brain disorder, but that is another matter. Which is hardly surprising for if you really annoyed the man, he could crush you through Hamlet's voice, 'O, it offends me to the soul to hear a robustious periwig-pated fellow tear a passion to tatters, to very rags, to split the ears of the groundlings, who (for the most part) are capable of nothing but inexplicable dumb shows and noise.' You have been warned.

End of day, to quote rusticated Congressman Sanjay's Jha's go-to phrase, one cannot place any value judgement on whether the usage of the double negative in our regular discourse is kosher or not. The jury is out and unlikely to return in a hurry. Ultimately, it is all a matter of conditioning. If you are an Indian who is well versed in the intricacies of the English language, it all depends on whether the American way of speaking appeals to you more or the British. I am specifically referring to Indians born and bred in India, and not people of Indian origin such as Rishi Sunak or V.S. Naipaul. Shashi Tharoor can be in the mix. Though he was born in the UK, he spent his early years in India, till he went to the US for higher education and, strangely, there acquired a British brogue. Those ringing, plummy tones would have raised his stock at the United Nations. And therein lies the rub. Had the estimable Tharoor returned to his home country to pursue a career in politics, armed with a Yankee twang, we would not have given him the time of day. But a clipped, British accent, *a la* Alec Guinness? Ah, now that is entirely different. That, we Indians like.

A caveat. I feel it incumbent upon me to explain, just to set the record straight, that the double negative variant starting with the words 'until you don't...' is of uniquely Indian provenance, whereas the Pink Floyd offering, 'we don't need no education' is a typically American figure of speech, finding favour in various parts of the globe.

Screenwriter Robert McKee got it just about right, 'In life two negatives don't make a positive. Double negatives turn positive only in math and formal logic. In life things just get worse and worse and worse.' Speaking for myself, until you don't tell me otherwise, I won't speak in double negatives. Ain't nobody can do nothin' about it.

GERIATRIC GOSSIP

Old friends, old friends / Sat on their park bench like bookends.
– Simon & Garfunkel

There were these two elderly gentlemen, hang on, what the hell, let's call a spade a shovel, there were these two old gentlemen taking their early morning constitutional at their nearby park. Early to mid-eighties, if I am any judge. One of them was somewhat bent over with a walking stick for support. The other was relatively sprightly with an easy gait. Then there was me, an elderly denizen, an apt description for one who was giving the two oldies about twelve years, if a day, at an educated guess. The two spavined gents seemed to be involved in an animated conversation, which aroused my curiosity. After a short while, an inviting park bench beckoned and the two senior citizens decided to sit themselves down to continue their chinwag. As there was no other bench in the vicinity, I too parked myself at the edge of the bench, closed my eyes and did some deep breathing, apparently oblivious to any other goings-on. While my pretend posture was yogic, my actual intention was that of an inquisitive fly on the wall. Only, this was a fly sitting on a park bench. The oldies were unmindful of my presence, which was just as well, and my auditory canals were sharply attuned to the slightest chesty cough. Thus, I was privy to this fascinating chit-chat between the two gnarled, self-appointed wiseacres.

'I say Chandran, what a lovely morning eh? The lark's on the wing; the snail's on the thorn; God's in his heaven - all's right with the world.'

'Nice one, Mathew. Is that one of your own, or is it something you lifted from one of the Wodehouse novels?'

'I wish. You are right about the Wodehouse bit Chandran, but the Master of farce himself took it from Robert Browning's *Pippa's Song*. He was always doing that, Wodehouse. Quite often, deliberately misquoting.'

'Right, so what you are telling me is that this lark and snail quote is probably a line that can be drawn from Bertie Wooster through Wodehouse and the copyright resting with Browning.'

'That's about the size of it.'

'Right, let's put all this poetry and literary stuff to one side, shall we? Tell me Mathew, what's your take on this godawful brouhaha about the BBC documentary on our revered PM?'

(Now we were getting somewhere. I was beginning to tire of Browning, Wodehouse, Wooster et al).

'Look here Chandran, you will need to speak up a bit. You know I am a bit hard of hearing in my left ear. What was that about the BBC?'

'The problem is your right ear is worse. Not that my ears are in any great shape either. Why don't you get one of those hearing aids that are so widely advertised these days?'

'What, and let the whole world know I am deaf as a doorpost? No, thank you! What is more, those hearing aids are pretty useless. They make awful sounds that drive you insane. Let's get back to the subject, Chandran. What has the BBC gone and done now?'

'They have produced a documentary film trashing our Prime Minister.'

'Why did they have to do that? There are enough and more people in our own country doing that on a daily basis.'

(Good point, Mathew. Nicely put.)

'That's all very well, Mathew, but no one takes a blind bit of notice when opposition parties make a song and dance about these things in parliament. However, when a foreign news channel, particularly a reputedly hallowed institution like the BBC, takes up the cudgels, then the opposition goes to town making a song and dance about what the BBC said. Get my meaning?'

'Sort of, but what is BBC's beef against our PM?'

'I say old chap, don't use words like beef when we are discussing the PM. Not done, not cricket. Anyhow, to answer your question, the government will have us believe all this is motivated propaganda, raking up the past when the highest courts in our land have cleared the PM of any wrongdoing. They have a point, but the opposition, thanks to this BBC film, have got the bit between the teeth and are going hammer and tongs. State and central elections not far away, see what I mean?'

(This Chandran pensioner is quite something. Follows politics closely and is able to see both sides of the argument. The kind of chap we need as a TV anchor instead of the one-dimensional ghouls we have).

'It's a pity, Chandran. I mean, Britain has an Indian at Number 10 and although he makes simpering noises about what a nice bloke our PM is, he just shrugs his shoulders when it comes to telling the BBC where to get off.'

'Look Mathew, Rishi Sunak is no more Indian than Narendra Modi is an Englishman. So, stop calling him an Indian and his wife, who was an Indian is now totally English, and she has the papers to prove it. As for the BBC, it is a law unto itself and that's that.'

'I guess, but I loved those old BBC programmes on their world service radio. My school English teacher would encourage us to listen to their news just to be able to speak "propah" English.'

(By now, I was growing weary of this BBC discussion and hoped the fogeys would turn to something else. And right on cue, Chandran obliged).

'Listen Mathew, let's dump the BBC subject, you will hear a lot more of it from our media, social and conventional, every day. My lungs are also protesting having to shout into your left ear. Tell me, what do you think is going on with this Adani fiasco and the Hindenburg report.'

'Heidelberg? Didn't they produce those great offset printing machines. I worked at a printing house once upon a time.'

'No, no. Not Heidelberg, Hindenburg.'

'Never heard of them. Must have been a small printing outfit.'

'Negative, nothing to do with printing. Where have you been, Matt? This is a hole-in-the-wall American company that tinkers around with corporate houses' stocks and makes a lot of money. The owner is a short seller.'

'What has the owner's height got to do with anything?'

(By now, my yogic breathing had gone for a six. I was desperately trying to avoid breaking out into raucous laughter).

'Are you trying to be funny or just being dumb?'

'All right Chandran, you're the clever git. What is a short seller?'

'Ah, now that's asking. Something to do with buying long and selling short, then selling it again and making pots of money.'

(At this point I burst into an uncontrollable fit of laughter and managed to pretend I was coughing).

'Thanks for that Chandran, now I know everything. But how does all this tie in with Adani?'

'Look Matt, you must have read that Adani is a big fish with massive interests all over the world. He even owns a port in Israel. So, this Hindenburg chappie found a few, big holes, real or imagined, in Adani's businesses and splashed it all over the place. Net result, Adani shares came tumbling down like a ton of bricks. The markets exploded, like the Hindenburg zeppelin disaster in 1937 that slayed 36.'

(This Chandran fellow can enter any quiz competition and show all the others a clean pair of heels).

'And the Heidelberg shark had already bought and sold Adani's shares short.'

'Brilliant Matt, at your age, with just one functioning ear, you cracked it straight out of the box. And for the last time, it's Hindenburg. Don't sully Heidelberg's fair name.'

'Then there's plenty of stuff in the papers about tax havens, Cayman Islands, shell companies, the role of SBI, LIC, SEBI, RBI, Finance Ministry and so on. With the PM's benevolent shadow always in the background. And the opposition are again trying to make a hearty meal of it. That really sticks in my craw. How am I doing Chandran?'

('Sticks in my craw.' I like that, must use it sometime).

'You are really cooking, my friend. And don't forget, once again the timing is impeccable. Nirmala ji presented what most people thought was a budget for the ages. But the Adani fiasco and the Hindenburg nutter decided to rain heavily on her parade. The government is crying conspiracy and the opposition is crying JPC.'

'And the common man is crying hoarse. I think I have had as much of this as I can take for one day. Let us get back home. One last thing, if I may, Chandran. Can you email me in about five easy steps how to buy shares, sell them short and make a bit of moolah on the side? My pension, coupled with the present rate of inflation, is killing me.'

'That makes two of us Matt. We will do this together. It is perfectly legal, by the way. However, we will not throw mud at anyone. I will call my grandson to help us out at my desktop. Much better way to spend our time than worrying about osteoporosis, dental work, prostate, health insurance etc, don't you think?'

'You said a mouthful there, Chandran.'

The two of them wended their weary way back home. I watched their receding behinds with unabashed admiration. Shakespeare said 'sweet are the uses of adversity.' These two gentlemen, in their sunset years, showed me it is never too late to learn, even from somebody else's misfortunes.

CALLING OUT NAMES IN MEGHALAYA

The assembly election results for three important north-eastern states of India, namely, Tripura, Nagaland and Meghalaya are just in. And surprise, surprise, the incumbent BJP has come up smelling of roses in all the three states. They won by a comfortable margin in Tripura and Nagaland, bagging the requisite number of seats, along with their allies and romped home. In Meghalaya, however, they could barely scrape together two seats off their own bat, and still ended up on the winning side! As one BJP foot-soldier was overheard stage-whispering to a friendly (is there any other kind?) television reporter, 'You win some, you win some!' They are a winsome lot, the BJP party workers. And why not? It appears all they need to do is turn up for an election and the results are virtually a foregone conclusion, barring in a handful of states. I am stretching a point here, but what the hell, in politics exaggeration is the name of the game.

Mind you, it was strongly rumoured that the erstwhile Chief Minister of Meghalaya, Conrad Sangma, had a run-in with one of the BJP bosses and decided to part company prior to the assembly polls. However, when the results came in and the guitar-strumming Conrad found himself a few seats short he, like any astute politician, decided to make nice with the BJP and they are friends again. Politics throws up strange bedfellows, even if the lay public feels like throwing up now and again. Still and all, in the words of that lovely Burt Bacharach song, *That's What Friends Are For.* Bottom line, 'the double-engine sarkar' is enjoying a lip-smacking, flavourful triple sundae in the north east and it will stay that way for the next five years. To the victor go the spoils.

Meanwhile there are more assembly elections on the anvil. Word on the street is that bell-weather state Karnataka will be difficult to hold on to by the ruling dispensation, and with stacks of cash being found recently under the beds and floorboards in some BJP MLA's home, the opposition will get its chance to rub it in, good and proper. Time for some good, old fashioned whataboutery to fill the airwaves. And Rahul Gandhi is helping the BJP in that regard with some strange statements in Cambridge, of all places, about seeing 'eye to eye' with militants in Kashmir, his stunning discovery of harmonious China as a force of nature, Pegasus spyware in his phone *et al.* Wonder who his speech writer is. In passing, I must say the now not-so-young scion's decision to trim his erstwhile, outrageously straggly beard is a welcome change. The optics just went up a notch. Contrarily, it's a bit rich his branding the BJP as a 'suit-boot ki sarkar.' He was dressed to the nines at Cambridge, suited and booted to the gills. Spiffy. Savile Row?

That said, let me get back to the north-east. Like most other people in our country, I plead guilty to not knowing very much about this bountiful and beautiful region. Evidently, even most of our political parties in the past paid scant attention to the 'three sisters,' Meghalaya, Tripura and Nagaland. Now that politics has seen to it that these almost-forgotten states are dominating, at least for now, dining room conversations in many parts of India, we are all frantically searching websites to learn more. However, what has caught my attention is not so much the unspoiled beauty and grandeur of the region, though that alone is worth the price of an air-ticket to Shillong, but the evocative names of the people who belong to these states. In elaborating on this somewhat unusual theme, I leave out Nagaland and Tripura for now, and concentrate instead on Meghalaya. This is because most people's names in Tripura are of familiar origins from other parts of India, and those of Nagaland, while interesting, don't quite have the exotic magic or music of those who have been christened in Meghalaya. Christened, incidentally, being the operative word, given the Christian dominated nature of the state. My observations include names of some of the small constituencies as well.

Let us then, you and I, dive in and examine these names that I, for the most part, have not come across before. To employ that horrendous present-day expression, 'my bad.' First off, let us get the common or garden Sangma and Lyngdoh out of the way. It appears that you cannot hurl a brick in Meghalaya without beaning a Sangma or a Lyngdoh. Rather like a Chatterjee or a Banerjee in Bengal. Not that one wishes to, heaven forbid. Hurl a brick, I mean, but you get my drift. Instead, let us feast on some of the other incredible names, shall we? For starters, there's Dr. Wanweiroy Kharlukhi, which is such an evocative name. Had I been on first name terms with him, I would probably have called him 'Wanny' or perhaps just a vanilla 'Roy.' Incidentally, I cannot blithely assume that the name belongs to the male and not the female of the species, for there's no way of telling until I come across a picture. We move on to Prestone Tynsong and Hamleston Dohling, whose names put me in mind of church bells chiming. Come One Ymbon must surely vie for the top three spots if one were to rank these names in terms of favourites.

Not that it is easy to pick favourites. One is spoilt for choice in Meghalaya. Take Matthew Beyondstar Kurbah or if you must, Brightstarwell Marbaniang. Clearly the stars are propitiously well aspected for these bright candidates. They will go far. The stars are the limit! Methodious Dkhar reminds me of American jazz legend, Thelonious Monk and don't ask me why. If you know your jazz, I wouldn't at all be surprised if Methodious trumpets his political success most melodiously, with Conrad Sangma accompanying him on guitar. Politicians are expected to be ardent and keen about their work and who better than Ardent Miller Basaiawmoit to deliver, whichever portfolio he might be offered. If the CM needs some heavy lifting to be done on his behalf, he need look no further than Heaving Stone Kharpran to do his bidding. The Red Indians of yore had names like this.

In case you thought the Lalus of the world came only from Bihar, Meghalaya says 'what the heck, we have our own Alexander Lalu Hek.' Legend has it that revered Greek statesman Demosthenes was one of the world's greatest orators. Who is to say that Meghalaya's very own Sosthenes Southun is not inspired by the oratory skills of the ancient Greek? Questions, questions. I am not betting against Walmiki Shylla being named after the great Indian sage, Valmiki, who gave us the epic, Ramayana. I love Gavin Miguel Mylliem and Gabriel Wahlang, whose names remind one irresistibly of colourful Latin American and Spanish flavours. Remington Momin's ancestors may have introduced the first typewriters to Meghalaya, but that is just an educated guess on my part.

Those are just a handful of glorious samples of the names of the beautiful people of gorgeous Meghalaya, and let us just take a quick peek at some of the constituencies that these worthies represent. Sutnga Saipung, Mowkaiaw, Mawrengkneng, Pynthorumkhrah, Nongthymmai, Rambrai-Jyrngam, Chokpot, Mawthadraishan, Bajengdoba and Rongieng. Those are just a soupçon mined from a field of infinite, if unpronounceable, riches. A vowel or two, casually thrown-in between the consonants, would have helped but hey, we shouldn't be fussy. I am sure the Meghalayans will be similarly up against it with Madal Virupakshappa, the BJP MLA who is drowning in his own, ill-gotten hard cash. By the way, just to show there is no ill-feeling, Nagaland's likely Chief Minister is called Neiphiu Rio. Not bad, but wouldn't stand much of a chance against his Meghalayan neigbhours in an 'exotic name' competition.

That said, it strikes me that the BJP can consider themselves fortunate that their representation on the Meghalaya cabinet will be barely skeletal. Had it been otherwise, the likes of our Prime Minister and Home Minister attempting to wrap these amazing Meghalayan names round their tongues would have been a task well beyond their levels of articulation. It is well beyond mine! They will do well to stick to 'Good morning, Mr. Sangma. Would you like another airport?'

In conclusion, I would like to share an amusing, personal anecdote, entirely true, of my own experience with an unusual north-eastern name. I made an appointment with my local salon for a much-needed haircut a few days ago. They gave me a pleasant, industrious, young lady, clearly from the hilly regions, to take care of my grooming. I have to say she did an extremely competent job – hair-cut, shampoo, head-massage, the works. I felt like a million dollars at the end of it all. Out of courtesy, I thanked her profusely and inquired as to her name for future reference. 'So So,' she replied.

'I beg your pardon?' I responded, somewhat baffled.

Once again, she repeated the words, 'So So.'

'Ah so, I get it. Your name is So So, but your hair-dressing skill is anything but. Glad to meet you So So. My name, as you might have gathered from the booking slot, is Suresh Subrahmanyan, but you can call me Su Su.'

So So merely giggled as I strode confidently out of the salon.

TO 'SIR,' WITH RESERVATIONS

The Oxford dictionary defines the respectful appellation of 'Sir' as follows, 'used as a polite way of addressing a man whose name you do not know, for example in a store or restaurant, or to show respect viz., Good morning, Sir.' The operative phrase here is 'way of addressing a man.' From the time we were toddlers in school, we have grown accustomed to addressing male teachers or masters as 'Sir,' while lady teachers were invariably referred to as 'Miss,' irrespective of their marital status. Now, why am I at pains to belabour this rather obvious point? The reasons are not far to seek. My newspaper this morning carried an arresting headline, 'Woman or man, address judge as "Sir."' This confusing instruction was given by the Chief Justice of the Gujarat High Court.

Reportedly, the hoary, old subject of whether judges should be addressed with the deferential, some may even say obsequious, British-era-hangover 'My lord' or 'Your Honour' was resurrected in the Gujarat High Court, presided over by a lady Chief Justice. The honourable lady passed a verdict in favour of 'Sir' as a gender-neutral alternative. The vexed question of what is the proper way of addressing judges of either gender has been raised in earlier years, but there has been no clear-cut direction such that lawyers or the accused can find themselves on safe ground when they clear their throats to address their Lords or Ladyships. I can hardly say 'to address their Sirs,' which quite frankly, sounds ludicrous.

You see my quandary here, readers? The problem arose in the first place because a lawyer, addressing a division bench comprising a lady and a gentleman judge, decided that discretion is the better part of valour, took the chivalrous approach and addressed both of them collectively as 'Your Ladyship.' It is my guess that that was what he naively intended to do, though the chagrined judges took the view that he was addressing only the distaff member of the bench, and was peremptorily told, if not actually reprimanded that he should be acknowledging both of them and not just the lady judge. In short, the unfortunate lawyer found himself between a rock and a hard place.

Thus chastised, the lawyer meekly apologised, lest he should be found in contempt. At which point, in order to put this issue to bed once and for all, as the debate over terminology issues was eating into precious time of court proceedings, the judges declared that 'Sir' would be an acceptable and gender-neutral way of addressing their Honours. In order to arrive at this facile conclusion the judges, as is the way with judges (and with lawyers and solicitors), proceeded to quote several precedents drawn from past learned judges to buttress their case and declared their verdict. 'Sir' it is and 'Sir' it shall be. Case closed.

Some interested, or even disinterested third party do-gooder could contemplate approaching the Supreme Court and seek the opinion of their Lords or Ladyships or Sirs as to how they felt about the whole rigmarole. However, our courts are already at bursting point and facing considerable pressure to hear important cases expeditiously and will not look kindly upon being asked to pass judgements over what they will doubtless regard a trivial matter.

Let me now declare, straight off the bat, that I feel a great sense of unease over the Gujarat High Court's view on how judges ought to be addressed. While I have no wish to bring back practices that would smack of our colonial past, I have to say that this decision could have unintended consequences for the larger sphere of general discourse. The way I see it is that, if judges wish to become neutral-genders (sounds weirder every time I utter it) and have no issues with being addressed by a 'one-size-fits-all' appellation of 'Sir,' that is their business and good luck to them. However, one should also have some consideration for the wider Indian populace, or 'the great unwashed' as somebody (perhaps a judge) once described them.

For decades now, we the people of India have grown accustomed, thanks to Bollywood, Tollywood and all other filmy 'woods' regaling us with emotionally charged scenes of Dilip Kumar, Amitabh Bachchan and Sivaji Ganesan addressing our wigged sentinels of jurisprudence dramatically with a thunderous 'Objection, My Lord.' Are we going to be denied such heightened histrionics with a lame 'Objection Sir'? In any case, I cannot get my head round the prospect of having to address a lady judge as 'Sir.' My English teacher in school, Mrs. Scott, would have administered 'one hit on the back of the head' if I called her 'Sir.' Just not cricket, Your Honour. To think that a lady Chief Justice has actually suggested this is all the more befuddling.

Writers sometimes face a unique problem when referring to a person in the abstract (gender-neutral), and choose to be politically correct by writing 'she' or 'her,' only to lapse reflexively later on into 'he' and 'him.' As in, 'a person is expected to be resourceful if he seeks to be successful.' Why could that not have been a 'she'? Or, if you wish to hedge your bets, you could say 'he or she,' which over several sentences and paragraphs, can get tiresome. Old habits die hard.

If I were to do a quick sketch for a short one-act play dealing with judicial nomenclatures, it would go something like this.

Defence Counsel – 'Your Worship, my client is innocent of all charges levelled against him. The prosecution has failed to provide any substantive evidence. I humbly request your Lordships to dismiss this farcical case. With costs. Thank you, Your Honour.'

Male Judge – 'I would strongly urge Defence Counsel to make up his mind whether to address the bench as "Worship" or "Lordship." We cannot entertain both.'

Lady Judge – 'Counsel also added "Honour" for good measure. In my view, none of these terms is suitable. With due apologies to my learned colleague. Why call us "Worship?" We are not Gods.'

Defence Counsel – 'No? Not Gods? You could have fooled me your… your… your… Sirs? You see how tame that sounds? On your banging of the gavel and pronouncing "Guilty" or "Not Guilty" depends the future of so many undertrials. In a sense, you *are* Gods and rightly worshipped. Not unlike doctors and surgeons.'

Male Judge – 'What is wrong with "Sir?" It is respectful and as my colleague keeps reminding us, it is gender-neutral. What is your problem with "Sir?"

Defence Counsel – "With due respect Sir, to address a lady as "Sir" is both conventionally, technically and grammatically wrong. An abomination. The term gender-neutral also, unfortunately, brings to mind people of an indeterminate sexual orientation. If you are against terms like "Lordship, Worship, Honour" etc., then we have no option but to address a lady judge as "Madam." In school we used to call them "Miss" but that will not be appropriate here in court.'

Lady Judge (stage whispers to her male colleague) – 'I should hope not. I did not come prepared for a tutorial on terminologies and court etiquette. Not from this chit of a lawyer, at any rate. Can we get on with the case and forget about how we are addressed for the moment? We can meet separately with our other colleagues and issue a set of instructions approved by the Supreme Court on this matter. Yes, Sir?'

Male Judge – 'Yes Sir. I mean, Yes Madam. Oh, what the hell! Even I am dithering. Let us deliver a verdict and be done with it. I have had it up to here with name calling.'

You see what is happening here, readers? Confusion confounded. We may have noble thoughts in wishing to gradually divest ourselves of painful reminders of our British colonial past, but in trying to set things right in a hurry, we could be digging a bigger hole for ourselves. Even

'Sir' is still an English word and, for the most part, court proceedings are still conducted in English. It would be better if our legal luminaries bent their minds to the expeditious disposal of cases, (the ever-growing pending litigations are as long as several arms), rather than getting hopelessly mired in how they should be addressed. 'Judge not, that ye be not judged,' say I. A smidgen of humour won't hurt. Your average denizen on the street cannot fathom what all the fuss is about, 'I don't understand why judges get paid so much. Others judge me for free.'

I guess what I am striving to say is that, there are more bizarre pronouncements we have received from judges than an obsession with how they should be addressed. Personally, my favourite, laugh-out-loud, throwaway line from the bench occurs in a brilliant satirical sketch by the late comedian Peter Cook, portraying a judge. During his summing up, he winds up his long peroration with this sage advice to the jury, 'You will now retire and carefully consider your verdict of "Not Guilty!"'

Now that is something for their Lordships, Ladyships, Right Honourables, Worships and Sirs to mull over. After all, what's in a name?

A FLY ON THE WALL TAKES THE MINUTES

It is given to only a select few to sit in on meetings involving the most powerful personages of the land, those that guide our destinies and chalk out our futures. We, the hoi polloi, come to learn of these earth-shattering proceedings much later in a carefully orchestrated form. However, the common-or-garden house fly suffers from no such deprivation. It sits inconspicuously on a wall and absorbs everything that is being deliberated upon. The fly's discretion is legendary. It speaks to no one and disturbs no one, barring the occasional foray over a sugared bun or jalebi, only to be harmlessly swatted away, whereupon it settles back at its appointed place on the wall. All ears, in a manner of speaking. We were extremely fortunate that one such fly, let us call him Lalloo, agreed to write up the Minutes of this high-powered meeting for our delectation.

The Prime Minister was at his wit's end. He summoned his Lieutenant and, if you will pardon the coinage, Rightenant, for an emergency meeting. It had just gone past midnight and the PM's two startled henchmen scrambled out of their beds, as did their chauffeurs, and they were at their boss' residence before you could say Naya Sansad Bhavan. The sudden call from the big man had unforeseen and unfortunate grooming consequences. Hurried and harried as they were at the unexpected call at an unearthly hour, though they should have been accustomed to it by now, the Rightenant's hair was in complete disarray as he had absent-mindedly failed to run a comb though it prior to rushing out. The Lieutenant, on the other hand, being follicularly challenged, was less conspicuous in this respect, but his understandably crumpled clothes left him in a state of *déshabillé*.

They were ushered in to the PM's private chamber, where he entertained only his closest confidantes. One is happy to report that the PM, as is his unfailing wont, was perfectly groomed and looked as fresh as a daisy. However, his brow was furrowed with worry lines as he motioned to his Lieutenant and Rightenant to be seated. The PM was so preoccupied with his own thoughts that he paid scant attention to his visitors' slovenly appearance. Refreshing cups of hot, masala chai materialised out of nowhere as a Jeeves-like *khansama,* who appeared to float on thin air, placed the steaming cups in front of them.

The PM kicked off the proceedings. 'Gentlemen, I apologise for dragging you out of bed at this late hour. That said, if I can be staying awake this late with weighty issues to disturb my beauty sleep, I do not see why you two should be snoring peacefully.'

The Lieutenant was the first to give utterance with a few hesitant words. 'What is it Sir, that is bothering you? You appear distrait. And distraught. Please tell us. We are here to help with anything you need.'

At which point, not to be left out of the proceedings, the Rightenant weighed in with, 'Oh, absolutely Sir, anything at all. Just say the word, Sir. Your wish is our command.'

The Supreme Leader sat back and absorbed these usual obsequies with an accustomed air and spoke. 'There is too much talk going on all over the country, particularly through the media channels, that I am beginning to lose my magic touch. And if things continue like this, we might be looking at the wrong end of the result when the General Elections come round in less than a year. Any thoughts?'

The two helpmeets spoke as one. 'No, no, Sir. That is untrue, Sir. Vicious lies. Perish the thought. Please do not pay any heed to these media wallahs.'

'Why should I not? After all, I am told they are all supposed to be under our thumb. Or should that be thumbs? Even one or two television news channels which were sitting on the fence have now hopped on to our side. And yet, and yet, there is talk of research on the mood of the nation revealing some disturbing trends. Of course, it goes without saying that I am still cock of the walk as far as popularity goes, but that is not nearly enough. That other upstart of a fellow seems to be catching up merely by walking all over the country and growing an unkempt beard! And how did we allow Karnataka to fall? I burned the candle at both ends there and look what transpired? Very dispiriting. Then there are elections coming up in Madhya Pradesh, Chhattisgarh and Rajasthan, and I ask myself, "what will the harvest be?"'

The Rightenant was on his feet. 'Sir, I take full responsibility for what happened in that state, but our vote share did not fall. The JDS sank without a trace and the Congress benefitted. We will correct that in 2024. Not sure what you meant by the harvest question, but all indicators point to a normal monsoon. So, we should expect a bountiful harvest all over the country.'

The PM looked exasperated and turned to his Lieutenant. 'Please explain to our Rightenant in words of not more than two syllables, what the import of my harvest comment was.'

'Do not worry Sir. I shall do that later. For now, I would like to assure you that all those three states you mentioned, where assembly elections are due, we shall win hands down. As for 2024, the result is a foregone conclusion. All our plans and strategies are in place.'

'You always say that we shall win hands down. It is the hands-up, palm symbol that I am currently concerned about. They will do anything to win. Freebies being distributed like every day is Christmas, Holi and Ramzan combined. Their young leader always chooses to bad mouth me outside the country, this time in California. First, he claimed God can take tips from me on how the universe works. Then he called me a specimen. What exactly *is* a specimen?'

The Rightenant was up in a flash. His had taken English as an elective at university. 'I can answer that, Sir. A specimen is an individual animal, plant, piece of a mineral and so on, used as an example of its species or type for scientific study or display. The term is also used humorously and pejoratively to describe a person.'

The PM was not impressed. 'Sounds like a great description of the young erstwhile MP! However, I can clearly see that the specimen reference was meant to be an insult. Humorous? I am not laughing. I can choose to ignore all this, but with elections coming up, we need to develop a counter strategy. I am still waiting for you people to come up with something, and believe you me, my patience is running wafer thin.'

The Lieutenant attempted to strike a soothing note. 'PM Sir, I understand your concern. Rest assured we are wrestling with these challenges and are fully confident we will come up trumps.'

The PM angrily thumped the table, spilling some of the masala chai and staining the polished mahogany. 'Never, I repeat, never ever use that word again in my presence. I mean it, or there will be consequences.'

'What word, Sir?'

'Wrestling. I do not wish to hear that word. All I have been hearing these past few weeks is about these wrestlers who even threatened to steal the thunder from my New Parliament House inauguration. I understand the proper expression is raining on my parade. Right Sirji?'

'Understood Sir,' said both the deputies. We shall look for some synonyms to replace the word "wrestling." Sorry, I had to use the word just now only to demonstrate that we shall not be using that offensive term again.'

The Rightenant made a quick interjection with, 'That was excellent Sir, "raining on my parade." I could not have put it better myself.'

'Thank you. I am flattered. I can take cold comfort from being able to impress my two confidantes at one in the morning. Adding insult to injury, someone likened our beautiful new parliament building to a coffin! The sheer audacity. Yet you wonder why I am worried? And before I forget, what a palaver over this *Sengol* business. Frankly, until a few months ago, I did not know what a *Sengol* and its significance was. Then this wonderful Bharatanatyam exponent from Chennai wrote me, explaining all about it. At least, now I know it is not a walking stick, as claimed by some famous people. If it was good enough for Rajaji Ji, Nehru Ji and his buddy Mountbatten, it is good enough for me. End of.'

The PM's Rightenant was so moved his eyes had misted over. 'Such a perfect summation, Sir. And again, "palaver." How many people use beautiful words like that.' He reached out for a tissue and emotionally blew his nose accompanied by a massive honk.

The PM winced and rose, as did the other two. 'Gentlemen, I must get some sleep. I take it we can call it a night and reconvene tomorrow, if you have no big-ticket idea to share. Go to bed. You both look like train wrecks.'

The Rightenant nearly jumped out of his skin and urgently stage-whispered into his boss' ears, 'Sir please, do not talk about train wrecks either. Like wrestling, very sensitive subject right now.'

'Oh sorry, how remiss of me. *Mea culpa.*'

The Lieutenant cleared his throat. 'PM Sir, we think we have an idea that will change the entire mood of the nation in one master stroke. Your ratings will zoom stratospherically, and you could end up with more than 400 seats in the Lok Sabha come May 2024.'

'Yes, yes, but what is this big idea of yours. Cat got your tongue? Spell it out, man.'

'Sir, immediately announce that you are awarding the Bharat Ratna to one of India's greatest cricketers, and right now, the undisputed darling of the entire nation. I am referring to the one and only Mahendra Singh Dhoni. Strike while the iron is hot. You will be the toast of the nation. Your ratings will go through the roof.'

The PM sat down again and his furrowed brow uncreased itself. He beamed for the first time. He stuck both his hands out to his senior functionaries. 'What a brilliant idea! Toast of the nation, eh? Lightly buttered, as well. At least, I won't be toast. And so simple, like all great ideas. They had their Sachin, we will have our Mahi. Of course, we shall make M.S. Dhoni a Bharat Ratna. Why did I not think of it? Please get my staff to prepare all the necessary ground work. We shall announce it on Independence Day. As per time-honoured custom, our President will give away the award, in case anyone starts wondering. Thank you and good night.'

The PM left with a satisfied smile.

Postscript from Lalloo the fly: Meanwhile, the young scion traipses the globe seeking new ways to put down our PM, but ends up only adding more grist to the PM's mill. His stabs at irony and sarcasm lack punch and fall flat but he bashes on regardless. Perhaps I need to shift my location to his family HQ to pick up some juicy tidbits. They speak highly of the walls there. Love, Lalloo.

BHARAT, SANATANA DHARMA, ONOE ET AL

India is a fascinating country. Dear me, did I just unknowingly drop an inadvertent brick? Should I have said Bharat is a fascinating country? Or, to hedge my bets and err or the side of caution, should I have said India, that is Bharat, is a fascinating country? Keep both sides happy? Damned if I do and damned if I don't. That seems to be the predicament in which I find myself. As do many others who are trying to figure out what this India and Bharat palaver is all about.

How did this controversy over our beloved nation's nomenclature erupt suddenly out of the blue? If media reports are anything to go by, and that is a big 'if,' it all apparently started with an innocuous invitation for dinner. The moot point is that the invitation, which was from our President, no less, to the visiting Heads of State and VIPs attending the G20 Summit in New Delhi, was issued by and captioned 'The President of Bharat.' This set the cat among the pigeons. I should mention, in passing, that the official logo unit of the G20 Summit incorporates both the names of Bharat, calligraphed in the traditional Devanagari script and India, capitalized in English. An even-handed approach ensuring both terms co-exist harmoniously side by side, as blessed by the Constitution. Pitchforking Bharat to the forefront, almost seamlessly (some may even say slyly) via the Presidential dinner invite was clearly the brainchild of the Government without drawing ostentatious attention to itself. That did not quite work as it stood out like a sore thumb. The Cassandras, read the Opposition parties, spotted it quickly enough and all hell broke loose.

I have no wish to go into the alleged chicanery of the Government in bringing Bharat into the spotlight in this fashion, nor do I have any interest in expounding upon the inconsistencies involved in the argument adduced by those who smell a big, fat bandicoot behind this move, claiming that it is to divert attention away from the Opposition's political combo, the collective I.N.D.I.A, which appears to be gaining some traction. Keeping Adani off the headlines was also casually thrown into the mix. On balance, whatever the motive, the Government appears to be perfectly within its rights to employ the term Bharat, which has been enshrined in the Constitution.

Patriotic songs in the vernacular including the National Anthem, extol the virtues of Bharat and not India. That is such a no-brainer it does not even need to be explained. There are enough examples from the north of the Vindhyas to bolster this thought, both in classical and film music. Even in the more arcane world of Carnatic music from the South, a certain Mayuram Viswanatha Sastri composed a song called 'Jayati Jayati Bharata Mata' in the raga Khamas which was popularised back in the day during the 50s by Carnatic music's then poster boy and genius, G.N. Balasubramaniam. One can hardly imagine anyone rendering this song as 'Jayati Jayati India Mata,' God forbid. Any more than you can chant 'India Mata ki Jai.' Other famous doyennes like Bharat Ratna (not India Ratna) M.S. Subbulakshmi and Padma Vibhushan D.K. Pattammal have rendered numerous songs on Bharat on either side of our Independence, particularly those composed by freedom fighter, social reformer and poet, Subramania Bharati. The name Bharati, incidentally, was an affectionate and respectful appellation, and he was often referred mononymously as simply Bharatiyar. His songs and poems moved millions. At least, they did in south Bharat.

Proponents of the more elaborate use of the term Bharat also point to various cities in India having been named differently with nary a whimper raised. Madras and Chennai, Bombay and Mumbai, Calcutta and Kolkata, Trivandrum and Thiruvananthapuram are frequently cited.

This trend is not confined to India alone. There are many similar examples on the global map. As is his wont, if we are to 'credit' the Prime Minister with this move, he has given no indication that there is a concerted effort to amend the name of the country officially, which will also most likely involve a constitutional amendment, to be approved by Parliament. A headache he can do without. Then again, he is known to play his cards close to his chest. The Opposition's quandary is that it can only criticise the Government for its real or imagined motive behind the move, and not for freely using the name Bharat. Astute intellectuals opposed to the idea, who have committed their thoughts on the subject to print, need to be mindful that they do not paint themselves into a corner from which it might prove problematic to wriggle out, the ruling party ever ready to pounce and brand them as unpatriotic.

Where Hindustan that is Bharat that is India fits into all this, I do not know, but should be fit for another hornet's nest of a punch-up. I have little doubt some learned historian has explained all this in considerable detail. For now, we should be grateful the discussion has been confined to just two names.

While fanatic followers of the Indian cricket team often chant 'Indiaaaa, India,' in unison on cricket fields around the world, when our fans decided to take a leaf out the English cricket groupies' brand 'Barmy Army,' our patriots hit upon the idea of calling themselves 'Bharat Army,' the name boldly emblazoned on the tricolour. The two terms, India and Bharat have coexisted harmoniously and interchangeably. One might add here that some famous Indian cricketers like Gavaskar and Sehwag have weighed in behind the Idea of Bharat. M.S. Dhoni could not be reached for a comment as he was enjoying Alcaraz's brilliance at the U.S. Open followed by a round of golf with President Donald Trump! (Is there more in this unusual pairing than meets the eye?) The Bharat vs India debate is a capacious bandwagon onto which everyone can jump. Trust our politicians, irrespective of party affiliation, to put a vicious spin on the whole issue allowing the matter to literally spin out of control.

The political pot, always simmering, boiled over last week when actor-turned-politician, Tamil Nadu's DMK Chief Minister M.K. Stalin's son Udayanidhi, likened our core Hindu philosophy, *Sanatana Dharma,* to rampant diseases like dengue, malaria and the corona virus, asking for its eradication – the Dharma that is, not the diseases. As the terms 'eradicate' and 'disease' are by way of being joined at the hip, it was an unfortunate choice of words by the young scion. Having reflected on his outpourings and deciding he had to go the whole hog, he has now called the BJP 'a poisonous snake.' Expect more fireworks. Simply put, Udayanidhi's intemperate remarks have got him into hot water, landed him right in the soup. Or to put it in terms that he is more likely to be familiar with, dunked him in some hot and spicy *rasam.* However, he and his paterfamilias are digging their heels in and refusing to budge from their stated position. Reverting to the old ruse of claiming he has been misunderstood and is being quoted out of context. Poor lamb.

To add fuel to the fire, senior DMK functionary, A. Raja, no stranger to controversy himself, went one better and gave it as his considered opinion that *Sanatana Dharma* is as bad, if not worse than AIDS and leprosy. One wonders what drives these motormouths to utter such arrant nonsense. It was at best politically inept and maladroit, possibly politically suicidal - something the I.N.D.I.A collective, of which the DMK is an important cog, needed like a hole in the head. It is hardly surprising that other major constituents of I.N.D.I.A are rapidly distancing themselves from this fracas. To add to the confusion, any number of scholars and Indologists are expansively and contrarily holding forth on the *real* meaning of *Sanatana Dharma.* Net result? Nobody is any the wiser.

As if all this were not enough to keep us fully occupied and entertained, enter stage left One Nation, One Election ('but you can call me ONOE.') Pursued by a bear or not, I cannot be sure. The aim is to hold Assembly and Central elections in one fell swoop, and be done with it. The Prime Minister, in his usual way, came up with a googly while his opponents were expecting the ball to go straight on. It was announced, taking everyone aback, that a special session of Parliament has been called later this month, agenda unspecified. Our speculation factory then went on overdrive, particularly by the print and electronic media. Topping the bill was the ONOE issue (with the Women's Reservation Bill and possibly the Uniform Civil Code to follow), which has been informally talked about for some years now, and irate members of the Opposition went to town writing reams about the unsuitability and unworkability of the scheme.

The silver-tongued, articulate Congress MP, Shashi Tharoor led the anti-ONOE brigade, writing columns on the subject. That said, he has been unstinting in his plaudits for those in the Government who burned the midnight oil to achieve a favourable outcome at the G20 Summit. Tharoor's party leader, Rahul Gandhi, revels in taking pot shots at his homeland from a safe distance outside the country, and not for the first time. Others followed suit, presumably in a bid to pre-empt and thwart any such attempt by the ruling party. One assumes Rahul Gandhi will soon return to resume his I.N.D.I.A Jodo Yatra. And we still haven't a clue what these special sessions are all about. Spewing fire and brimstone was the order of the day, which has been doused somewhat by the enormous optics offered by the G20 Summit (Yippee, the Delhi Declaration happened, Putin and Xi notwithstanding).

Clearly, the main talking point from the Opposition has been to establish that the ONOE policy is impractical and will result in a huge waste of national resources, which runs counter to the Government's USP on the subject, viz., achieving economies of scale being the primary selling point. It is worth reflecting here that till 1967, both State and General elections were conducted simultaneously. The point appears to have been lost somewhere in the dense thicket of mass verbiage. So what are we dealing with here? A special session of Parliament in the offing, for which no one even remotely knows the agenda. But everyone is happy to fly kites, play guessing games and shoot in the dark and hope some stray bullet will hit the target. Right now, everyone is shooting blanks.

We can only hope that the Opposition members participate in a lively discussion, if at all ONOE is placed on the agenda, and not stage a walk-out in a huff because the PM is not addressing the House on Manipur.

Whatever be the outcome of all these issues that constantly keep us on our toes, I daresay there will be many more to come. We in India, that is Bharat, will never lack for something to talk and write about. With State and General Elections just around the corner, our cups of joy should be overflowing. I rather feel like S.T. Coleridge's Kubla Khan, *For he on honey-dew hath fed / And drunk the milk of Paradise.* That is a bit of a stretch but put it down to poetic license.

Bring them on, I say. I am all ready and agog in front of my television set, my favourite dailies rustling by my side, and a large tub of popcorn or spicy snacks to keep my gastric juices flowing smoothly. It is going to be one heck of a ride, folks. Lie back and enjoy it.

WHAT'S IN A NAME?

One of the most exciting tasks that a married couple anticipates is the arrival of the proverbial stork with their first born, or for that matter, second or even third born. Rarely in our straitened times do couples go for more than two kids, three being a bit of a stretch, probably accidental. Unless, of course, you are Elon Musk, in which case after the announcement of the birth of the eleventh baby, he has just got down to spitting on his hands and getting into his stride. More of Musk anon. It is superfluous to add that in our enlightened age, marriage is not a necessary pre-condition to add to the world's head count. In fact, as a wedded couple you are not even called upon to be of a different sexual orientation. Same sex couples can have children, just like anybody else. That should cover the whole gamut, unless some new development has taken place in the sphere of human behaviour and physiology that has escaped my attention.

My preoccupation this week is more to do with how couples and their near and dear ones get into a right, royal tizzy over what to name the impending arrival along with the patter of little feet. Those who do not wish to know in advance the sex of their bundle of joy that is still blissfully swimming in its mother's amniotic fluids, run around with reference books while frantically Google searching, scouring names of boys and girls. In any case, Indian law does not allow parents to know the baby's gender in advance. Depending on which religious denomination you belong to, Hindu, Christian, Muslim, Sikh, Parsee, Jain, Buddhist or any other, there are loads of names for you to sift through during those nine months of cozy captivity for our little wonder.

Fierce debates rage in the homestead as all kinds of names are scattered about like so much confetti. If it happens to be a boy, Amar, Akbar or Anthony or their variants should do just fine. Sticking with the Bollywood motif, if it's a girl, one could turn to that notorious vamp Bindu's cabaret dance line from the 1971 hit film *Kati Patang,* 'Neena ya Meena, Anju ya Manju, yaaa Madhu!' Not that it makes a blind bit of difference, but the vamp's name in the film is Shabnam, though she is affectionately called 'Shabbo.' That is a translation from the opening line of the song. The context is different but still, I think you can see where I am going with this.

To further complicate matters, many couples are keen on nailing both the official registered name for the baby as well as a nick name or pet name. 'Right, we have all settled on Krishnamoorthy Venkatasubramanian as the final name, if it is a boy, as it incorporates in some shape or form the names contained in the father's and mother's family genealogy. However, he shall be known as Kittu to the world. If he migrates to the United States and becomes a billionaire software czar and covets the White House, he shall change his name to Kittu Venky. The same rules apply if the arrival is a girl. Full name, Anahita Ambegaonkar, converted in America to Annie Amby.' This principle will hold irrespective of which religion the child belongs to. As an aside, I find it rich when Americans moan about difficulties in pronouncing Indian names with more than three syllables, and find the need to shorten them, Yank style. What about former U.S. National Security Advisor Zbigniew Brzezinski, then? Wrap that round your tongue.

The process of naming a child, in this modern age when the world is our oyster, or as the poet Wordsworth had it, 'the world is too much with us,' has become somewhat universalised. Westerners, who notoriously make a fuss about pronouncing names from the southern hemisphere, have become just that much more familiar. They still behave as if the cat has caught their tongue, but they muddle through. Kamala Harris poses no problem, that's easy-peasy, Vivek Ramaswamy is rapidly gaining currency with frequent appearances on American television debates. Britain's Prime Minister Rishi Sunak is a walk in the park, though his first lady Akshata Murty could prove a handful, if not a mouthful. To the native Brit that is, not to the Asian migrants.

For reasons I am unable to articulate, Indians in India celebrating the impending new arrival with a 'baby shower,' a western concept, seems little more than something the marketing mavens of the gifting industry have showered upon us, to expand their business by showering the baby with gifts. Not unlike the ad blitz inflicted on an unsuspecting world on Valentine's Day. There are those that aver that the idea of a baby shower was originally inspired by ancient Greek and Egyptian rituals. In traditional India, there are certain ceremonies held when the woman is still 'carrying,' but we tend to go a bit soft on the gifts!

Now that we have turned to the subject of names in the western hemisphere, I cannot but talk at greater length about Elon Musk and his rapidly expanding familial empire. While I have touched briefly upon the Indian diaspora and the unique challenges that their names could pose to a western audience, the Twitter now X mogul, Elon Musk, has blazed a new and enthralling trail when it comes to naming his eleven offspring. Across three partners (Justine, Grimes and Shivon Gillis), the prolific Musk has fathered eleven children, and I would not bet against more in the pipeline – more partners and more children.

While one gasps at the great magnate's fecundity, it is more the names his children were burdened with that is noteworthy. Try these on for size. Nevada Alexander Musk, twins Griffin and Vivian Musk which was more conservative, Kai, Saxon and Damian Musk, X AE A-XII Musk (I kid you not), Exa Dark Siderael Musk, nicknamed Y as X AE A-XII had already appropriated the nickname X (makes sense), Strider and Azure Musk and the latest arrival, Techno Mechanicus, nicknamed (what choice did they have?) Tau. Somewhere along the way, they sadly lost Nevada, then resorted to IVF, Vivian declared she was a transgender, the IVF a second time produced triplets, the abovementioned Kai, Saxon and Damian.

At which point Elon and his first wife Justine decided she had had enough and separated, something the Americans do with elan. So with Elon. Presumably Grimes and Shivon Gillis are still in the frame, but honestly, my guess is as good as yours. If you have been able to make cogent sense out of all that, you are a better man than I am, Gunga Din. Overall, not that I am much of a Bollywood follower, but I can't help but paraphrase one of their big hit numbers in doffing my hat to the productive Elon, 'Tu cheez badi hai Musk, Musk.' Loosely translated, in case you are reading this Elon, it means 'You are great, awesome, awesome!'

One thing that really gets my goat with Americans is when the father and the son are given the same name, as in George Bush Sr. and George Bush Jr. It gets no easier when both of them become President of the U.S.A. Obviously not at the same time, but still. In casual conversation at a party for instance, someone says something like, 'That was a quite a victory for George Bush.' Your natural riposte to that comment would be, 'Which George Bush are you referring to? The one that freed Kuwait of Saddam Hussein's occupation or the one that smoked out Saddam from a hidey-hole somewhere in Iraq, leading to his execution?' See what I mean? Merely affixing a Sr. or a Jr. just doesn't cut it. That is taking the lazy way out. I know there is an H.W. and a W that splits the difference between father and son, but that doesn't help. And why John Kennedy was called Jack at home is even more of a mystery, what with his wife being called Jackie. Ours not to reason why, I suppose.

If it was just the newborn's name that parents and elders tear their hair out coming to grips with, that is nothing compared with the argy-bargy that goes on in relation to how to spell the name. This is particularly relevant in the Indian context where superstition and old wives' tales count for a lot. The baby arrives on schedule, spittle generously foaming around the mouth, gurgling away while everybody goes coochy-coo. The father rushes in, brandishing a sheet of paper and announces with much fanfare, 'I have it. From this day forth he shall be called Nikhil. I have checked it out with the priest. It's all kosher and official. We can always call him Nikki or Niks at home.' The mother then peers at the sheet of paper, smeared with sacred ash and *kum kum*, bearing the bold legend NIKHIL, scrunches up her face and says calmly, 'The H will have to go. We cannot go beyond five letters, and my family guru says H, being the eighth letter of the English alphabet, portends ill luck. So let us settle on NIKIL.' Given that the change suggested was not drastic, everyone agrees with a sigh of relief. This is a common occurrence in millions of households around the country. If the baby is a girl, the name could be Riya, Ria or even Rhea. It is all written in the stars.

When all is said and done, the newborn is the victim here, having no say in the matter whatsoever, lumbered with a name he or she will have to live with forever. Techno Mechanicus for crying out loud, you want to change your name? You can, but have a care. Your super rich dad could cut you out of his will and where will you be? What is the point of changing your name to John Doe if you are going to be left skint? Remember what Shakespeare said? 'What's in a name? That which we call a rose, by any other name would smell as sweet.' Though on this occasion, I would prefer to sign off with James Joyce, 'What's in a name? That is what we ask ourselves in childhood when we write the name that we are told is ours.'

Way to go James, or should that be Jim?

A BIT OF A CHAT

'What we've got here is failure to communicate.' *Cool Hand Luke.*

(This story is being narrated by a retired government servant).

I am experiencing a few issues conversing with people below the age of 40 these days. Which is a dead giveaway that I am above 40 years old. As to how many years above 40 is for me to know and for you to preferably not find out. Don't get me wrong. The sub-40 age groupers do speak English perfectly well, no problems there. I cannot vouch for their Tamil or Bengali. Even the words and phrases they use are ones that I am quite familiar with. So where is the hitch? Or glitch, if you prefer. I am not fussy, either way. It is the context that stumps me. The thing of it is, the way in which they employ their vocabulary drives me up the wall. I hear the words, I know the words, yet their import escapes me. You see what I just did there? I am already lapsing into a we / they binary, and that is not desirable while conversing in the same language with fellow humans. Sometimes I think I am losing it, then I tell myself if I cannot figure out what *they* are saying, then surely, *they* must be struggling to follow *my* conversational methods. That puts us on an even keel, and I must brace myself and be up for the challenge.

It is with such conflicting thoughts swirling around my head that I had the somewhat dubious pleasure of meeting a young gentleman, a chit of a lad really, while waiting at our friendly neighbourhood bank for the teller, or whatever they are called these days (cash dispenser?), to call me up for transacting my business. This young man, it was impossible for me to guess what his age might have been, sat next to me immersed in his mobile. Other than the inescapable fact that he was younger than me. Most people are. He was prematurely bald, which is the way with many of the younger generation nowadays, what with all the multi-tasking across time zones, shattered love lives and multiple woes besetting them.

In which respect I had a head start over him, being blessed as I was with a full head of hair. Distinguished silver grey is my preferred description of my thatch, if that does not sound too vain. He was wearing a pair of faded denims with holes at the knees and his canary yellow tee-shirt had this bold legend, GO F*** YOURSELF! The three asterisks after the F were not typed by me to hide my queasiness, that is exactly how the tee-shirt announced itself and, by implication, announced the young wearer. Of course, he was completely absorbed in his iPhone. What did you expect? However, he turned towards me, smiled broadly and introduced himself.

'Good morning, Sir,' said he, 'you can go before me, if you like. Like, I am just chilling.' I was chuffed at the respect he was showing, but I declined. The air-conditioning at the bank was effective and I was not averse to a bit of chilling myself.

Ever so pleased he did not address me as Uncle. 'No, no, you were here before me. Let us adhere to the time-honoured queueing tradition.' I hoped the word 'adhere' did not confuse him.

'Are you sure Sir? I am in no hurry. It is my off day from work.'

'Day off, off day, that makes two of us. It is my day-off-day too. Every day is my off day. I am retired from service. I just need to be back home for lunch, which is still three hours away.'

The young man was not quite sure whether he should be happy for me or console me. I mean, in India many people feel it is the end of the world when they retire. 'Well Sir, I guess you are enjoying your retired life. Must be cool, being able to watch all the cricket matches all day long.'

What's with this affinity towards arctic climes? – cool, chill and so on. 'There are more things in life than cricket matches,' said I tartly. 'Tennis, for a start. Anyway, what line of work are you in?'

'I work for a software company here.'

'But of course, why did I even bother to ask? You cannot throw a stone in Bangalore without striking some software chap or the other. But what is it that you do exactly in this software company? If that is not betraying confidences.'

He looked dubiously at me and proceeded to clear his throat, as if to say, you asked for it. 'I write code, design apps for a variety of digital platforms, monitor their effectiveness on a continuous basis, and make course corrections, as and when. All this on behalf of various clients, our inputs uniquely tailor-made and applied for specific purposes. We charge them a bomb. By the hour.' He then turned back to his mobile as if he had just told me what the time was.

'Is that all?' I asked, 'or are you keeping things from me? Anyhow, if you will pardon a personal question, what are you paid for doing all that stuff that you just rattled off? Sounded most impressive, though I might need an English translation.'

'It is a personal question, but no sweat. It varies from company to company but on average, perks and everything included, I would say I clean up around Rs.35 lakhs per annum. By the way, that is just my salary. The company charges the client in numbers you don't want to know.'

'How old are you? 21? And why are you bald? And why do you wear torn clothes? Can't you afford something better? At that salary?'

'So many questions. Let us just say I am older than 21 and leave it at that. We are all suffering from hair loss and IBS, that is irritable bowel syndrome, given the hours we keep and the tension involved. We work crazy hours, aligned to American timelines. As for the torn clothes, you won't understand. Why are they taking so long? There are just two people in front of us.'

'What is the hurry, young man? Plane to catch? Relax. You seem all frazzled. If you like, I will stand you a *café au lait* at the coffee shop next door, after this. You could use one. Cup, I mean. Or mug.'

'Sorry, just a bit knackered. Yeah, coffee. That's a thought.'

'Fine, by the way what is your name?'

'Rabindranath. You can call me Robbie.'

'Bengali?'

'Everybody asks me that. No, Kannadiga. It's just that my parents hero-worshipped the Bengali bearded bard.'

'Ah, where the mind is without fear etc. Bengali bearded bard, eh? Nice alliteration! By the by, I am Narasimhan. Call me Nari. Hooray, just one left in the queue. Last question Robbie, and I don't mean to embarrass you. What is that printed on your tee-shirt?'

'I am not embarrassed, Sir. You might be. What do you think that is, printed on my tee-shirt? Which part of it do you not understand?'

'I couldn't bring myself to utter that word.'

'What word?'

'That one starting with F and then blank, blank, blank. I mean, GO F*** YOURSELF! I am all for freedom of expression, but surely there are limits, young man. This is a bank. You can't go around flaunting stuff like that on a tee-shirt.'

'What? GO FREE YOURSELF!? What is your problem with that? Seriously.'

'Is that what it is? Then why bother with the riddle, Robbie? Why not just spell it out?'

'Where is the fun in that? It is called a teaser. You certainly got teased, didn't you? Now I know how your mind works, begging your pardon.'

'Thanks for nothing. Your number is flashing. And the coffee date is cancelled.'

Note: This retired person and the young software geek at the bank were all set for what at first seemed a love feast. The more they tried to talk to each other, the more things started breaking down. They spoke the same language, but they spoke in different tongues. The generation gap is a cliché, but it has a ring of truth to it. I am reminded of that great line from jazz singer and guitarist George Benson's song *The Masquerade,* 'We tried to talk it over, but the words got in the way.'

BOTTOMS UP!

I do not wish to seem fashionably blasé or anything and, crucially important as these issues are, abrogation of Article 370 with the Supreme Court putting its rubber seal of approval on it, and the Hitchcockian suspense surrounding the appointment of Chief Ministers to the three Hindi heartland states bagged by the BJP in the recent assembly elections, concluding with the ultimate denouement, i.e. the names being named – there simply was so much of it on television that my head is still swimming. Sorry about that very long and convoluted opening sentence, but I am just keeping in step with the way political developments unravelled last week in India.

As for the eyebrow-raisingly surprising names of those new Chief Ministers appointed in Chhatthisgarh, Madhya Pradesh and Rajasthan, ask me again in about three months' time and I just might be able to recall them. For now, the Prime Minister, with his penchant for pulling rabbits out of hats, could well be quoting south Indian superstar Rajinikanth, 'Enn vazhi, thani vazhi,' or loosely translated without transliterating, 'It is my way or the highway.' I am sure Modiji, who never misses a trick, would make the effort to learn that line in Tamil, should he get the opportunity while campaigning next in Tamil Nadu, but the 'zh' sound as in 'vazhi' could prove to be his Achilles heel, as many other Indians have discovered, Tamilians included. Not that that will stop the great man. He will bash on regardless. He recently loosed off a couplet or two in Telugu, while addressing his party faithful in the capital, willing his words to be heard in distant Telangana. One can only take his word for it that he was speaking in Telugu. Two marks for effort!

That said, I am giving a wide berth to the election results and Article 370 (or 35A, come to that) for the time being. Instead, I am turning my attention to the all-important subject of bottom pinching, touching or patting. Yes, you heard that right. Before you get the wrong impression about me, allow me to explain. I am not a weirdo. I am only responding to a prominent news item in a prominent daily headlined, *'Man held for a day for touching woman's bottom.'* Now, in the normal course of things, if such an announcement were to occupy a couple of lines at the bottom (that word again!) of a page under 'Miscellany' or some such section, that would be understandable, but only just. However, perverted behaviour of this nature to be hogging the headlines was a bit much. Tantamount to scraping the bottom of the barrel. I am on a roll here!

So what was it that so excited one of our leading newspapers to find this salacious morsel worthy of making banner headlines? While it would be up to the editor to answer that question, he or she not being readily available to answer flippant questions in response to their flippant headlines, I have taken it upon myself to speculate on the motive behind the newspaper's thinking. This is entirely from my fevered imagination and most likely bears no relation to the actual facts. Then again, truth is stranger than fiction.

We are in the conference room of the esteemed daily and all the editors, sub-editors and cub reporters gather round late in the evening to discuss the next day's issue and topics that merit attention. I have not actually worked in a newspaper organisation but I am reliably informed that this is the normal practice to prioritize the contents for the following day's issue. To add verisimilitude, I would have liked to say that it was a smoke-filled conference room, the men and women dragging on their Wills Filter fags or some fancy hand-rolled tobacco and downing cups of coffee to keep their frayed nerves under control. However, that romantic Raymond Chandler inspired image would be grossly inaccurate. These days, smokers are treated as *pariah* outcasts, banished to the streets where they can finish their smoke and get back, huffing and puffing their carcinogenic lungs out and sidle bashfully back to the meeting. Coffee (or tea), however, will be consumed at the rate of knots. And so to the meeting.

The editor opens the proceedings. 'Good evening, ladies and laddies. We have no time to waste. We have to put the paper to bed by 11 pm, so that the early bird can catch the worm, if you get my meaning.'

Some of the junior subs break into titters, but the editor resumes. 'This is no laughing matter. Right, what am I bid for state election results taking pride of place on the front page?'

At this, one of the bright sparks pipes up. 'You mean sir, after the actual front page carrying the party-political advert? Followed by the second front page featuring the Christmas / New Year Sale advert from one of our largest retail brands? Not to forget the vertically-cut half front page carrying some news which no one reads?'

'Cheeky,' the editor interjects. 'I like someone with a bit of spunk, but don't cross the line. Let us get back on track. State elections, it is. The Israel / Hamas unending conflict can take a back seat. Ditto the Russia / Ukraine imbroglio. We will paper over them, ha ha.' As the editor laughs at his own weak joke, the others join in awkwardly.

The boss man continues. 'While we are about it, will someone arrange a quick survey, and I mean really quick. Talk to about 100 people on phone and project what these state elections could portend for the forthcoming general elections in May. What was that? Not a representative sample? Who cares? We won't reveal the sample size. People like surveys. Let us give it to them. TV channels are feasting on them. Right, that's pages 1 and 2 taken care of. Moving on to page 3. Any thoughts?'

The senior deputy editor draws the meeting's attention to the crypto-terror attack on the Lok Sabha. 'In my view this should go on the front page.'

The editor, irritably. 'Look we are through with the front page. And we have received feelers from the Home Ministry not to play up the security breach affair in Parliament. Crossing the Home Minister is not good for health. Not for my health, at any rate. Don't we have anything exciting to play up?'

A young girl in jeans and a bright, yellow 'I love SRK' tee-shirt clears her throat. 'If I may Sir, this bottom patting incident needs to be highlighted.'

'How much?' The editor was slightly shocked. 'Did I hear you correctly? Speak up, young lady.'

'I am not sure what you heard, Sir. I am talking about this nasty incident on one of our Mumbai trains, where a man was caught and handed over to the cops for repeatedly patting or pinching a lady's bottom.' She had everybody's attention.

'What was it? Patting or pinching? We need to be accurate. Or was it just accidental touching? Crowded train, sudden braking, people keeling over each other. That sort of thing.' The editor was quite animated, his eyes gleaming.

'Not accidental, Sir. The guy was a perv. There were witnesses, including the victim's husband, who helped in apprehending and handing over the criminal to the police. I do believe, with due respect to all concerned, that this should be highlighted properly in our paper.'

One of the other colleagues intoned, 'But this sort of thing happens all the time in our country. I think a brief mention should suffice.'

'Rubbish,' cried the editor. 'I completely agree with the young lady. Let us place it on top of page 5, and a minimum of two columns of copy. Anything else? You can write this story.'

'Thank you, Sir. I already have.' The young reporter was quite flushed. 'In fact, I have information that the Metropolitan magistrate was severe when the case was brought to his notice. He said with reference to the victim's complaint and I quote, "No lady will put stigma upon her merely because somebody touched her buttocks and without any reason."'

The editor was impressed. 'The Magistrate's English may not have been up to scratch but he makes a telling point. People cannot go around touching or patting other people's buttocks, with or without reason, and that's that. We have our story. Well done, dear lady. You have distinguished yourself. It's getting late and you will have to burn the midnight oil and post the story for tomorrow's edition. Someone kindly see to it that she gets a drop home. That concludes the meeting. Rest of you can take care of sports, film reviews, business page etc.'

As the meeting broke up, the editor turned to his deputy, 'It's things like this that make my day. Bottom pinching, eh? That will take care of another 10,000 copies, d'you think?'

'Actually, it was patting or touching, not pinching.'

'All right, let us not split hairs. I want you to keep a close watch on that girl's progress. I can see her rising rapidly. Bottom pinching today, interview with the PM tomorrow. She gets preferential treatment. I do not want some rival tabloid pinching her. Ha, ha ha!'

The two of them walked out of the conference room, the editor laughing his guts out, his deputy looking wan and pale. His hands were itching to pinch his editor's bottom. Wiser counsel prevailed.

FORTY WINKS WITH MY DOCTOR

Some people talk in their sleep. Lecturers talk while other people sleep.
– Albert Camus

I was at my general physician's chamber a few days ago for a routine check-up. I had my latest blood reports, ECG, chest and spine X-rays at the ready. He waded through them perfunctorily, as doctors are wont to do, intoning a 'Hmmm' and an 'Aaah' or a 'Tsk, tsk' now and then. He would also squiggle some unintelligible markings on the pages (another fad of doctors), while you watched silently and a tad apprehensively. Then he views the ECG and mutters something that sounds like 'arrythmia,' but as he is muttering to himself, I am still unable to get a word in edgeways. A man of few words, my doctor, playing his cards close to his chest. Finally, he slots the chest and spine X-rays on to a wall-mounted light box and stares at them for what seems an eternity. I too keep him company and gape at the grey images with no idea of what I am looking at, my pulse starting to elevate by now at an alarming rate. If only the man would say something.

At last, he is done and I wait for his pronouncement. Instead, he asks me a question.

'Are you in the habit of sleepwalking at night?'

I thought that was a silly question, as if anyone sleepwalks during the day. How could I possibly know if I am in the habit of sleepwalking if, by definition, I cannot be aware of such nocturnal perambulations? Then again, he is the doctor so I had better attempt an answer.

'I could not possibly say, doctor. If I am walking while sleeping, then I am not aware of it. Stands to reason.' I thought I had made a good point, but doctors are made of sterner stuff. He was not to be deterred.

'Surely, your wife would have noticed,' he said.

'In the dead of night? She herself would be deeply resting in the Land of Nod. Even if she had been awake, they say you should not wake up a sleepwalker as things could turn ugly. She could alert me the following morning, but as I have heard nothing from her, the sleepwalking theory can be put to bed. Unless, of course, she was also sleepwalking. Then we are in big trouble.'

'You don't suffer from sleep apnea, then.'

'Is that a question or a diagnostic statement? I don't even know what apnea means.'

'Never mind. What about getting up in the middle of the night to do your small job? All elderly people go through this nuisance.' The doctor was clearly adamant. He was pursuing a line of questioning leading to an unpleasant destination. Prostate issues, perhaps? I was getting a bit miffed.

'Doc, if I needed to get up in the small hours to do my "small job" as you so colourfully put it, then I would have been fully conscious of it. On the other hand, if I am sleepwalking, I have no recollection, until the cook complains next morning that the vessel containing the almond soufflé in the fridge is conspicuous by the complete absence of any soufflé. The empty glass bowl stares accusingly in my direction. In my defence, I am allergic to almond soufflé. Somebody wolfed it down and it was not me. The needle of suspicion points to the cook. She should be grilled, speaking metaphorically.'

My doctor stifled a yawn and continued. 'Right, so you do not walk while sleeping. Let us turn to other matters. Do you snore at night?'

Another daft question. 'Doc, which sleeper ever admits to snoring at night? I might as well ask you the same question. I will vehemently deny that I snore, but my wife will hold a diametrically opposite view. The same is true if one reverses the roles. It is an age-old verity. I am one with author Anthony Burgess *(A Clockwork Orange),* who said, "Laugh and the world laughs with you, snore and you sleep alone."'

'In other words, you snore. Why don't you just say so, instead of rambling all over the place? Anthony Burgess, bah!' I could see he was getting a trifle tetchy.

'Sorry Doc, but what has all this sleeping and snoring business got to do with the price of fish?'

'I am coming to that. Price of fish, eh? Nice one. I must use it sometime with one of my other patients, preferably a strict vegetarian. One last question before I can arrive at a definitive diagnosis. Do you generally sleep on the right side, left side, or flat on your back?'

Again, with the sleeping. What is this obsession with my sleeping habits that seems to so fascinate this physician? I was now certain that he was going to start on the subject of dreams. And there, right on cue.

'Do you have dreams while you sleep or are you blessed with being able to sleep dreamlessly? Dreamless sleep, as you will agree, is a consummation devoutly to be wished.'

Shakespeare creeping into his conversation now. However, that did not reduce my growing sense of unease. I was beginning to feel my doctor needed to consult a different kind of doctor himself. 'Physician, heal thyself,' about sums it up. Jesus Christ said that, and he knew a thing or two about healing. While I did, like everyone else, have dreams while I slept, not counting day dreaming, I did not want to encourage this doctor any further. Had I done so, he might have taken off on Calpurnia hearing her husband moan and so on. I had to find a way to put a stop to this nonsense.

'Doctor, can we please move away from the subject of dreams and fitful slumber and all that kind of Freudian stuff? Just tell me what my blood reports and X-rays reveal and I will be off before you can say 'now is the winter of our discontent.'

The doctor appeared somewhat mollified by my own contribution from the Bard's canon and reason returned to its throne. 'Listen, your blood readings are all within the normal limits, so you don't have much cause for concern on that count. However, your spine appears to be slightly wonky?'

'Wonky? Meaning? Scoliosis?'

'Pardon the slang. And please stop self-diagnosing. You have a cervical issue which is what is leading to your having bad dreams, walking in your sleep and so on. I will send you to an orthopaedist for further investigation.'

'For the last time Doc, I do not walk in my sleep and when I do have dreams, I have usually scored a double century at Lords or just beaten Djokovic in the final at Wimbledon. And I sleep like a baby. If it's all the same to you, I do not wish to see a bone doctor. I will bid you good day.'

The doctor had the final say. 'That will be Rs.1000/-. Cash, card or UPI?'

As I left his chamber, I could faintly hear him reciting Hamlet to himself, 'O God, I could be bounded in a nutshell and count myself a king of infinite space. Were it not that I have bad dreams.'

'Checkmate,' I said to myself.

MURDER MOST FOWL

Just for a change, this week I decided I will take a bird's eye view of various happenings around the country, particularly those that had something peculiar or ridiculous to comment upon. Fortunately, in India we are never short of news items culled from our dailies that amuse and / or startle us. Whether these nuggets should be classified as 'funny peculiar' or 'funny ha-ha,' is largely up to you, dear reader. Comedy lies in the sensibilities of the beholder. Truth to tell, most times funny does not even come into it. A person being put to death or gangraped can never be funny or amusing. The circumstances leading to such a heinous crime, however, can befuddle and even amuse, in a dark, macabre kind of way.

Take what happened in the garden city (that tired moniker is quite funny) of Bangalore. Mubarak Pasha, a 30-year-old businessman comes home from work, his wife sets the table for dinner. 'Dinner's ready, come and get it,' she coos invitingly, presumably in the vernacular. The bread winner of the home sits down to eat, examines the fare on offer, scrunches up his face and looks extremely displeased. 'Where is my fried chicken?' he demands. Evidently this Pasha is a bit of a fried chicken freak, and cannot bear to go through a meal without sinking his teeth into some succulent chunks of the local equivalent of KFC. 'I specifically told you to cook fried chicken for dinner and you have arrogantly disobeyed my orders, and not for the first time either.' Clearly, the couple have had foul words before over fried fowl. Now whether his dutiful wife gave him a rude retort or merely walked away in a huff, the news report was not forthcoming. What happened next was what grabbed the headlines.

The short-tempered Pasha flew into a fit of rage, looked for the nearest lethal log of wood, and proceeded to bash his wife's head in. Before you could say Kentucky Fried Chicken, he had become a widower and their three children were left motherless. The fact that he trotted off to the nearest police station later and confessed to his crime is neither here nor there. My plea to housewives, therefore, is to be ever vigilant. Today it is fried chicken, tomorrow it could be mutton biryani or masala dosa. I am not suggesting you should be ready to serve your lord and master's favourite cuisine day in and day out, at his whims and fancies. I am merely advising you to be on guard, keep your own weapon of choice handy, be it a log or a well-honed axe or meat-cleaver, just in case your husband starts acting up violently. Forewarned is forearmed.

Let's move on to another horrific incident. The Home Minister of Karnataka upbraids a young university student and her boy friend for straying out and wandering around in the vicinity of the picturesque Chamundi hills near Mysore well after dusk, as a consequence of which the girl was waylaid and gangraped by a bunch of six inebriated goons. The boyfriend had been neutralized. Not to be satisfied, the criminals had actually made a video of the assault. 'What was she doing there at 7 – 7.30 pm? Why did she go to a secluded place with her classmate after sunset?' asked the minister. At a very basic level, the minister's scolding, rather like an irate parent's, would have been reasonable (just about) if the victim had returned home safe. In the face of a ghastly incident, not to have first-off, condemned outright the venal crime and targeting instead the victim's apparent carelessness, the minister was at best unbelievably naïve and at worst, criminally callous. To be fair, he did describe the incident as 'unfortunate' and that drastic action will be taken against the culprits. Naturally, the opposition political parties, always with an eye to the main chance, rightly deplored and condemned the minister's insensitive remarks. Later on, the state's Chief Minister tried to assuage matters by strongly condemning the home minister's tasteless comments. Whether the matter will end there or take on a more incendiary form, only time will tell. Meanwhile, the unfortunate victim's life has been irretrievably damaged while the goons, at the time of going to press, are still at large lurking around for another quarry.

Still on the subject of rape, the Chhattisgarh High Court had an interesting take on the subject. Wait for it and fasten your seat-belts. This is what their honourable justices of the court had to say on a plea from a wife claiming intolerable sexual harassment by her husband. 'The complainant is the legally wedded wife… therefore sexual intercourse or any sexual act with her by the husband would not constitute an offence of rape, *even if it was by force or against her wish…*' (my italics). The court, as per the news report, did add a proviso that the 'victim' should not have been under 18 years of age. We should be thankful for small mercies! Naturally all manner of sections, sub-sections and clauses were quoted by the High Court in extenuation of their archaic judgement. My heart goes out to the poor wife, the complainant, who will, in light of the judgement, not be able to proffer the age-old excuse of suffering from a headache to ward off the lascivious advances of her husband. The horrible man will whip out the rule book and point to the loopholes in the IPC Section 376 of the relevant act, as deemed by the esteemed court, and demand conjugal satisfaction – headache or no headache. Perhaps the act ought to be amended to provide relief to the unfortunate wife, in case she is suffering from a migraine or some other ailment to which women are prone. That will serve the wanton hound right. Otherwise, every other male in the country will quote this judgement and make his wife's life a living hell. Come on, all you lords and ladyships, can we have some amendments please?

I conclude this ignominious round-up of bloodthirst and unbridled lechery with yet another sleazy account that simply refuses to go away. A basketball coach, who preyed on his young female wards and who was briefly incarcerated under the POCSO (Protection of Children from Sexual Offences) Act, was recently released on bail to roam free. while his alleged teenage victims have been coming out of hiding to narrate horror stories of forced sexual advances, inappropriate touching and all manner of unsavoury acts. Some of the descriptions trotted out by over 20 girls, all aspiring basketball players, were quite graphic and does not leave much to the imagination. That the local police authorities were unable to explain precisely why the accused was allowed to leave the suffocating confines of his prison cell continues to baffle. Evidently all this happened in the state of Karnataka which also witnessed the fried chicken murder and gangrape. Not that I am suggesting that Bangalore and its mother state own sole copyright on salacious crimes (it happens all over the country), but that is the way the cookie crumbled this time round. In passing I must add that the photograph of the alleged offender, the basketball coach, in the newspaper, a passport mug shot, would make any mother want to welcome him home as a son-in-law – pleasant, trustworthy and good-natured was the impression created. Who knows, perhaps the photograph was inappropriately touched up to give a favourable impression! This should be a lesson to all those matrimonial match makers who go superficially by an exchange of photographs. *Dig deeper.* A picture may be worth a thousand words, but those words could reveal more than you had bargained for. Pramodh Kumar, that was the disgraced coach's name, is presumably in hiding somewhere,

HELL HATH NO FURY LIKE A WOMAN SCORNED

There is a tendency amongst many of us hack writers to attribute any slick proverb to Shakespeare. The Bard of Avon came up with so many smart lines befitting any occasion, that one can be excused for giving him the credit for aphorisms he did not even write. My proverb of choice for this essay is 'Hell hath no fury like a woman scorned.' I diligently researched the saying to ensure it was not one of Shakespeare's nuggets. In fact, it was William Congreve who came up with this beauty in his Restoration play, *The Mourning Bride,* way back in 1697. Congreve is also credited with the other famous quote, 'Music has charms to soothe a savage breast,' which has often been misquoted as 'Music has charms to soothe a savage beast.' Dear reader, I can see you getting all fidgety and going, 'That's all very well about Congreve whoever he was, but where are you going with all this? We haven't got all day, you know.' My apologies. I will come straight to the point.

I recently came across a news item that a woman in the city of Pune was so incensed with her thirty-something husband that she punched him in the nose, so hard that the poor fellow died. Probably of nasal asphyxiation, if there be such a term. She almost certainly did not mean to total her hubby but that, tragically, is what happened. Apparently, it was the young lady's birthday and she had set her eyes on a shopping trip to Dubai. When it became clear that no air and hotel bookings for Dubai had been made, and that the husband was planning to fob her off with some flowers and a dinner date at a nearby restaurant, all hell broke loose. You would not be far wrong in saying the gloves were off.

The better half, for want of a better term, hauled off and delivered a vicious right hook to the unfortunate chap's nasal bridge that would have made Mike Tyson proud. She punched his lights out and not only did the husband see stars, he was soon one among the stars! Evidently, the husband had also promised her expensive jewellery and luxury perfumes, but nothing was forthcoming on the big day. You can see where the hellish fury was coming from, but hey, she could have confined her aggression to a few tight slaps or something less fatal than a bleeding, blocked nose resulting in the bread winner's last breath. The police are now trying to piece together the whole unpleasant episode. The killer widow must be full of remorse and crying her eyes out. Next time, if there be a next time, she must learn to go easy on the wrist work and follow through while delivering the punch. Better still, the stomach would have been the least fatal target what with its natural cushioning and inherent give. Which is sooner said than done. 'Heat of the moment' will be her plea to the cops and the courts. My own take is that she will not face the ultimate wrath of the law, though a verdict of manslaughter could well be on the cards.

In a reversal of roles, an irate husband in Bangalore hurled a pressure cooker full of boiling sambar at his wife, causing severe burns and injuries. I am not making this up, cross my heart and hope to die. This after not being able to push her over the balcony or finding a knife handy to stab her mortally. And the provocation? Apparently, the family was skint, unable to pay the rent and living from hand to mouth. The man of the house was an electrician and the distraught wife requested him to help a neighbouring senior citizen with some electrical repairs, thereby earning an honest wage and keeping the wolf from the door. Why this perfectly reasonable suggestion should have shocked the electrician to such an extent that he should himself have turned into a werewolf, reached for the sambar-filled pressure-cooker and performed a discus throw with it, is a moot point. His wife was rushed to hospital.

Last heard, the wife was recovering and the husband was headed for the hills, tail between legs, being pursued by the local gendarmerie. So here we have an instance of a woman, not quite scorned, but scorched and scarred by sambar. I would suggest she follow her Pune counterpart, viz., find the blighter, and with hellish fury punch him with all her strength right on the nose. And let the devil take the hindmost.

For the most part, domestic physical violence has a been a conspicuously male preserve. Never a day passes without the media reporting a man abusing his infinitely better half for the flimsiest of reasons. Like the chappatis were too cold or the tea was too hot. Once in a rare while, we get refreshing news of the tyrant getting his comeuppance, bobbitised by his partner in the dead of night. Such cases are few and far between. However tragic the consequences of the Pune lady's pugilistic approach towards her husband, she was probably taking out her frustration for being ignored or rebuffed over long periods of time. The anger was building up to a crescendo. However, that is only me playing guessing games. I do feel a pang of sympathy for the unfortunate husband who was merely trying to keep the home fires burning by not splurging on expensive foreign travel and shopping sprees in Dubai. Truth will out. It is one thing to literally have one's nose put out of joint, quite another to have the breathing apparatus rendered *hors de combat* forever.

Moral of the story. Next time your wife insists on a foreign holiday and a visit to Cartier or Gucci in Paris or Venice, keep your guard up and stand at a safe distance away from her before saying 'No.' Above all, learn how to duck and weave.

THE RIGHT TO REMAIN SILENT ETC.

There can be little argument that the genre of crime fiction, whether in book or film form, is the most addictive avenue of diversion that most readers and viewers long for. To be curled up in bed on a cold and wet evening, thumbing through a P.D. James or a Dorothy Sayers mystery with a mug of hot chocolate is a consummation devoutly to be wished, to employ an expression culled from Hamlet's most celebrated speech. Depending on personal preference, it could also be a Sherlock Holmes or an Inspector Morse that you might take a shine to. One is spoilt for choice when it comes to crime. There are still others, if crime is not your bag, who might plump for a light-hearted Jeeves and Wooster caper, as I often do myself but for the moment, I am focused on crime, as I have some pertinent, if offbeat, views to share. Do I see a hand going up? No Sir, nobbling Lord Emsworth's noble sow, the Empress of Blandings does not qualify as serious crime. Not in my book, anyway.

I have lost count of the number of crime-related movies or television serials I must have watched. Books as well, and for the purposes of this essay, the terms books and films can be used interchangeably. Brilliant as most of these films are, they tend to fall prey to a clutch of well-worn tropes which is pretty much unavoidable, but pose interesting questions. Incidentally, as an entertainment form the British do crime with greater subtlety and finesse than anyone else, and not too many people will take umbrage with that assertion. Getting back to the cliché, imagine if you will, the following scene. A murder suspect has been brought in by the police for questioning. He is anxiously waiting in the interview room, chewing his finger nails, sweat beads beginning to form on his brow. That is exactly how the inspector and his deputy want him, as they watch the probable killer through the one-way mirror, before entering the room. It would also not have escaped anyone's attention that the inspector's sidekick is invariably portrayed as one who is slightly challenged intellectually, is patronisingly put upon by his boss and thus carries a sizeable chip on his shoulder. Once in a rare while, he gets his own back, which adds greatly to the charm of the narrative. Holmes' Watson and Morse's Lewis are fine examples of this genre of underlings.

The following exchange then takes place, after the junior police officer formally records the interview formalities. For the sake of verisimilitude, I shall dub the pair of police officers Morse and Lewis. With due apologies to their creator, Colin Dexter. Inspector Morse opens the proceedings, addressing the suspect in the time-honoured fashion, 'Please state your full name for the record.'

'Hyde, Edward. Inspector, you have got the wrong man. I was nowhere near the scene of the murder.'

'So you say, Mr. Hyde, so you say and I don't, for a moment, believe that is your real name. Tell me, where were you on the evening of the 27th of July between 6.30 and 7.45 pm?'

I have yet to come across an episode without that question being posed to the suspect. Bear in mind that this interview is being conducted roughly three months after the date of the murder, and the suspect, who allegedly committed the dreaded deed, is initially out of his depth faced with this query, but rallies well and is equal to the task.

'With respect Inspector, I can hardly remember what I was doing yesterday afternoon, leave alone something that I am suspected of having done three months ago. Have a heart, Sir. Come to that, can you tell me what you were up to on the 10th of July between 7 and 9 am? Hmmm? Foxed? I rest my case.'

Inspector Morse bridles. 'Now look here, Mr. Hyde. I ask the questions around here, so let's have none of your cheek. "Rest my case," indeed! I am talking about a ghastly, premeditated murder, one in which you strangled the victim to death in her bathtub. Surely, anyone would clearly remember the date and time of such an event?'

At this point, Morse's deputy, Lewis shoves his oar in. 'If I might interject Sir, ever since Alfred Hitchcock's blockbuster *Psycho* was released, murders in bathtubs and under showers have gone up by leaps and bounds; 33% to be exact.'

'Thank you for that priceless input, Lewis. Can we get back to the strangling? I am pressed for time.' His boss' sarcasm is lost on Lewis, but he acquiesces.

At this point, the suspect pipes up. 'Alleged strangling, Inspector, alleged. You are forgetting your police etiquette. I am here as a suspect, an innocent victim of mistaken identity. I have the right to remain silent, but I am cooperating. You are going to be the laughing stock with the judge and the public at large when we go to court.'

'We shall see about that. And you talk too much.' With that Morse flounces out of the room, Lewis in tow.

That was an impressionistic sketch of a situation I have frequently come across in crime fiction, where the cops have invariably been found to come up short against a fast-talking suspect who is probably guilty, but knows there is no concrete evidence even if his own alibi is dodgy. I harbour a sneaking sympathy for the suspect, because I can never recall what I had for lunch a couple of days ago, if called upon to reveal the menu. Which brings me to another situation in the police interrogation room, in which the suspect's solicitor plays an active part.

Inspector Morse opens a fresh line of attack. 'Mr. Hyde, you were seen loitering with intent in the vicinity of the crime just an hour before the murder took place. What do you have to say for yourself?'

The suspect is about to answer when his solicitor urgently whispers something into his ear and proceeds to reply. 'My client is not obliged to answer that question on the grounds that it might incriminate him. Furthermore, it was 11 in the morning in a crowded street corner and your CCTV cameras would have captured several other people strolling by in the area. Why should my client be singled out and brought in for questioning? Rather invidious, wouldn't you say, Inspector?'

Morse was now at his ironic best. 'Perhaps because he was the only one in that crowded street corner who was seen running away from the crime scene at the speed of Usain Bolt, with a knife soaked in blood in his right hand? And, by the way, you can't impress me with fancy words. Invidious, shinvidious!'

Lewis could not let this pass. 'Sir, invidious means to give rise to offence. In fact, the judge in an earlier case, *Carlill vs Carbolic Smokeball,* employed that exact word when…'

'My dear chap, can you kindly put a sock in it? I have enough problems to deal with here without your asinine interruptions.' The deputy crawled back into his shell like a salted snail.

At this point, the suspect butted in, 'Officer, I was only…'

'Shut up, Hyde,' snapped his solicitor. 'I will take that question. Forgive my client, Inspector. He is new to your interrogation techniques. The fact is, my client was helping his friend at a nearby eatery to cut some vegetables and accidentally cut his middle finger which started bleeding profusely. Your cameras caught him when he was rushing out to get some urgent medical attention and first aid at a nearby nursing home. He was in such great pain that he even forgot to leave the kitchen knife behind at the eatery.'

'Left or right?'

'Pardon?'

'Which hand?'

'Er, the right hand. Are you playing mind games with me, Officer? Surely, you can see that from the CCTV cameras.'

Morse's brows furrowed. 'Curiouser and curiouser. Nice try, my friend. And you call that a bandage? Let's get serious. I want the name and address of this fictitious eatery.'

And so the long day wears on, the police team is unable to break through the suspect's defences. Here's the thing that always tickles me. What exactly is behind the legal mumbo-jumbo in saying, 'I won't speak on the grounds that it might incriminate me?' I have never understood that. In my books, just saying that alone should indicate that you are trying to hide something, which sounds extremely incriminating. I am sure some legal boffin would put me right on that, but speaking as a layman, it has always been something that puzzled me.

Finally, I touch upon the 'no comment' scenario. When all else fails, the suspect is had by the short and curlies and has nowhere to hide, he falls back on the tried and tested 'no comment' strategy.

Inspector Morse goes for the kill. 'Mr. Hyde, the murdered victim was a very wealthy man. How do you explain scanned copies of his last will and testament and bank statements turning up in your laptop?'

'No comment.'

'We found traces of the victim's blood on your shirt sleeves. Would you care to explain? And don't give me some applesauce about tomato sauce from your friend's kitchen.'

'No comment.'

'Mr. Edward Hyde, what is your name?'

'No comment.'

Lewis is amused. 'That was quite funny, Sir.'

'We are not amused,' says Morse in regal fashion. 'For the last time Lewis, cease and desist or I will order you to leave the room.'

The detective inspector again turns to the suspect. 'Mr. Hyde, let me caution you. There is a limit to exercising your right to remain silent. You are not a trappist monk. For the last time, this 'no comment' tactic will not help. My assistant and I are going to leave the room for ten minutes. I strongly suggest you consult with your solicitor and come up with some answers. I expect a full confession.'

That is about the size of it. When a suspect goes on repeating 'no comment' like a well-trained parrot, it kind of stymies the long arm of the law. What kind of defence is that? Clearly, from a legal standpoint, there is more to this than meets the eye. Like the earlier examples, this too had me struggling for answers. On balance, it is not the worst option to take a leaf out of the suspect's book and stick to 'no comment.' Seems to work wonders for criminals. A lawyer might disagree. After all they are, likely as not, paid by the word. As Franz Kafka observed, 'A lawyer is a person who writes a 10,000-word document and calls it a brief.'

AND GOOD LUCK WITH THE SPRING CLEANING

I have come to grips with one of the great verities of life. It is that your desire to get rid of detritus collected over the years at home, deliberately or inadvertently, grows in inverse proportion to the intention of doing away with it. Like Topsy from *Uncle Tom's Cabin,* I think it just 'grow'd.' I use the word detritus somewhat loosely. When you have lived for well nigh seven decades and a bit, all kinds of things tend to accumulate. Not really detritus, but possibly timed-out. At the time, they are considered precious and indispensable. Having salted them away, you have barely had the time to revisit the cache. They are kept carefully in shoe boxes, biscuit tins, dark corners in cupboards and drawers, secreted away in suitcases caked with grime and dust, that have not seen the light of day since Noah's Ark opened its doors to its varied paired fauna. Times without number you have said to yourself, and to your wife, 'I must get down to do some serious spring cleaning. There's just too much stuff lying around taking up space.' The sardonic laugh is from the wife, who herself has much to think about when it comes to cleaning out her invaluable collectibles.

With that pious thought and fully aware that the road to hell is paved with good intentions, I start attempting to sort out the various accumulated articles and knick-knacks. This is how they stack up, category-wise, and I spend more time thinking about what to do with them than in actuality accomplishing anything in the way of discarding them.

Books. There are now so many books around the house, literally bursting out of every nook and cranny. Our staircase to the terrace could be in danger. Let me get cracking. The local lending library will be pleased to get a trunkful of these books. Let's see. There are 61 novels of P.G. Wodehouse. Can't touch them. I would rather commit *hara-kiri* than part with any of Plum's masterpieces. As far as I am concerned, they are all masterpieces. I must admit many of the Jeeves / Wooster and Blandings Castle escapades are coming apart at the seams, the white-ants have got to them, but I am damned if I am giving any of them away.

What's this? *The Golden Treasury of Longer Poems,* presented to S. Suresh, winner of the school elocution contest 1963. You see what I mean? Then there's Amis, Kingsley and Martin, Spike Milligan, The Complete Works of Italian crime writer, Andrea Camilleri, Christopher Hitchens, Julian Barnes, Ian McEwan, some old Perry Masons, Louis L'Amours and Agatha Christies, learned volumes from my advertising days and so much more. Not to mention books written by my friends and relatives (everybody is publishing books these days). Tell you what, all the fat Encyclopaedias can go far a start, ditto voluminous autobiographies (they are so full of themselves), don't need so many Wisdens (I can get all the cricket statistics from Google). That should be a decent start for clearing up. I can review the situation a year down the road.

Lest I forget, there is an Eng. Lit. topper at home, namely, my better half whose books occupy several shelves. From Austen and Bronte to Camus and Turgenev, Dumas to Dickens and Eliot – George and T.S. to Mann and Salinger. And that is barely skimming the surface. Shakespeare's Complete Works is not a space saver either. Can't touch any of them. And here's a laugh. I too have published books comprising a compilation of my pieces. Since no one buys them, barring a handful of diehard loyalists, I purchase boxfuls of them at volume discounts and periodically gift them to unwary friends and visitors to our wee home (you are duly cautioned). Those boxes take up space as well.

Finally, the airport pot-boilers for flights. Follet, Baldacci, Cook, Clancy, Francis – you get the drift. From the sublime to the ridiculous, there's also a stack of comics and Mad magazines to deal with. Net result, after spending over two hours, I have managed to cull out a measly 17 books to dispose of. If I must buy a book in the interim, it will have to be Kindle or some such. More's the pity.

Compact Discs & DVDs. Music and all manner of film entertainment is a passion with me. Having graduated from vinyls, spool tapes and cassette tapes, VHS tapes and finally CDs and DVDs, I felt I had reached the apogee of technology delivering hi-definition music and drama for home entertainment. Then came the audio and video streaming devices delivering the best of music and films the world had to offer, rendering all my CDs and DVDs redundant overnight. I am now sitting on a mountain of over 700 CDs and DVDs of some of the best and brightest, not knowing what to do with them. Barring a handful of titles, pretty much all of them are streaming on Spotify, Amazon, Netflix, Apple and several other channels. It breaks my heart to throw them all away as the market for same is worse than bearish, and every time I pick up a CD of Bob Dylan or Joan Baez or the Fawlty Towers DVD box-set, I hastily slot them back into the shelf. It's a good job I stopped buying CDs over five years ago. Incidentally, my CD player went on the blink recently, and there's no one to repair it. This is a quandary I will have to live with. Does not help the space problem, but that is my problem.

Letters. No one writes letters these days, not for the past 15 years, give or take. I mean with a pen on sheets of paper. It's all on email or junk mail. However, things were different way back when. Postcards, picture postcards, inland letters, bulky letters arriving in buff envelopes, starting from school friends writing in during holidays, parents writing to us when we were incarcerated in boarding school, pen pals, letters from across the seas and so much more. Because of the effort and trouble taken to sit down and write these letters, we could never throw them away. They are all there in various boxes. It is now time to take stock as you may not want these personal missives to be lying around when you are no longer amongst those present. But when you get down to re-reading them in order to start tearing them up, nostalgia claims you for its own and instead, you start tearing up! In the words of the Bard, 'letting "I dare not" wait upon "I would," like the poor cat i' the adage.'

Miscellany. If books and music have the capacity to give us everlasting pleasure, I am not sure of some of the gewgaws that seem to find their way into every available space around the home. A weathered Cotswold stone from somewhere in those picture-perfect Cotswold villages, some sea shells and pebbles from a beach in the Costa Brava (I have seen more shells on the Marina Beach in Madras), a withered feather from I know not where that serves as a bookmark, theatre and cinema tickets *(The Absent-Minded Professor,* The Minerva, Calcutta), bus and train tickets from all parts of the globe, even a 20p tram ticket from Calcutta (the no.24 that ferried me to college at the crack of dawn), my late Cocker Spaniel's dog collar and identity badge – there's no end to it. Photographs, tons of them. Need to get them digitised. Soon as I put this article to bed, I will be slapping my forehead exclaiming, 'Gosh, I forgot to include Christmas and New Year greeting cards with all those twee messages, two large-size envelopes full of them. And like letters, greeting cards are also now an almost extinct species what with all the moving images we can conjure from the internet.

In conclusion, I guess what I am striving to communicate is that we humans are inveterate collectors of things. Any 'things.' Trying to get rid of them is a mug's game. It's over four years since I last examined my hidden treasures. One of these days I will get down to it, but the result will be the same. I will come over all misty-eyed and shove them all back. Someone called Josie Brown is credited with saying, 'The key to spring cleaning is to be ruthless. Throw out anything and everything you never use.' Sooner you than me, Josie, sooner you than me.

'THAT FELLOW DOWN UNDER'

The President of the United States of America, Joe Biden, recently had the world in splits, embarrassingly so, with a stunningly casual throwaway line while addressing the Australian Prime Minister, Scott Morrison. It happened at a joint live video communique announcing the formation of an important defence strategic alliance between the United Kingdom, Australia and the United States. Joe Biden took over the microphone, virtually that is, from Britain's PM Boris Johnson, thanked Boris, tactfully refraining from commenting on why Boris had not combed his hair that morning, then turned to the screen displaying the Aussie PM and said, wait for it, 'And I want to thank that fellow Down Under, thank you very much pal.' Collapse of stout party, as the venerable Punch magazine used to put it. To Scott Morrison's credit, he was very diplomatic about the whole *faux pas,* and in statesman-like fashion, dismissed the incident as one of those things that happen, and that one should not make much of it. That was very large of him but the media had a field day, wondering if Biden's shocking memory lapse was a portent of more sinister things to come.

One would have normally credited former US President Barrack Obama with tact and good sense and the ability to mind his Ps and Qs. However, he too fell victim to the 'hot mic' syndrome on one occasion at a G 20 conference during a private chat with the then French President Nicolas Sarkozy, just before the scheduled press conference. The assembled reporters were handed translation boxes but were told not to plug their headphones in until the leaders' backroom conversation had finished. Several people ignored the instructions and heard Mr. Sarkozy talking to

Mr. Obama about Israeli Prime Minister Benjamin Netanyahu. 'I can't stand him anymore, he's a liar,' Mr Sarkozy said.

'You may be sick of him, but me, I have to deal with him every day,' replied Mr Obama drily, clear as a bell for every reporter to faithfully record. *Sacré bleu,* about sums it up.

In case, dear reader, my observations thus far have led you to believe that American Presidents have cornered the market on public brick dropping, that is far from the case. 'Even the normally understated and extremely tactful Queen Elizabeth of Great Britain had a blushful moment some years ago. The then 90-year-old longest reigning British monarch made a blooper when, in a rare diplomatic solecism, she was caught on camera referring to Chinese officials, characterising them as being 'very rude' during President Xi Jinping's state visit to the UK. Coming from the Queen that was almost the equivalent of top swearing. Unfortunately, her remarks were recorded by the official Royal cameraman, which then raises the pertinent question as to how it was leaked to the avaricious British fourth estate. Doubtless the concerned cameraman would have been rigorously questioned by the Palace, his camera taken away and sacked. *'You will never hold another camera in front of royalty ever again.'* So, he scoots off and joins The Sun or Daily Mirror, tasked with shadowing the royal family wherever they go, armed with a state-of-the-art, long-focus telephoto lens camera. Many a royal has been caught unawares by prying cameras doing unroyal things they would rather the public be blissfully ignorant about.

India has had its own share of prominent personalities who did not quite think through what they were saying, and tended to come a cropper under the unremitting glare of the media. Former senior Congress leader, the much- respected Ghulam Nabi Azad, provided an original twist to the concept of family planning and how best to execute his ambitious programme in a hugely populous country like India. During his tenure in 2009 as Health and Family Welfare minister, he turned the spotlight on the implementation of a massive rural electrification programme to achieve the desired results. You heard right. Electrify the nation and our population growth will decline dramatically! Give the man his due. He had a credible explanation. The minister gave it as his considered opinion that in many backward and rural areas of our country, the lack of electricity meant people had nothing better to do after dusk and invariably resorted to sex for entertainment, which is a necessary precursor to a burgeoning population. If electricity was widespread, people in small towns and villages can visit community halls and watch television till late into the night, the minister opined. By the time they return home they will be too tired to indulge in love making and will make straight for bed to catch up with their beauty sleep. A truly original thought! One wonders why successive governments waste their time and resources towards educating our folk on family planning, contraception and the like when all it needed were millions of television sets placed across the country and the requisite power feed to run them for the diversion and delectation of our outback, small town denizens. Unfortunately for the minister, the numbers indicated no dramatic fall in the population figures. In fact, one could go so far as to say that the romantic antics of our film stars and starlets only enhanced their innate tumescence.

On the subject of population control, here is a quick aside. The late Sanjay Gandhi was 'credited' with promulgating the disastrous *'nasbandhi'* or forced sterilization programme during the late 70s to keep India's population growth in check. This was during the infamous Emergency and the policy had his mother, then Prime Minister Indira Gandhi's blessings. Free transistor radios were distributed to those who offered themselves to be thus humiliated. Informed reports also attributed the aggressive intervention by 'western loan sharks' like the World Bank and the IMF in the government's misguided programme, which cost the Congress Party dear at the hustings.

Saving the best for last, three of my favourite gaffes come from the late Prince Philip, the Duke of Edinburgh, who was famously adept at saying the wrong things at the wrong time. For which reason, the British media declared him a national treasure! In 1969, on an official visit to Canada, he quipped, 'I declare this thing open, whatever it is.' On a state visit to China in 1986, he told a group of British students, 'If you stay here much longer, you'll all be slitty-eyed.' Later in 2003, he told the President of Nigeria, who was attired in his traditional, flowing robes, 'You look like you're ready for bed.'

In sum, we should all be grateful when our leaders go off script, as it gives rise to so much mirth and merriment.

HOW LONG IS A PIECE OF STRING?

Of late, I have been receiving a few friendly comments from a handful of readers who have my best interests at heart, to the effect that my columns tend to be a tad too long. Happily they are in the minority, but I tend to take any feedback seriously. I reflect. If not exactly riddled with self-doubt, I contemplate and cogitate. Rather like Macbeth, I am not even sure if it is a dagger that I see before me or something less lethal. Do many of the others in my circle feel the same way, and are only keeping their counsel out of a sense of propriety? The very fact that someone has bothered to write in and comment at all, is generally a welcome sign. In order to be even handed, I should also mention that there are many who write extremely nice things about my blogs, and thank you very much indeed. You know who you are. You buck me up no end.

Getting back to the vexed issue of the length of my blogs, I responded to one of my good friends' comments about the piece being too long with a snappy, philosophical, almost Kierkegaardian 'how long is a piece of string?' To his credit, he responded with a terse 'long enough to become a noose.' On my part, this was not taken amiss. This is good-natured banter, but he had given me food for thought. Not that I had entirely agreed with him, but still, something over which to chew the cud.

Now here is the thing. On average my columns tend to weigh in at around 1500 to 1600 words. I go in for what is fashionably called 'the long form essay.' I could add here that, as long-form essays go, mine will come under the shorter version of the category. There are many distinguished, and some not so, writers who think nothing of spitting on their hands and dashing off four to five thousand words! Without batting an eyelid. Almost the length of a not-so-short story. So, I repeat my cardinal question, 'how long is a piece of string?'

In the past, when I used to contribute regularly to a few newspapers, I had to cut my coat according to my cloth and restrict the verbiage to around 1000 words or less. Which is not something to be sneezed at, but one was constantly worried about having to curtail one's natural instincts to spread oneself high, wide and handsome, in a manner of speaking. On the odd occasion that I erred in length, to employ a cricketing terminology, I darkly visualised some junior sub sweating under a naked light bulb in front of his desktop till late at night, burning the midnight oil and resenting the fact, sadistically wading into my piece with a hatchet. Apostrophes going haywire, semi-colons where none should exist, transferred epithets being re-transferred ruinously, sentences and paragraphs getting mixed up. It was a nightmare. Next morning, I would scan the broadsheet with trepidation. Furthermore, it did nothing to enhance my reputation when folks opened their newspapers of a morning with their hot cuppa. At least, now if a hawk-eyed reader swoops down on a clumsy mixed metaphor or a grammatical solecism, I can gallantly put my hand up and say, *'mea culpa.'*

Back to the topic on hand. You see, that is another thing. One aims to stay on the straight and narrow path sticking to the essentials of one's subject, but every now and then, the main path leads us on to some interesting side roads, turn-offs and alleyways that require a bit of explaining. That is how, without even being conscious of it, the words tend to multiply. I could, of course, suggest to some of my readers that if ploughing through 1600 words feels like a steep climb, perhaps they ought to read my burnt offerings in two easy instalments. 800 words a day should be a leisurely stroll in the park. The downside, however, is that the suspense involved in the wait to get at the second instalment might be too stressful. Was it the butler who put the strychnine in the soup or was it the housemaid? So much simpler to read the whole, damn thing in one go and get a good night's sleep. Incidentally, it was the squint-eyed gardener!

I am not sure how many of you have heard of the late Miles Kington. He was on the editorial staff of Punch and contributed prolifically to many of Britain's leading newspapers and magazines. His stock-in-trade, as one would expect of a Punch staffer, was humour. I discovered him during my early days in a reputed advertising agency in Calcutta, where the librarian had the good sense to subscribe to Punch. More for the glossy adverts than anything else. I devoured the magazine and Miles Kington was my favourite columnist. In more recent times, I have been fortunate enough to access his books online and not a day passes when I don't read and re-read his delightful musings.

The reason I brought his name up was that he apparently wrote *a column a day*, anything from 1000 to 2000 words. Yes, you read that right. For nearly forty years, almost till the day he breathed his last, this indefatigable humourist wrote a piece every single day! It would greatly surprise me if he is not featured in the *Guinness Book of World Records*. What is more, his editors swear Miles' quality never wavered, and his choice of subjects could be just about anything under the sun or nothing at all. So here I am, wondering how to manage to write one column every week, huffing and puffing, without being gently rapped on the knuckles for contaminating my mailing list's inboxes with tiresomely long pieces, when good, old Miles Kington could do it on a dime.

There is a personal postscript to the Miles Kington story. A story I might have told before, not that anyone will recall, and at my age, repeating myself is an occupational hazard. In my callow, ad agency days, people like Miles inspired me to write little snippets purely for my own pleasure. On one occasion, I decided to write a longer snippet, if that is not a contradiction in terms, and in a rash moment of bravado, despatched it *par avion,* by registered post to Miles Kington 'for favour of publication in your esteemed magazine.' Which, of course, was Punch. We are talking mid-70s here. The post office charged me a pretty penny for the stamps to London. Rather ambitious, you might say, but what the hell. Young blood. Nothing ventured, nothing gained. Or, if you prefer, in for a penny, in for a pound.

Nothing was precisely what I heard for quite a few weeks. Just when I had all but given up the ghost, a light blue envelope with a postage stamp bearing the Queen's silhouetted bust arrived. Next to that was franked the Punch logo in black. My heart leapt upstream like a young sockeye salmon in season. I opened the envelope with great care, lest I should inadvertently damage part of the precious contents, took the letter out with trembling fingers and opened it. There it was, a Punch letterhead with a brief, handwritten note from none other than MK himself, which I reproduce from memory. *'Dear Suresh,'* it read. *'I found your contribution most interesting, but the format needs some working and as such we will, regrettably, be unable to carry it. Keep writing. Best wishes, Miles.'* A bit of a blow of course, but I do not believe I have received a regret letter that made me happier than this one. It is preserved in aspic. If only I could find it. For what it is worth, that article which Punch declined to publish carried approximately 1600 words. As you can see, I am wearing Miles' polite *nolle prosequi* like a badge.

Eliza Doolittle, the charming, Cockney flower girl from the hit musical *My Fair Lady* (born out of G.B. Shaw's *Pygmalion*) tells off her language guru, the irascible Prof. Henry Higgins with these opening lines of a memorable song, 'Words, words, words / I am so sick of words / I get words all day through / First from him, now from you / Is that all you blighters can do?' She makes a powerful point. Today, you switch on your television set to any news channel and what do you get? The Tower of Babel. Perhaps the Tower of Babble would be more appropriate, given how all the participants shout in complete disharmony and we grope to make any sense out of the proceedings. We are on far more civilized ground when it comes to words in the written form.

So, there you are. I had very pious intentions of making this a short and sweet piece, in order to please my friend who first pointed out the lengthy error of my ways. Once, however, I started putting pen to paper, speaking metaphorically, the urge to let myself go was too great. The blog took on a life of its own. You might say it is a kind of affliction, this craving to be long-winded but, as Novak Djokovic said recently, it is what it is. My English teacher in school during the swinging 60s would have approved, but in this day and age of short attention spans, the same teacher would probably have given me detention, six of the best and ordered me to write 500 times, 'From now on, I shall not write an essay consisting of more than 500 words.'

There you have it. I have crossed the finishing line. Breasted the tape. The verdict is in. 1639 words. Au revoir.

THE LAW AND THE BIG SQUEEZE

The law is an ass
– Old English proverb

I am at odds with the Karnataka High Court, which recently ruled that the act of a 38-year-old man opting to squeeze another man's testicles during the course of a heated argument cannot be regarded as an attempt to murder. Now, in the normal course of sitting down to write my weekly blog, the subject of testicles would be the very last thing on my mind to expound upon. I leave that kind of stuff to urologists and others in the medical profession to mull over. Apart from which, strait-laced members of my family are apt to look askance at this sudden, unsavoury departure in my choice of topic. Which is probably the way it should have stayed, were it not for this morning's esteemed daily newspaper. There it was: the headline, bold as brass, plumb, spang in the middle of the front page, *Squeezing testicles in fight not 'attempt to murder': Karnataka High Court.* Well, I mean to say! What are our newspapers, or our judiciary for that matter, coming to, I ask rhetorically. Stopped me dead in my tracks. After that, I had to read the whole, sordid bulletin.

This is what their lordships of the High Court had to say on the matter. The prose is untidy but the point gets across. 'There was a quarrel between the accused and the complainant. During that, the accused chose to squeeze the testicles. Therefore, it cannot be said that the accused came with an intention or with preparation to commit murder. If at all he had prepared or attempted to commit murder, he would have brought some deadly weapons to commit the murder.' One presumes the good judge said all that with a straight face. Sounds logical enough, if a tad naïve. After all, bare hands can also be used to strangle a person to death. Overturning an order of a trial court, the High Court, in their wisdom, reduced the punishment earlier meted out, from seven to three years imprisonment. Did not the prosecuting lawyer try to convince the court that if a man's genitals are squeezed long and hard enough, it might well lead to death? Who can say? At the very least, his self-worth could get hit for six, and he will become a spent force, in every sense of the word for the rest of his miserable life.

So why am I not joyously strewing flowers and doing my version of the *Naatu Naatu* at this remarkable judgement? Why has my local High Court, by virtue of this verdict, given me pause? There is this great concept called precedent, much loved by legal eagles. They pass a judgement on some subject or the other, in this case that of testicle squeezing, and next thing you know, a precedent has been set. One is now free to go about picking up a fight and without so much as a by-your-leave, aim straight for your opponent's family jewels. No questions asked. The poor victim runs to the courts, if he is able to run at all, seeking justice for the indignity caused. Not to mention the pain suffered, and is fobbed off with an 'All right, we can feel your pain, but he was not trying to kill you, was he? Now be reasonable. Where was the gun? Where was the murderous machete? We will put him in the cooler for three years, with two years remission for good behaviour. That should straighten the blighter out.' 'But judge, where does that leave me?' bleats the victim. 'Next case,' bellows the judge, bringing his gavel down hard on the much-abused high table.

My point, quite simply, is this. Why is a reduced jail sentence going to act as a deterrent to this habitual squeezer of the unmentionables? Which incidentally, the courts have mentioned in excruciating detail. He sits in jail for the minimum period accorded to him, his palms itching to get at some poor sod's nether regions, because that is what gives him the jollies. He is a pervert. The whole insidious habit builds up into an uncontrollable desire, and the moment he steps out of prison, a free man, no one is safe. The warders lolling around at the prison compound better watch out. That's all I can say. Why could he not have behaved like a normal idiot involved in a street brawl? Some violent fisticuffs and kicking one can understand, but squeezing testicles? That's a no ball in any language. A sensible referee would have stopped the fight instantly.

Now here is the problem we need to bend our brains to. There could be any number of thugs in the country who would have read the fine print of the Karnataka High Court judgement with glee. And, presumably, with a fine-tooth comb. I know most of them are illiterate but word gets around. Then there's always television for those that cannot read beyond 'the cat sat on the mat,' or its Indian equivalent. The television set is called idiot box for a reason. The upshot of it all is that these sons of Belial go around seeking whom they may devour, screaming 'Your money or your balls,' in the full knowledge that their heinous act will not attract anything more than a light sentence, or better still a caution, if at all they are apprehended.

Street crime will now acquire a new avatar. It is being suggested, at least I am suggesting it, that innocent and unwary male strollers protect their private parts with those abdominal guards we employed while playing cricket. In school they were colloquially referred to as 'ball guards.' In case you don't have one or the old one has seen better days, you can always order it on Amazon. I know I have one somewhere up in the loft. I will need to fish it out and give it a Dettol wash and leave it out to dry. Never know when it might come in handy. As an interesting aside, here is a question for the ages. Why do people always laugh hysterically when a batsman suffers a painful blow in his crotch? It is no laughing matter.

This judgement has left me quite distraught. Or do I mean distrait? Never mind. Suffice it to say that you would not be far wrong in describing my current mental state as being discombobulated. One reason for that is that if ordinary men like you and I are in ever-present danger of being assaulted in unusual anatomical areas of our body, I dread to think what will happen to our good women. There are, I admit, some fundamental differences in our bodily make up, men and women that is. However, it is the principle of this ghastly affair that bothers me no end.

It seems to me that these no-good yobbos who roam our streets looking for cheap thrills, need never fear the law anymore. If they are caught in the act by a cop and challenged as to what on earth do they think they are doing, grabbing someone's breadbasket (as I have heard it described by English cricket commentators) in broad daylight, and that they had better come to the police station handcuffed, the criminal will have a ready response. 'Look Mr. Plod, the judge has already spoken on the matter. Am I carrying a sharp knife? No. A pistol? No. Then what is all the fuss about? I was merely having a friendly chat with this gentleman who was reluctant to part with his bulging wallet. As a means of gentle persuasion, I proceeded to apply the squeeze to those parts which will elicit a positive response. You can escort me to the station by all means, but you will get no joy out of it. Probably a suspension for your troubles.'

The befuddled cop goes cross-eyed with confusion. He decides not to get crotchety about someone's crotch. 'I could not follow a word of what you just said. Now you just run along and we shall say no more about it. So saying, they all part company, leaving the poor victim of physical abuse abandoned, his wallet gone and facing the gargantuan task of initiating an infructuous court case. As a final nail in the coffin, so to speak, his baritone voice has shockingly turned into a shrill soprano. How was he going to explain that to his wife?

Honestly, those eminent judges at the Karnataka High Court have a lot to answer for. Perhaps we need to knock on the doors of the overburdened Supreme Court for a second opinion. A real testing affair, this issue of the manhandled testicles. A right, royal balls-up, if ever there was one!

Footnote: As if all this was not enough, a court in Gujarat recently sentenced a man, *with heavy heart,* for raping a minor. Just to be clear, it was the court that bore a heavy heart, not the rapist. I understand there were extenuating and mitigating circumstances, but still, *with heavy heart?* Clearly, there are many bleeding hearts in our judiciary!

As I am about to post this comes news from Bihar that a woman sliced her rapist's goolies in the dead of night with a sharp knife. A surgeon's knife and complete castration, without an anaesthetic, would seem to be the order of the day. If one might paraphrase the Queen of Hearts from Alice in Wonderland, 'Off with his nuts.'

IT IS WRITTEN IN THE STARS

Let me get one thing straight off my chest. I do not understand the art or science of predicting the future. Do I believe in it? Do I repose blind faith in its mysterious and arcane ways? I do, when the predictions go in my favour. Else, I am dismissive. This is not to suggest that I am scornful of it, it simply means I haven't quite got my head round how someone could possibly predict that a particular horse would gallop home in a canter, at handsome odds of 20 to 1 and make me a very rich man. Provided, of course, on a reckless dare I decide to plonk my hard-earned money on said horse.

I am aware that there are experts who study form, past results on the turf and all that kind of equine sporting stuff. *There is science and reasoning involved.* That being the case, I can understand plumping for the favourite at pretty low odds. That is how the form book is meant to operate and how racing experts provide odds. However, when some oily geezer sidles up to you and hoarsely whispers, 'Put everything you've got on *Break a Leg*. You will clean up,' it gives a man pause. 'But that horse has a broken leg,' you expostulate, 'how do you figure?' The geezer smiles enigmatically and vanishes. So, you do exactly what he said, assuming there are factors at play that are beyond your ken, and promptly lose all your money. A sucker is born every minute.

Betting on the horses is just one of many illogical things we human beings indulge in, in the fond hope that we can get something for nothing. In many countries, not in India of course, you can legally bet on just about anything your heart takes a fancy to. Just walk into a betting shop in London, and they will give you odds on sporting events of every description, election results, a political leader being assassinated within a week, an impending divorce in the royal family (at very low odds) - you name it, they have the odds. Why, you can even open your own book at the shop and provide odds on the next chap entering the shop being bald, of Oriental origin, walking with a limp and wearing a charcoal grey three-piece suit. If, however, it is discovered that the said bald, Oriental chap and you had conspired to arrange that extraordinary coincidence, you may find you are literally minus an arm and a leg and rushed to Emergency, if you are lucky.

Let me move away from horse racing or come to that, dog racing, another lucrative pastime in the western hemisphere. Here in India, we set much store by predictions of a different kind altogether. Indians are big on such predictive hobbies as astrology, astronomy, the spirit world, Extra Sensory Perception (ESP), palmistry and other related mumbo-jumbo activities. Did I say hobbies? It is for some, but for many others it is a highly profitable business. From the richest to the poorest in the land, pretty much everyone wants to know what the stars foretell this coming week, month, year. The newspapers unfailingly carry a column every Sunday, where all the signs of the Zodiac are given the full treatment. American astrologer Linda Goodman became a worldwide celebrity with her books on astrology rivalling J.K. Rowling's Harry Potter novels on the sales charts.

We in India have had our own Bejan Daruwalla, now residing among the stars, and his ilk filling our heads regularly with things to 'watch out for' in the near future. Even the cynics among us ('I don't believe in all this nonsense') take a sly peek at what the experts and charlatans have to say about our Zodiacal sign when nobody is looking. It is a kind of addiction, perhaps an innocent pastime. Let me quickly check on Gemini, my sign of the Zodiac. 'Your dual personality could get you into trouble this week with a lady you will meet for the first time.' Ominous, but tantalising. I spend the entire week looking at any strange lady who may or may not have smiled at me, wondering if there is more to this than meets the eye. However, nothing happens, the week passes, and next Sunday, it is a man from my dim past who is set to haunt me. I will say this for astrology. It keeps you involved and curious, but since you are a non-believer, you keep mum and anticipate silently.

I touched briefly on election results earlier. No general election in India is ever complete without some pundit or the other displaying his punditry with incisive predictions on which party is likely to win how many seats, cross his heart and hope to die, or whatever that expression's Indian equivalent is. All this in mainline dailies and national television, watched avidly by politicians, psephologists and voters alike.

When I lived with my parents in Calcutta during my university days, every once in a while, a spooky looking man from deep down south in Tamil Nadu, would show up at our doorstep, his forehead liberally caked with sacred ash and some prominent scarlet powder. Unannounced. If memory serves, his name was Tirumalai (or Tirupathi) or some such. Why and how he should turn up in Calcutta with a list of addresses of many prominent Tamilians working in the city, was an unfathomable mystery. Nevertheless, when the doorbell rang, and the formidable Tirupathi (or Tirumalai) stood there, grinning from ear to ear, I was surprised to see him being warmly welcomed by my pater and mater.

When I came to learn that his visit was by appointment, I became fidgety. He was treated with great respect (filter coffee at the ready) and was asked to consult his moth-eaten books, strange-looking shells and some dried leaves bearing barely legible inscriptions in Tamil, along with horoscopes, to predict what was going to happen to each one of our family members. He could also read palms. He was versatile. My mother was dead keen that my future, including marital prospects (particularly that), should be laid bare. That is when I made my excuses and bolted for the great open spaces. My mother could have been yelling after a deaf mute. Damned if that put the brakes on this Tirumalai (or Tirupathi) character from providing chapter and verse of my future career prospects and my life partner in sickness and in health. To say nothing of evil omens I should watch out for. A black cat did cross my path as I scarpered from the scene, but I merely stopped to scratch its chin and move on. The cat purred in satisfaction.

There are also a couple of fortune tellers who live in some remote village or the other, possibly in a mud hut, who are regularly visited by all kinds of people from far and near, some of them extremely well-heeled. Apparently, this soothsayer asks precisely one question. 'What time of the day or night were you born?' No date, place or any other detail asked for. Most of us haven't a clue what time we were born, unless the clock struck midnight as you emerged mewling and puking, in which case you are very special. Was it 2.17 am, 3.24 pm or perhaps, 8.31 pm? When I asked my mother the time of my birth she replied, with sturdy common sense, that she was in too much pain to recall. And yet, thousands of people approach these magic men with 'My daughter was born at precisely 6.18 am. Please tell me, oh all-knowing savant, when will she get married?' The savant casually pulls out a leaf from a crevice in his hut and declares, 'In precisely 11 months your wish will be granted, and she will bear two sons and a daughter.' Elated, the parents stuff some undisclosed currency notes into an earthen pot, and go away beaming with joy.

I can go on. In our country we have our own version of tarot cards that can divine the past, present or future. If tarot cards won't do it for you, there's always parrot cards. Haven't you seen an old Indian pot-boiler film lately? The local astrologer sits under a peepul tree armed with a stack of portentous cards, unlocks his cage, and Polly the parrot goes hop, hop, hop and pulls out a card that has, metaphorically or perhaps even literally, your name on it. In any event, the parrot's red beak ensures your goose is cooked, in a nice way, if you will excuse the avian mixed metaphor. Invariably, the parrot unfailingly predicts good things in the offing, that keeps the revenues flowing for its master and everyone happy.

Ah well, the westerners and the Chinese have their fortune cookies, we have our parrots and palmists. To each his own. As someone whose name escapes me once said, 'The future can be changed. The psychic reads the map, but free will decides the path we take.' Hear, hear!

SHALL I COMPARE THEE TO
A SUMMER'S DAY?

It has always been a matter of wonderment to me why, in the overall realm of things, poetry has invariably been placed a notch above prose in the pantheon of English Literature. I grant you that this is more a perception than a reality, but that is the general feeling one takes away. For instance, excellence in certain forms of sport is often likened to poetry. 'Roger Federer's backhand crosscourt is sheer poetry,' you will hear television commentators gush. Ditto Diego Maradona's 'Goal of the Century' against England in the 1986 World Cup in Mexico City. It was a close-run thing between Maradona's magical goal and the Uruguayan television commentator, Victor Hugo Morales who went poetically berserk describing it. Similar poetic praise is reserved for a Virat Kohli cover drive, though we have not been seeing much of that in recent times. The late American poet and music critic Amiri Baraka (previously known as LeRoi Jones) once said, 'Poetry is music, and nothing but music. Words with musical emphasis.' He was a jazz enthusiast and an avowed admirer of the legendary Miles Davis, whose trumpet playing has often scaled poetic heights.

We all know that Shakespeare wrote many beautiful sonnets, but he is justly celebrated for the sheer magnitude and magnificence of his immense body of plays. We quote the Bard, day in and day out, consciously or otherwise, whenever we speak or write in English. And yet, to a lay person of the present generation, his plays read more like poetry than prose. Perhaps that is one of the reasons why it is more enjoyable to watch an enactment on stage of *Hamlet,* than to actually sit down and read the entire play, as you would a novel. After all, wasn't it Shakespeare himself who said, 'The lunatic, the lover and the poet are of imagination all compact?' And just to drive home the point, the great man adds, 'The forms of things unknown, the poet's pen / Turns them to shapes and gives to airy nothing / A local habitation and a name.' This is perhaps one reason why heightened sensations in any field of activity draw comparisons with poetry, whereas things more mundane tend to be described as prosaic. That's just my impression and I am open to be taken issue with. Gently please, don't land on me like the proverbial ton of bricks.

If I were to reel off a few names of great poets at random, say, Donne, Dante, Blake, Keats, Shelley, Wordsworth, Coleridge, Eliot, there would be a tendency on the part of people to roll their eyes heavenwards and heave a deep sigh as if to say, 'those men knew what life and beyond was all about.' Whereas if I were to invoke the names of a few great novelists, say, Dickens, Hemingway, Kafka, Conan Doyle, Austen, Brontë (all three of them), Waugh (the Elder), Wodehouse, V.S. Naipaul, the general reaction would be one of awe and respect. The crucial difference lies in the ability of poets to evoke a kind of ethereal ecstasy while novelists, though hugely revered, tend to be viewed in more down to earth terms. This is not to put one literary form over the other. As I said earlier, it is just the way I perceive them. Truth to tell, I have never been much of a one for poetry. The poetry fanatics from English Literature classes would wax eloquent about Free Verse, Blank Verse, Sonnet, Acrostic, Villanelle, Limerick, Ode, Elegy, Haiku (you can never keep the Japanese out), to say nothing of sub-categories like Quatrain, Cinquain, Couplet, Sestet and several more. In more modern times, we have seen the emergence of Rhyming Slang, which the British hoi polloi is pretty adept at. Once the conversation gets into things like Iambic Pentameter, I scoot for the hills. Who knows, it is entirely possible that when John Keats felt a thirst coming on, he made a beeline for the nearest pub and declared to the bewildered bartender, 'O for a beaker full of the warm South / Full of the true, the blushful Hippocrene / With beaded bubbles winking at the brim.' Whereas a simple, 'a large tankard of your finest ale please, bartender, and here's a shilling for your troubles,' would have more than met the case.

I felt, therefore, that I should set the record straight and turn my hand to a bit of poetry, if this be the first and last time I attempt it. I have tried my luck with limericks earlier, and according to most experts, I came a cropper. This time, I shall curb my ambition and go for a straightforward four-liner verse format. Quatrain, is it? Let's just call it poetic license. So, here goes nothing. With apologies to all poets, past and present.

Let's hear it for poetry
Though I am partial to prose
If I can't quite rhyme it
Don't think me gross.

In India, politics is all
If Modi can't crack it
We are up the spout
And Rahul just can't hack it.

Then there's the doughty Mamata
Forever crying hoarse
With an eye on the PM's chair
Is it with her, the Force?

Yogi quietly watches the fun
Some say he is next in line
If Modi drops a hint
Watch the saffron sadhu shine.

What of the beleaguered Sonia?
On all sides being corralled
Can she find a way out
Of the mess that is the Herald?

All the while Tharoor speaks
Nineteen to the dozen
No one understands a word but
In social media he is buzzin'.

In Bengal the TMC frets
Over ill-gotten moolah
Arpita cries, 'Not me, not me'
While Partho da swings on his jhula!

Over in bustling Mumbai
The ED closes in on Raut
'I'll see you in hell' says our Sanjay
But for him it augurs a rout!

Arnab brings the roof down
On the Vadra-Gandhi clan
Rajdeep does much the same
Only with far more elan.

The Opposition was up in arms
'Let's talk GST, let's talk inflation.'
The Treasury turned the other cheek
And said, 'Why not corruption?'

China threatened to blow up Pelosi's plane
Xie tried hard, the visit to stall
But Biden held firm
The lady sure has some gall.

Meanwhile, the US took out al Zawahiri
Who didn't know what hit his shack
Biden celebrated from his secure White House
And told all Americans, 'Watch your back.'

In old Blighty, the race is on
To see who will let the cat out
Nightly at Number 10
Is Rishi still in with a shout?

Russia's shelling of Ukraine is unceasing
No one knows when this will end
Putin is pulling out all the stops
But Zelensky will not bend.

They say cricket and politics don't mix
Ha, ha, who are they kidding?
Ask ex-skip Virat Kohli
Whose career is up for bidding.

The legend MSD they left alone
With him they had no beef
Captain Cool was too clever
From whose book they should take a leaf.

India is playing in the Caribbean
Is anybody following?
Does anybody care?
Only the BCCI seems to be wallowing.

What about the Commonwealth Games?
Some say we shouldn't be there
Shuttling and wrestling for a few medals
Ah well, let's dream to dare.

Shed a tear for poor, old Djoko
They said 'no vax, no Slam'
'No way, Jose,' said the champ
'I am Novak(s), you can all scram!'

Covid, please make up your mind
Are you coming or going?
Monkeypox has its foot in the door
It's our minds you're blowing.

And that's where I'll end this try
Tilting at poetic windmills
I am no dab hand at it
Only prose will pay my bills.

I told myself at the outset that poetry is not my bag, but I am not very adept at taking good advice. Not even my own. But what the hell, one has to try something out in order to plumb the depths, as it were. Nothing ventured, nothing gained. Not that I have gained much from this exercise, but I have to say it was fun. I shall now proceed to inflict these rhymes on an unsuspecting world, and hope they will be a wee bit more charitable than I have been on myself. A few luminaries from the Dead Poets' Society could well be turning in their graves on reading my overwrought rhymes. Serve them right, I say, for making me go through all that stuff in school about Skylarks, Country Churchyards, Highland Lasses, Mists, Mellow Fruitfulness and so on. They were all compressed in very small print in a fat, red book called *Golden Treasury of Longer Poems*. By the time we got to the 17th verse, we couldn't wait for the end-of-class bell to ring. The only time the boys got excited was during Coleridge's *Christabel,* when the eponymous heroine watches her well-endowed, dodgy pal Geraldine disrobe herself, and our English Master quickly turned the page to avoid having to read, at least for us impressionable teenagers, some graphic anatomical descriptions. Not content with this, Coleridge got right up our noses and proceeded to write his longest poem ever, *The Rime of the Ancient Mariner.* Poor Coleridge. Poor English Master. Poor students. All said and done, I shall stick steadfastly to prose, barring the odd poetic quote punctuated here and there, to show there's no ill feeling. And finally, if someone can explain to me why (and how) 'the mirror crack'd from side to side' as Tennyson's *The Lady of Shalott* cried, 'The curse is come upon me,' I should be much obliged.

CHANDRAYAAN-3 AND PRAGGNANANDHA OVER THE MOON

Two events occurred, serendipitously, over the past week, gazillion miles apart, that had pretty much the whole of India's 1.4 billion people on the edge of their seats. The Indian Space Research Organisation's (ISRO) pride and joy, Chandrayaan-3, was hurtling towards the south pole or the dark side of the moon, orbiting closer and closer to the landing site of the golden orb, as we waited with bated breath. While that historic space journey was nearing its completion, here on God's good earth in the city of Baku in Azerbaijan, an 18-year-old chess prodigy from Tamil Nadu, Grandmaster Rameshbabu Praggnanandha, now fashionably Pragg, was creating his own history by pushing Norwegian chess maestro Magnus Carlsen to the limit for the FIDE world title. From India's point of view, a fairy-tale script would have visualised Chandrayaan-3 make a smooth landing on the moon's surface, and barely 24 hours later, the young teenager from Chennai checkmating the wizard from Norway. While it did not go exactly according to script, it came agonisingly close to doing so, and India's cup of joy truly runneth over. Chandrayaan-3 and Vikram Lander had India and the world agog with a perfect touchdown for the first time ever by any nation on the south pole, while the precocious teenager Pragg lost to a more experienced opponent by the skin of his teeth. India celebrated both these events as seminal landmarks. And rightly so.

The wonderful thing about the ISRO saga and the boy wonder's brilliance was that both these milestones were blessedly free of any kind of political taint. However, our political earthlings can hardly be expected to let momentous happenings pass without diving, deep end first, into a messy, me-too maelstrom. The imbroglio started with the television coverage of the moon landing. As Chandrayaan-3 was nearing its appointed destination on the lunar surface, our idiot box screens were split into two. While one half stayed with the historic descent towards the moon, the other half unveiled our Prime Minister, taking time off from the BRICS summit in Johannesburg, eyes glued to the history-making satellite. Waving our national flag, the PM watched with swelling pride and perhaps a touch anxiously, that all would be well if it ends well. Well, it did and the PM did what he does best. Took centre stage and spoke eloquently and at length, praised all concerned particularly the scientists at ISRO, and did not miss a trick to ensure his own Government's inspiring, leadership role was not lost on the populace. Some may aver that the word Government is surplus to requirements, but I will let that pass.

With a plethora of state elections in the offing, culminating in the magnum opus General Elections in May 2024, the ruling party will doubtless take every opportunity to blow their own trumpet, *fortissimo*, to extract full mileage from any event that positively redounds towards favourable optics. That is only to be expected of any ruling party that has one eye firmly cocked on the forthcoming hustings.

That being said, the opposition parties were quick to denounce the PM's television appearance at the crucial hour of the moon landing, as little more than a brazen publicity-seeking stunt. In the somewhat low-key (thankfully) verbal slugfest that followed, if slugfests can ever be low-key, the opposition bench took exception to the PM hogging all the limelight, after showering fulsome encomiums on ISRO, and not acknowledging the role played by past leaders like Jawaharlal Nehru in India's march towards becoming a technological power, driven by science and technology. The nation's 'scientific temper' owes much to the founding fathers of the nation since India's independence, they cried in unison.

The usual cut, thrust and parry that we have been witness to on a number of occasions in the past, continued apace. The names of Nehru, Indira Gandhi, and Vajpayee were taken in vain by both sides of the political binary. May their departed souls not stir restlessly. The Prime Minister's name was taken, as is the party apparatchik's wont, at the drop of a hat to bolster his stature as a leader of unparalleled dynamism and integrity. What all that has to do with the moon landing is neither here nor there. In politics anything and everything goes, so long as we can fit in 22 talking heads at the same time on our news channels, along with a hyper-ventilating anchor frothing at the mouth.

The opposition worthies, just by virtue of being in the minority, find themselves stranded to defend the vigorous onslaught of the treasury bench wallahs. They have no option but to sing hosannas to ISRO, as that august and noble body is beyond the pale of humdrum politics, and the ruling party will always be controlling the narrative just by *being there.* Bengal Chief Minister, Mamata Banerjee even comically referred to Bollywood actor-director Rakesh Roshan in recalling India's past space heroes, when she meant to say Rakesh Sharma. If the BJP are all over the place like a rash, the Congress counters by putting out full page adverts showcasing Nehru, Sarabhai and, incongruously, the local Chief Minister and Deputy Chief Minister of Karnataka, and the stellar role played by all of them leading up to the success of Chandrayaan-3, not to mention INDIA without the intervening full stops, but subliminally flagging the opposition alliance. I am speaking only of the Bangalore papers here, where ISRO's HQ is based. Obviously, no mention of the honourable PM can be expected in what is clearly a Congress party political campaign.

Not to be outdone (when is he ever?), the PM landed in Bangalore at the crack of dawn on Saturday week, feted the entire ISRO team and was in turn fulsomely feted. Sensitive to every nuance, the PM had special words for the women at ISRO *(Naari Shakti)*, and their stellar contributions to the success of the project. Never one to miss a trick, a natural born brand guru, the PM anointed the precise points on the moon where Chandrayaan-2 nearly landed and Chandrayaan-3 successfully touched down as – *Tiranga* and *Shiv Shakti* respectively. What is more, Chandrayaan-3's date of landing on the moon, August 23, 2023, will now be celebrated as National Space Day. That is a full plate to savour and the opposition has already started aiming its barbs.

Lest we forget, on November 14, 2008, Chandrayaan-1's lunar probe had 'impacted' at a point near the south pole, whatever that means. The impact point was named *Jawahar Point*. November 14 also happens to be India's first PM Jawaharlal Nehru's birthday. That should set the cat among the pigeons.

On the flip side, a proposed road show in Bangalore was cancelled at the last minute. An eminently wise decision. It would have been too much of a good thing and would have undoubtedly added more fuel to the simmering flame. However, we can expect to hear more on this subject. A bit of argy-bargy surrounding the issue of why Karnataka's CM and Dy. CM were not on hand to receive the PM at Bangalore and attend the ISRO function, was doused by the PM himself who had requested them and the Governor not to inconvenience themselves at the crack of dawn to pay their obsequies. And did the CM and his deputy hurriedly visit ISRO earlier to rub some of the sheen off the PM's visit. Dear, oh dear! Will the carping never end?

A totally needless distraction was the BBC's not-so-veiled criticism, four years ago, of India's 2019 Chandrayaan-2 venture, which was raked up and our media went into overdrive. The BBC was rightly chastised for clinging on to a colonial mindset, stereotyping India as it was several decades ago, struggling to feed its starving millions, yet splurging money on space missions it could ill afford. Unless I am missing something, I was unable to understand why the BBC's 4-year-old broadcast resurrected now, adding greatly to the noise levels and detracting from our hour of glory. Ironically, I do not recall the subject being discussed when it was first aired. To the best of my knowledge, the Chandrayaan-3 triumph was lauded by most western nations and media, though a tad guardedly.

One thing is clear. The political by-play from the sidelines has been confined to the Chandrayaan-3 mission. We must thank heaven that Pragg's dazzling moves over 64 squares in Azerbaijan have not attracted any political one-upmanship thus far. Let us hope it stays that way. The PM was one among many dignitaries from across various walks of life who extended his good wishes to the young man from Madras. Doubtless his home state, Tamil Nadu, will shower him with riches and encomiums beyond the dreams of avarice. Here's wishing that he is not distracted by all the hoopla that will surround him. He looks a well-grounded youngster imbued with solid, middle-class family values. Coincidentally, those values are almost a mirror image of the personality profile of the entire ISRO personnel. That said, it will not be long before Pragg is seen on our small screens endorsing any number of brands. You will get very long odds from a bookmaker if you bet against that prediction.

It is significant that having landed safely on the moon, Chandrayaan-3 mission's Rover Pragyan rolled down from the lander Vikram to commence its various scientific investigations. A mechanical Prag, scientifically and technologically driven, is surveying the lunar surface with the proverbial fine toothcomb; here on earth a human Pragg, strategically and mathematically hardwired, is forever scouring 64 squares on a chess board, inspired by tales from the Mahabharat and the *Chaturanga,* an early version of chess which also served as a brainstorming exercise for ancient war games.

If only our politicians don't ruin it all.

THE PREMIUMS ARE KILLING ME

There are worse things in life than death. Have you ever spent an evening with an insurance salesman?
– Woody Allen

By any yardstick, insurance is a sound concept, predicated on the principle that should any misfortune befall one, be it health, life, property, accident, theft, fire – in fact, pretty much anything that you possess which is valuable and vulnerable to damage or loss, can be insured and you can claim compensation. Provided, of course, that you have not been tardy with your annual premium payments. It must be conceded that getting some money back after losing a limb or two in a road accident or being charred beyond recognition in a fire is scarce comfort, but it is something, the *raison d'être* for taking out an insurance policy in the first place. Then again, be of good cheer. You are also liable to benefit by something called 'no claim bonus' whereby, if you have been a good boy (or girl) and paid your premiums without making any claim year on year, the value of your insurance increases by leaps, if not bounds. That, as I am sure all of you know, was a thumbnail sketch of the basic principles of insurance and why every right-thinking individual should buy into it. I am not even getting into the area of big-time, big bucks corporate insurance involving space travel, airlines, railways, maritime and the like.

Insurance can also be taken out against specific body parts that can affect a person's livelihood. Take musicians, for instance. The likes of Bruce Springsteen, Keith Richards, Tina Turner, Madonna and many others have insured their voices or their fingers (if one plays an instrument) for millions of dollars. Why, quite famously, country and western singer Dolly Parton insured her 40E breasts for a reported sum of $600,000. On the face of it, it would seem that Ms. Parton is more concerned about her décolletage than her singing voice. This (the insurance, not the décolletage) would apply equally to classical musicians and to top-of-the-line sportspersons who depend almost entirely on their hands and legs for their record-breaking performances. Similar information on celebrated Indian musicians, I have not been able to garner. Though it would not surprise me in the least if the likes of A.R. Rahman, Ilayaraja, the late Lata Mangeshkar and classical instrumentalists such as the late Pandit Ravishankar, Ustad Amjad Ali Khan, the late Lalgudi Jayaraman and others had taken out specific insurance policies for their body parts specifically involved in earning them their livelihood. The fact that quite a few of those I mentioned are 'late' is neither here nor there. This is over and above the normal health and life insurance policies that these individuals would have taken. Musicians can also be insured for 'opportunity loss' should their engagements be cancelled due to factors beyond their control, resulting in loss of income. Presumably athletics, tennis, football, boxing and other sports superstars would have also taken out similar policies. Lest I forget, add personal vehicles to that list. Given its limitless scope, I am not sure if film producers can insure their productions against flops at the box office, though I doubt very much that the insurance Scrooges will give them the time of day.

It is perfectly understandable that among the poorer classes, it is very difficult to convince people to part with meagre, hard-earned cash towards insurance, which they merely see as money going out of their pockets towards an eventuality that they do not or cannot visualize happening. A bird in the hand is worth two in the insurance bush is their philosophy. At a crude level, this point of view is quite understandable. We took out an accident insurance policy for our driver, who thought it was a sheer waste of money that could have been better employed by raising his salary. Tragically, he was involved in a fatal road accident and lost his life. We now hope the money his family would get from the insurance company would go some way towards alleviating their financial, if not mental, distress. Which brings me to the second part of the insurance dilemma, which is the process of actually getting the compensation and the hellish paperwork and torture involved in convincing the insurance monoliths that compensation delayed is compensation denied. The struggle to get things moving actually makes you wonder if it was all worth the while.

It is well known that the insurance business works on the principle that the greater the volume of clients insured, the theory of probability will ensure that the number of clients they need to shell out money to will be far less than the numbers actually insured. It is a fail-safe business model. Except when there are natural calamities or pandemics such as we have witnessed recently, when they have to dig deep into their resources, if not actually scraping the bottom of the barrel. More often than not, the attention given by insurance agents, the enthusiasm shown and promises made prior to completing an insurance sale, is directly in inverse proportion to the service one receives when one faces serious health or injury issues and makes legitimate claims on the companies.

The other oddity about personal insurance is that, from the quantum of premiums to cost of medical treatment, things get impossibly hard when you grow old which, ironically, is when you are most likely to need help. The form-filling alone can drive one up the wall. When you are young, fit and healthy with not a care in the world, the insurance agents will be all over you like a swarm of bees buzzing around a pot of honey. Everything is an absolute doddle. They will even take care of the form-filling. It's when those creaky, arthritic joints start playing up that you come up against the odds. Information overload kicks in. KYC, PAN card, Aadhaar, bank pass book, driving license, voter ID, present address, previous address, nominees – the list is never-ending, and you probably need to be insured against wrist damage owing to all the writing involved. What is more, since everything is expected to be done online these days, there is no question of a friendly face from the not-so-friendly insurance company to come home and help you; you are glued to your smart phone from morning till night – dial 1 for English, 4 for complaints, 6 for claims, 8 if you are dead and 9 if you wish to talk to 'one of our representatives' which may take some time as all of them are busy talking to someone else. Not clear who you should complain to if '4 for complaints' doesn't respond. You then hold on while they play Handel's or Chopin's Funeral March (souped up by A.R. Rahman) interspersed with repetitive commercial messages about the benefits of taking out an insurance policy with said company.

Now I do realize I may not be projecting an entirely fair picture of our friends from the world of insurance. Sweeping generalizations can be misleading and cynicism comes easily. That said, we have had some pleasant experiences, only over our mobile phones of course. But these have been few and far between. Nowadays you can count yourself lucky if you manage to even get a clear enough signal to follow what the person at the other end is saying. For the most part, even Kafka could not have written a more accurate account of the average Joe and his dealings with the world of insurance. The adjective Kafkaesque could very well have originated from the existential master's reflections on his dealings with insurance companies, but that might just be my imagination working overtime. I am guilty of going walkabout here, so let me get back to the point. I'll say this for our insurance friends. They leave absolutely nothing to chance. There is this 'Act of God' provision cunningly tucked away in very small print somewhere in their dossier, hidden craftily to ensure you miss it. Allow me to explain.

If your wee home gets washed away by flash floods that may be deemed an Act of God, you may or may not be entitled to cash in. Read the small print with a powerful magnifying glass. It is mystifying why the blame for natural disasters that cannot be properly accounted for should be laid at God's door and whether the Almighty concurs with this train of thought, but it is what it is. On the other hand, if your home is destroyed by fire due to an unattended electrical fault, the insurance blokes might be reluctantly willing to cough up provided the 'unattended' part escapes their eagle eyes. It's all about how you evaluate risk and the importance you attach to it.

In the final analysis, insurance is a bit like having to take a strong and bitter medicine. It is supposed to be good for you, but is awful to swallow. Here's Sylvia Plath, acclaimed poet and the tragic author of *The Bell Jar,* who was clinically depressed and took her own life, on the subject - 'My mother had taught shorthand and typing to support us since my father died, and secretly she hated it and hated him for dying and leaving no money because he didn't trust insurance salesmen.'

I rest my case.

THERE IS A CRACK IN EVERYTHING

'It always does seem to me that I am doing more work than I should do. It is not that I object to the work, mind you; I like work: it fascinates me. I can sit and look at it for hours.' Jerome K. Jerome, *Three Men in a Boat*.

Every once in a while, say about once in every four or five years, the distaff side of the family decides that it is time to do a spot of spring cleaning in our modest apartment. Now you might be forgiven for harbouring the impression that this involves some general cleaning up, perhaps a bit of polishing of the furniture here and there, and a lick of paint on some of the walls that may have developed a crack or two, owing to the inexorable ravages of time, as I once heard someone describe it. Perhaps a couple of days of minor inconvenience, but well worth the small effort and expense. And before you can say 'Mansion Floor Polish,' it's all done and dusted. Everything back to how it was, only much cleaner and more spic-and-span. With any luck, I should have been lolling back on my cushions, a bag of crisps and a glass of chilled beer at hand, watching Nadal and Djokovic slipping it across their rivals at the Australian Open.

That, of course, was the pious intention as we started out on our getting-the-home-shipshape project, but matters have a way of running a somewhat different course. Man proposes and the wife disposes. My goodness, you won't believe the amount of stuff there was to dispose, but more of that anon. I was all gung-ho for getting this job done on the quick-and-easy method, but I reckoned without my better half's cunning plan to lull me into a false sense of security. Now that we are well stricken into our 70s, it was always fully understood that hard manual labour will necessarily have to take a back seat even at the cost of minor compromises on the cleaning up, painting and polishing side of things. There are able-bodied men who can be paid to do the heavy lifting, quite literally. However, as The Beatles once so tunefully put it, *I should have known better (with a girl like you).*

It's a funny thing about cracks in walls. I am never able to spot them, however much I squint. 'Cracks? What cracks? Where?' Remember that memorable line from Leonard Cohen's song, *There is a crack, a crack in everything. That's how the light gets in.* That just about sums up my wife's side of things when it comes to blemishes on walls. Cracks, chips, peels, damp, discoloration – none of these apparent symptoms of degeneration catches my eye. My bad, as today's generation might inelegantly put it. And yet, there's my good lady wife, leading me by the nose with a powerful torch-light trained on those very spots which obviously need urgent attention. 'This will involve scraping the walls in the affected areas, applying putty, and finally painting the walls with two coats. Colour matching is vital and we will have to watch these workers like hawks.' The Oracle has spoken. Things are only going to get tough from here on in.

The thing of it is that, during my innocent childhood, stuff like wall painting, furniture polishing and redecorating the home never even remotely formed part of my consciousness. If such things did happen, I was blissfully unaware. I led a sheltered life. My wife came from a different background, where work was worship, preferably with hands - an article of faith. Her family members would speak with an easy familiarity about things like spirit levels, sandpapering, paint rollers, drill bits, steel wool, rawl plugs, putty knife and many more such items which were nothing less than Double Dutch to me. I was thrown into this mysterious, arcane world, which now became a part and parcel of our lives. I will leave it at that.

Wall painting (sounds so simple, does it not?) has many allied consequences of the temporary kind in order to enable work to proceed on an even keel. For starters, all the furniture has to be covered with every available bedsheet to avoid paint blotches from falling on the wood. The furniture must needs be moved to a central position in the room to enable the painters to move about without let or hindrance. More bedsheets must be found to cover all the curios and artefacts that we have collected over the years. To say nothing of our TV set, desktop computer, refrigerator and so on. And why on earth did I buy so many CDs, nearly 500 of them! Had I known that Spotify would have every piece of music for me to enjoy for just a small subscription (if I didn't want the intrusive adverts), I could have avoided all the expense. Then again, Spotify was not even a twinkle in the eye of its discoverers when I first graduated from LPs and cassette tapes to CDs way back when during the early 80s. When we travelled abroad, I would nip off to Oxford Street or Orchard Street, depending on whether we were in London or Singapore, and come back with an armful of CDs, sometimes hidden from my better half. These things tend to accumulate over time. Anyhow, the stacks of CDs needed to be covered as well to prevent dust from slipping through. And I haven't even started on the books yet.

Then there were the books, on cue. If you thought the CDs were coming apart at the seams, you ain't seen nothin' yet. Every available shelf space in our home is crammed with books. My wife is a student of English Literature, so she started collecting books long before we even got married. From Jane Austen to Kafka, Camus to Blake, Dickens to Chekov, Trollope to D.H. Lawrence and everything else in between. Not to mention the *de rigueur,* voluminous Complete Works of you-know-who. And given the amount of travel we had done over the decades, light reading in the form of P.D James, Robin Cook, Dick Francis, Robert Ludlum and their ilk as well. To start with, the space allotted to me among the tomes was small. Wodehouse and some books on cricket and tennis were my *oeuvre,* but as the years passed, I too dived into the reading habit with vigour. With online ordering making things easier,

I have been buying more books than I have been reading. I have now cried a temporary halt to this insane buying and decided to start reading some of the books that are still snug as a bug in a rug in their original Amazon packaging. There is Kindle of course, which is cheaper and only takes up data space on your mobile, but somehow it is not quite the same thing. The smell and tactile experience of a printed book can never be matched by anything that comes online. Rather like the look and feel of a brand, new long-playing record as opposed to the instant convenience and gratification of Spotify.

Now that I have taken your breath away with our in-depth love for music and literature, allow me to turn to art and nature through some of the canvasses that adorn our walls and thence, finally on to plants. Seriously though, the idea is to share the physical challenges of moving and protecting these precious possessions while sprucing up our wee home. To start with the paintings, and without dropping names, let me just say they are the works of some of India's finest artists who ever dipped a brush into a pot of paint. More to the point, in their glass frames, they are heavy. To remove them from their parent walls, place them delicately on an unoccupied bed and cover them with bedsheets is a task that can test the strongest. Once the walls have been given the once (or twice) over, the whole process is to be reversed, which is even tougher. And if we have been able to achieve all this without breaking or damaging any of these master works, we can sit back and take a long draught of iced Coke and heave a huge sigh of relief.

Finally, there's the plants, which require special attention. Shift them, if you must, but with care. One false move, a snapped twig and there will be hell to pay. They come in all shapes and sizes. Tall plants, ferns, creepers, small potted plants – these are all very much the good wife's area of competence. What I know about plants can be written on the head of a pin with a pneumatic drill. Oftentimes, she and the domestic staff do all the lugging and heaving, leaving me out of the action altogether. Her charitable explanation being that I have a sore back and should not risk a crick or two amidst the lower vertebrae. She does have a point, but I suspect the real reason is her concern over my tendency to operate on two left feet, and the disastrous results that could follow.

Now to the ultimate challenge, while all the painting and cleaning is being completed. 'It's a good time to get rid of some of the rubbish we keep sitting on purely out of silly sentiment. They take up too much space and it will mean nothing to whoever ultimately inherits all this.' That pearl of wisdom from the wife, naturally. She says that every time we do up the house. While I agree wholeheartedly, the actual process of getting rid of the rubbish is more challenging than we had envisaged. So, what else is new? 'How about this set of 32 volumes of the Encyclopedia Britannica, gathering dust for 32 years? The local library would love to have them,' I tentatively suggest. 'No, we can't give that away. It was a present from my much-loved aunt.' 'Right, how about those two rickety rocking-chairs. Nobody ever sits on them and the termites are feasting on them.' 'Yeah, they can go. Only I bought them on a charity sale run by my dearest friend. It will be a wrench. I can have them repainted.' 'Surely, that battered HMV record player can be given the heave-ho. It does not work and we don't play records anymore.' 'I agree, but it is a genuine antique, and that dealer down the street said he could crank it up again. Could fetch a decent price at an auction house. What's more, we still have those old Bach, Satchmo, South Pacific, G.N. Balasubramanian and M.S. Subbulakshmi vinyls on LPs and 78 rpms.'

Ten days on, our home looks as good as new. And nothing went into the scrap heap. We are sitting on our own scrap heap, greatly treasured.

AIM. SHOOT. POST.

Why are you on Facebook? Why do you care who is trending? Did you miss your 15 minutes of fame?
– Van Morrison

My participation in social media is negligible. I post my weekly blog on Facebook and Twitter and on occasion, I might make the odd comment, odd being the operative word, if some of my 'friends' happened to post something that I found particularly relevant or interesting. Other than that, zilch would be an apposite word to describe my contribution to these vehicles that so intensely involve and engage millions of people all over the world. At this point, I can faintly detect in the offing, a few of my readers bristling at what they might wrongly assume is a condemnation of social media and their active role in it. Or should that have been 'in them'? I have never quite come to grips with whether the word media should be treated as singular or plural. The singular medium or the plural media, if you get my drift. In such dodgy circumstances, I just go with the flow.

Leaving that grammatical conundrum to one side, in re: my imagined condemnation of the social media multitudes, perish the thought. I admire the amount of trouble people take to tell us all about their daily rounds of duties and concerns, their food habits and eateries visited, the music they lean towards, oftentimes breaking into song themselves, their travel plans, their pet hobbies as well as their pets and so much more. The downside is that a ghastly road accident becomes a target for instant clicking and posting, never mind extending a helping hand. Above all, politics. That is when biases, bile and invective combine in an incendiary way to give us agnostic, disinterested readers, some well-earned, if dubious, entertainment. Twitter is usually the vehicle of choice for verbal abuse. Therefore, I may not be an active participant, but I do commend the assiduous participation of people of all ages and denominations in social media, *per se.* Free speech and all that guff. More power to your shoulders.

As I spend on average, about 30 minutes or so browsing through Facebook, Instagram or Twitter every day, I have been able to arrive at some kind of categorisation of the posts that most engage social media freaks. I had already mentioned some of these heads, but I felt it would be an interesting exercise to elaborate on them, such that we get a more rounded feel for what confronts us on a daily basis. By no means a comprehensive list, I have merely cherry-picked a few that interest me. Now that Mark Zuckerberg has announced the launch of Meta's Twitter clone, Threads, taking Twitter head-on, there is much frisson in the air. Elon Musk is having kittens and is threatening legal action claiming infringement of copyright or similar. Let battle commence. Seconds out of the ring, first round, go for it chaps and hit below the belt.

The Travellers.

Indians are now arguably the most peripatetic race in the world. They are everywhere. Or in the words of that memorable Beatles hit song, *Here, There and Everywhere.* Europe, the Americas, Australasia, the Far East, the Silk Route, the Middle East and, come to that, even the North Pole. The Indian footprint spreads far and wide and is as firmly etched on diverse soils as the mythical Yeti's. Which, of course, means photo ops galore. In earlier times, we would lug our Canons, Pentaxes, Yashicas or Leicas and take careful aim at the Leaning Tower, the Pyramids, Sydney Opera House, the Niagara Falls, the Eiffel Tower, the Tower Bridge, Machu Picchu, the Statue of Liberty, the Empire State Building, and so on and so forth. Yank out the completed roll of film and hand it over to the nearest developer and in two shakes of a duck's tail, you will be poring over the glossy or matt prints with your near and dear ones. Plenty of 'oohs' and 'aahs.'

All that has changed now. We live in an instant world. Your mobile phone is your camera. Correction. Your camera is your mobile phone. Click away till you are blue in the face and keep posting for instant consumption by your publics, on Facebook and Instagram. That's you standing next to the Little Mermaid in Copenhagen. That's me sitting on a log somewhere in the dense Black Forest waving my trusty alpenstock. That's you again standing next to the lovable 400-year-old Mannekin Pis (the Pissing Boy) bronze statue in Brussels, and that's all of us biting into a juicy sirloin steak at Angus Steak House in Piccadilly Circus. The waiter took the picture. And hang on, is that Jeremy Irons walking past in Leicester Square? Shall I run and get a selfie? It's not Jeremy Irons? Aw shucks! 257 responses in less than 3 hours. Mostly emojis, hearts, smileys and kisses. If you are a foreigner (as opposed to an Indian), you will be doing the same thing in front of the Taj Mahal, the silvery beaches in Goa or the Madurai Meenakshi temple.

The posts I really marvel at are the ones where the traveller takes a picture of himself or herself in the plane, making sure the backdrop clearly establishes he or she (or both) are swanning it in Business Class. Or even First Class. Raise a flute of Dom Perignon. Cheers! Then there's the airline route map. Or flight path. Oh, the flight path! That is an absolute must. Just taking off from Mumbai. In nine hours, we will be landing at Heathrow. Will click and post the London skyline. After eight plus hours, London approaching, gradual descent. No skyline. No Houses of Parliament. No Thames snaking through the city. Only clouds. See the clouds! These are London clouds that rain on Wimbledon's parade. Bye for now, rushing off to Customs and Baggage Claims. Will post pictures from the black cab. Bye for the next forty minutes. That is so cruel. His family and friends having to wait for an agonising forty minutes.

Eating out.

Why so many social media devotees should be dying to know what you are eating on a daily basis is a matter for deep contemplation. Philosophers have said that you are what you eat, but still. Must we be subjected day after day, to photographs of restaurants visited and mouth-watering snaps of every dish ordered from soup to nuts, the wine list, and naturally, a close-up of the label of the exotic wine of choice, rounding it all off with the dessert? Othello's envious green-eyed monster roils my innards. Many even helpfully post a picture of the invoice so we know the damage incurred. On balance, if one were contemplating a culinary binge abroad, this is useful. Less ambitious folk in India are also happy to share with us the refined art of making curd rice at home and how not to screw up the delicate business of cooking up a storm with tomato *rasam* and the Kerala special, the mixed veg *avial.* Yum, yum. A short film of the entire procedure is *de rigueur.* Bon appetit!

Let's have a sing-song.

Never mind what your choice of music might be, it's all there on Facebook, Instagram or even WhatsApp. From precocious three-year old toddlers to spavined octogenarians, and every age group in-between, we are all closet warblers. And now, we are all coming out of the closet, in a manner of speaking, technology helping out with the pre-recorded background soundtrack. From Hindi and Tamil film songs of yesteryear, western pop hits of The Carpenters or Engelbert Humperdinck, Carnatic 'hits' like *Vatapi Ganapatim* or for that matter the infantile Geetham, *Vara veena mrudu paani,* a ghazal or thumri thrown in, if that is your bag – *there is no end to it.* Even your pet dog is encouraged to howl a few canine notes! All of it captured on your mobile for posterity, at times a pain in the posterior! I often wince with regret that we did not have mobile cameras fifty years ago, else many of our musical exploits would have been preserved for us to admire nostalgically, but after 'giving me excess of it' (to slightly paraphrase the Bard), I am not so sure. It might have been too much of a good thing.

The Twitterati.

Look, there is quite a bit of sensible and sensitive chat that takes place on Twitter, but you will have to search very hard to find it. Needle in a haystack. Mostly, it is dominated by trolls and bots, political mud-slinging, engineered by the rival parties themselves. Even observations on sports personalities can get pretty ugly. This freedom granted to us to punch in pretty much what we want without let or hindrance, and repent at leisure, is a curse that has come upon us, as Tennyson's Lady of Shalott might have put it. Those who would have found writing a 300-word essay with a fountain pen on a foolscap sheet of paper a gargantuan struggle, now fancy themselves as a latter-day Charles Dickens or Jane Austen. With due apologies to those two literary titans. For the most part, the posts are so full of bile and borderline toilet banter that it barely merits a second glance. So much so that the bitterness is spilling over into our drawing and dining rooms. Friends become foes overnight, and the idea of what is 'politically correct' to talk about or not has undergone a sea change. Better to simply sit back and sing a song, out of key.

Twitter? Speaking for myself, it is strictly for the birds. As former American basketball pro Charles Barkley put it pithily, 'Social media is where losers go to feel important.' He might have had an axe to grind and is probably guilty of making a sweeping generalisation, but one can see where he is coming from.

ABOUT THE AUTHOR

Suresh Subrahmanyan is a former advertising and brand communications professional, now based in Bangalore, with over 40 years' experience in the field. He is a keen connoisseur of various genres of music, closely follows cricket and tennis. He takes a lively interest in current affairs, which serve as cannon fodder for his weekly blogs. Some of his essays are autobiographical, with an eye peeled for the ridiculous. A regular columnist in various Indian publications, his forte is humour and satire. Unsurprisingly, his favourite author is P.G. Wodehouse, along with several British writers, past and present. This is his fourth volume of wry observations and recollections.

He can be reached at – sirsub11@gmail.com